5th Edition

The Market Guide for Young Writers

Where and how to sell what you write

KATHY HENDERSON

WRITER'S DIGEST BOOKS

CINCINNATI, OHIO

Excerpts from "The Nauga Hunters" on pages 54 and 55 are reprinted by permission of Matthew Cheney. The story first appeared in *Merlyn's Pen: The National Magazine of Student Writing.*

The poem, *We Are A Thunderstorm*, appearing on page 60 is copyright © 1990 by Amity Gaige, from the published book, *We Are A Thunderstorm*. Reprinted by permission of Landmark Editions, Inc.

The poem, *Opossum*, by Vicki May Larkin, appearing on page 61 is reprinted by permission of Vicki May Larkin.

The excerpt from *Genie of the Lamp* is reprinted by permission of Very Special Arts. *Genie of the Lamp*, by Beth Lewis, was the 1992 VSA winning entry.

The sample film and audio/video scripts appearing on pages 65 and 66 are reprinted by permission of Richard L. Rockwell, WOAK Station Manager, Royal Oak Schools (Missouri).

The illustrations appearing on pages 1, 122 and 191 were prepared by Jennifer Bolten.

Photo of Kathy Henderson (page iv) is copyright © Glamour Shots.

Other fine Writer's Digest Books are available from your local bookstore or direct from the publisher.

00 99 98 97 96   5 4 3 2 1

Library of Congress Cataloging-in-Publication Data

Henderson, Kathy
    The market guide for young writers : where and how to sell what you write / Kathy Henderson—5th ed.
        p.   cm.
    Includes index.
    ISBN 0-89879-721-7 (alk. paper)
    1. Child authors. 2 Authorship—Handbooks, manuals, etc. 3. Authorship—Competitions. [1. Authorship—Handbooks, manuasl, etc. 2. Authorship—Competitions.] I. Title.
PN171.C5H4   1996
808'.02'083—dc20   95-44903
                                                                        CIP
                                                                        AC

Edited by Argie Manolis
Designed by Brian Roeth
Cover design by Stephanie Redman

With kindness, love and appreciation to

Professor David S. Dennison

ACKNOWLEDGMENTS

I would like to express my appreciation to author Gordon Korman for sharing his young writer experiences; to Stephen King for his generosity in allowing me to reprint a short story written in his youth; to Amity Gaige for her inspiration; to David Melton and Nan Thatch for their dedication to young writers and artists; to Kent Brown for his vote of confidence; to Michael Eckert and all the other editors and contest sponsors for extra efforts they made in meeting my deadlines; to Dick Rockwell for sharing his Focal Point Tools and scriptwriting assistance; to Sandy Asher for sharing her playwriting expertise; to Debbie Ridpath Ohi for so enthusiastically offering to make information about the *Market Guide for Young Writers* available on the Internet's World Wide Web; to my new editor Argie Manolis for her patience, prodding and editorial skill; and to the many editors, contest sponsors, teachers, young people and fellow writers who have contributed information and ideas for this edition.

With special thanks to:

Alicia Gauthier	Kristin Thurston
Alison Turtledove	Michael Eckert
Sarah Feldman	Susan Currie
Mollie McDougal	Gwen McEntire
Mona Weiner	Sandra Haven
Michael S. LaFontaine	Raymond F. Pape
Amanda Lang	Janet McConnaughey
Greg Miller	Sandy Whelchel
Christy Anthony	Greg Sanders

ABOUT THE AUTHOR

 Kathy Henderson, originally from Detroit, developed an interest in helping young writers in 1984 when her daughter's eleven-year-old Oklahoma pen pal wanted advice on how to market the two hundred short stories and three science fiction novels he had already written. In addition to the *Market Guide for Young Writers*, first published in 1986, Kathy Henderson has written a dozen other books for young people. She is an active member of several national writer's organizations, and enjoys the many visits she makes to schools, libraries and conferences around the country.

TABLE OF CONTENTS

PART ONE

Chapter One
BEFORE YOU BEGIN

Chapter Two
ARE YOU READY TO MARKET?

Chapter Three
THE BASICS OF GETTING PUBLISHED

FROM THE AUTHOR

Dear Reader,

Have you ever watched racehorses as they're standing in the starting gate? They're full of energy, chomping at the bit, ready to burst out full speed the moment the gate swings open.

They remind me of the eager young writers I meet through the letters they write me or at the schools I visit. They, like you, I imagine, are full of energy and excitement, eager to burst out onto the track that leads to publishing success. If you rush out unprepared, however, the race to the finish line could be a sad, disappointing one.

This book was written as a training guide to help prepare you for the publishing tracks that excite you. Even if you are familiar with past editions, please take the time to read through this edition before racing to the sections where markets and contests are listed. While the basic advice remains the same, new information has been added, information many of you have asked for. Plus, a whole new stable of successful young writers and dedicated editors and contest sponsors share their experiences and advice.

Don't miss the special "guest celebrity" profiles of Gordon Korman and Stephen King, successful authors who first published as young writers.

Happy Writing!

Kathy Henderson

Kathy Henderson

FOREWORD

Once when I was in the fourth grade, our class was getting ready for Thanksgiving. I'm sure we heard stories about the Pilgrims and the Wampanoag Indians who befriended them. I can't really remember. In fact, even when I search my memory, I can't remember the name of a single classmate. I can only remember one thing about the entire fourth grade.

That one thing is a picture I drew of a turkey. The teacher hung it up high over the chalkboard. In front of the whole class she said, "Look how good Kent's turkey is."

I felt very proud at the time. Somehow that sense of accomplishment has stayed with me for almost forty years. The good feeling I had in being recognized for my creative work has been a lasting influence on me, and on my career.

I think there must be no better feeling than one that comes from the sense of creating something yourself. It may be a picture of a turkey, a rabbit made from clay or a story or poem.

Writing gives me great joy. I believe it is so with you also.

Over the years I've had the fun of seeing the poems and stories of thousands of young people. Some of these stories interested me as a reader more than others. A few we picked to publish in *Highlights*. There is one thing that I always remember when I read these—the writer's sense of accomplishment, the pleasure he or she gained through the experience of writing.

Writing is more than the activity of putting one word down after another. You cannot write without thinking. Good, clear writing is a sign of good, clear thought.

The process of writing helps you think. It helps you reflect on ideas and explore your thoughts. You can first try your ideas and words out on yourself. Then you can share them with others.

This book is about sharing your ideas and thoughts. It's about a good way to share a little bit of yourself with others. Your audience may at first be friends and family. After a while, you may want a larger audience for that bit of yourself.

The author of this book has been writing for a long time. She came to want a larger audience early on in her writing. She had felt the satisfaction and joy of writing, and she felt a strong wish to share with others.

We can imagine that Kathy Henderson found a number of ways to share her work.

Remembering the joy of sharing—as well as the difficulty of finding out how to share—prompted Kathy to write this book.

This edition is the result of a desire to refine and improve the information given in earlier volumes. By helping countless young writers, Kathy has given back some of the joy writing has given her.

In this book you will meet a number of young writers. Notice how much they are like you. You will meet here, too, a number of editors. Notice they seem like people with whom you could sit down and talk.

There is sound advice in this book—lots of tips on getting started, helpful pointers about the writing process and a host of ways to give yourself the encouragement. Rejection, a part of every writer's life, is explored in a sensible way.

The up-to-date listing of where to send your writing is the best I've seen, by far. Its completeness gives you a broad choice of publications and a wide number of contests. The publications and contests listed here will allow you to find your audience. It allows you to share your thoughts and talents.

This is a book to be used. On its pages lie the hard-won wisdom of an author who has learned how to share the joy of writing with others.

Kathy Henderson is offering young writers like you valuable knowledge about writing. By using the information in this book, you can increase that sense of personal accomplishment gained through writing.

Kent Brown, Editor
Highlights for Children

PART ONE

Chapter One

Before You Begin

Each month the work of dozens of young writers appears in publications all across the country. To do what these young people have done, you don't need to be at the top of your class in reading or writing, or be labeled "gifted" or "talented." You don't need to know somebody in the business or have lots of money or years of experience. You don't need to live in an unusual place or lead an unusual life. And you don't need any fancy equipment. As many young writers have proven already, you don't even need to wait until you are older to try.

There are only two specific things you do need to know beforehand: *who* publishes the type of material you like to write and *how* to prepare your finished story, poem, article, play or script before mailing it to an editor or contest. *Market Guide for Young Writers* has that special information plus a lot more to help you become a *published* young writer.

This chapter provides an overview of the marketing process. Combined with chapter four, which explains the proper way to format and mail manuscripts, and chapters nine and ten, which contain the names and requirements of markets and contests open to submissions from young writers, you'll have all the basic information needed to start submitting. If you have prior marketing experience, these chapters will refresh your memory and bring you up-to-date on who is currently publishing what.

If you aren't sure what marketing your writing means, or if you already know what it means but aren't sure if you're ready to try it, skip these first two chapters for now and start with chapter three. Then come back and join us here.

WHAT'S IN THIS EDITION

I encourage all readers, including those familiar with past editions, to take the time to read through this edition in its entirety. In addition to the revised and updated markets and contests, and profiles featuring a new group of young writers, editors and contest sponsors, this edition contains new and expanded information in many other areas. More importantly, from the standpoint of helping you as a young writer prepare and market your manuscripts, greater attention has been paid to explain what it means to be a writer, why it's important to work to continually improve your writing skills, plus how to research, study and evaluate opportunities. In particular, look for

- More detailed formatting directions plus examples for plays and scripts
- Examples of properly formatted poems
- Examples of query and cover letters
- Information on how to mail artwork and photographs
- The growing opportunities in electronic "online" communications, markets and contests
- More answers to the questions young writers ask most
- More detailed information on how to study markets and their guidelines
- Advice about markets and contests to avoid
- Expanded information and coverage of local and regional opportunities
- Additional resources about writing and marketing
- Insight to help you evaluate and develop your writing and marketing skills
- More than forty new market and contest listings
- Special "guest celebrity" young writers, Gordon Korman and Stephen King
- Special "Author's Tips," like the one on page 4, sprinkled throughout this book, which will alert you to recommended resources, additional information, warnings and reminders

The market and contest lists in this book are the result of a special survey of editors and contest sponsors across the United States and Canada. Their enthusiatic response made it possible

---

Author's Tip:
....

If you are serious about writing and plan to make it a career, I recommend that you read *The Young Person's Guide to Becoming a Writer*, by Janet E. Grant. This practical book will help you develop your talent, explore your options, find help and chart a course for success.

---

to group together a promising list of publications and contests that, for one or more reasons, are especially receptive to submissions from young writers. Many of the magazines have specific sections or whole issues written entirely by young people. Others, such as those whose readers are mainly adults, make a special effort to encourage young writers and are willing to consider their work, especially in the areas of essays, opinions, profiles and personal experience. Contests may be specifically for young writers, or they may have separate categories for them. A few markets and contests have no preferences or restrictions regarding age at all; however, they recognize that some young writers are producing work as good or better than many of the submissions they receive from adults. Remember, however, that only those markets and contests responding to my survey and agreeing to be listed are included. The main criteria is that they will seriously consider, for awards and/or publication, submissions made by young writers.

Why are so many editors interested in hearing from you? The answer is simple: Many of them were once young writers too! One editor expressed the feeling shared by many others when she wrote, "Your *Guide* is a great idea. I only wish it had been available eight or ten years ago for me."

MORE ABOUT THE LISTINGS
Many of these markets not only publish material from young writers but offer payment as well. Others offer free copies of issues containing your work instead of payment. Sometimes they offer both. As you search through the listings, pay special attention to entries marked with an asterisk (*). Markets and contests

bearing this symbol represent especially good opportunities for young people. They are the ones that have special issues, columns or departments featuring work from young writers and, therefore, are likely to accept more material from them than will other markets. If you are a very young writer (twelve and under) or are especially anxious to get published, these are the opportunities to stick with. If you are a young writer thirteen and up, especially one with little writing or marketing experience, you should also concentrate your efforts on starred markets and contests and consider other listings only after carefully studying the requirements and objectively evaluating the quality and maturity of your own manuscripts. Don't make the mistake of thinking these opportunities aren't challenging. Many are among the most highly respected in their fields. However, your work has the best chance of fitting in here. Submitting to other markets and contests now would be like trying to stuff Cinderella's stepsister's big foot into her tiny glass slipper. Highly unlikely!

Two new symbols have been added in this edition. The maple leaf (✤) has been added to indicate markets in Canada. The double cross (‡) indicates markets and contests that should only be considered by more mature young writers (fourteen and up) or very determined and experienced younger ones. Watch also for a special "Author's Note" that appears at the bottom of some of these opportunities. They are often highly specialized and maintain very sophisticated editorial preferences. Getting a manuscript accepted here can be very difficult even for adult writers. Still, the editors and sponsors of these markets and contests have said they are willing to consider manuscripts by young writers. Consider your options and your work carefully before trying these markets. Submitting inappropriate material that has little chance of being accepted is a waste of time and energy for both you and the publication.

A few starred (*) listings will also have a double cross (‡). This means that even though they offer young writers some type of special opportunity as mentioned above, competition is exceptionally tough. Sometimes, competition is tough due to the high number of submissions a market receives compared to the space it has reserved to print them. It stands to reason that an editor who receives one thousand submissions every month but only has space availabe to print ten during an entire year will have to reject the majority of the manuscripts received. Thus, well-written and correctly submitted manuscripts often get rejected.

A check mark (✔) indicates that a listing is new to this edition. It may or may not be a new publication or contest in the sense that it has recently been established.

DOLLARS AND SENSE

Be aware that a few markets insist that writers become subscribers before their work will be considered for publication. In addition, many contests require an entry fee. A dollar sign ($) will alert you to these listings. Entry fees for most contests are minimal and are normally used to help defray the costs of the contest, including payment for prizes and/or publication of winning entries. Many of these contests are also marked with an asterisk(*), meaning that despite the entry cost, they are still good places for young writers to consider. A few contests require more substantial entry fees, often five dollars or more.

You should not disqualify a market or contest from your submission list just because it has an entry fee or insists that only subscribers or club members may submit material. Take into account other factors as well. For instance:

- Who is sponsoring this contest?
- Is the entry fee reasonable?
- How are the fees used?
- How much competition will my entry or submission face?
- Will I be competing with others my own age or with similar experience?
- Do I need to subscribe first, or will the price of a subscription or membership be deducted from my payment if my work is accepted for publication?
- Would I enjoy being a member of this writer's organization?
- Have I studied the contest's rules or the market's guidelines carefully to determine if my planned submission would be appropriate?
- Are there any extra benefits that make the payment of an

Author's Note: Warning!

Beware of publishers and contests that ask you to pay to see your work in print or in order to collect your prize. Read all acceptances, evaluations and award notices *carefully*. You should *never* have to pay to have accepted manuscripts published or to collect awards from contests.

---

entry fee worthwhile? For example, does the contest or market offer writers professional critiques of their entries for no or little additional cost?

- Do I know other people who have entered this contest? What was their experience?
- Can I afford the fee?
- Are there other markets or contests that would be better for me to try first?

Remember that there is always some cost involved in submitting to markets and contests, even if it's just paper, postage and envelopes—one to send your manuscript and another (known as an SASE, or self-addressed stamped envelope) to have it sent back if not accepted. Entry and subscription fees add to that. No matter how minor the cost, make sure your material is not only good enough but appropriate to make the cost of submitting a worthwhile risk.

DON'T BE FOOLED BY OPPORTUNITIES THAT SEEM TOO GOOD

If you enjoy writing, the prospect of getting published or winning an award can be very exciting. Unfortunately, there are some publishers and contests that attract amateur writers with promises of publication and large cash awards, trophies or other prizes for a fee. You may receive information from such publishers and contests through the mail or see ads for them in magazines and newspapers. Oftentimes, you will not realize that a publication or contest expects *you* to pay to have your work published until *after* you have submitted your manuscript. This situation is similar

---

Author's Tip:

Many authors enjoy receiving letters from people who have read their books. I know I do. However, due to our busy schedules, we can't always respond as quickly as we'd like. Often we are asked for information that would not be appropriate or possible for us to give. For advice on writing to published authors, please see page 120.

---

to subsidy or vanity publishing, which is discussed below.

Be aware also that some literary consultants or agents—working independently or in conjunction with a publisher or contest—offer free evaluations and publishing advice in exchange for what's called a "reading fee." A reading fee may be one price, such as one hundred fifty dollars for a book manuscript, or charged on a per page basis according to the type of work submitted.

If you want advice or help with a manuscript, I suggest you look for less expensive, and often more productive, solutions. Find out if there is a writer's group that meets in your school or neighborhood. Ask for references from teachers, librarians or bookstore clerks. They can recommend books to read or may know of an experienced writer willing to work with you. Chapter five, "Opportunities Online," explains how to become involved with manuscript critique sessions and workshops conducted electronically. Many organizations, such as the National Writer's Association, include manuscript help as part of the yearly dues or for a reasonable fee. Some writers exchange manuscripts with other writers through the mail, with the writers supplying envelopes and postage to have their own manuscripts returned to them.

SUBSIDY PUBLISHERS AND VANITY PRESSES

Subsidy book publishers (also known as vanity presses) are publishers that invite you to submit your manuscript, accept it for publication, *then* tell you how much it will cost you. Often, they offer free information in the form of how-to-get-published booklets or other valuable-sounding gifts. Their ads may say that you can obtain a free, professional evaluation of your manuscript's qualities and potential without obligation. Sometimes, they cite the names of now famous authors whom they claim to have worked with in the past.

Subsidy publishers typically respond to submissions in one of two ways. First, they may praise your work and you as a writer who is obviously blessed with the talent of a potential best-selling author. They can't wait to sign you up as a client and help you get your work published. It will all happen quickly, they promise. Second, they may claim your work has merit but it isn't quite good enough to publish, yet. They will go on, however, and say that with their expert editorial help and publishing guidance, they can help you produce a published book. Whatever the exact words of their pitch, the catch is the same: *You* must provide all or most of the funds to get your book published. In other words, when you send them enough money, they will make the arrangements to get your book printed.

Selling your new book to readers is another matter entirely. Despite the promises they may make, subsidy publishers have little incentive to market the books they publish since all of their costs, plus a handsome profit, have already been covered by the authors themselves. Likewise, it may not matter to them if the book is well written or just a writer's ego on display. Since their primary purpose is to get *you*, the writer, to pay to have your book published, how objective do you think they will be when discussing the merits of the particular manuscript you sent them?

If you're a fan of the *Little House on the Prairie* television series, you may remember Charles Ingalls falling into this trap when he submitted his father's autobiography to a publisher. Grandpa Ingalls wanted so much to have his book published. And Charles, after reading the publisher's praise and not wanting to disappoint his father, sent the money he had saved for a badly needed new plow in order to get the book published. At first, everyone celebrated the publishing success of Grandpa Ingalls. But, before long, everyone realized it was a hollow victory. Grandpa Ingalls, in particular, was embarrassed and disillusioned, especially after bragging so much about his writing ability and publishing success.

WATCH OUT FOR CONTESTS WITH HIDDEN COSTS

Similar tactics are used by some contests. The initial entry fee may seem quite reasonable, perhaps only a dollar or two. Or, no entry fee is required at all. Sometimes, an entry fee will be referred to as "nominal" or "modest" even though they expect you to pay twenty-five, thirty, fifty dollars or even more to enter your work. Like subsidy book publishers, they may offer free information for a self-addressed stamped envelope (SASE). Typically, their ads boast of awarding thousands of dollars in prizes annually plus publication of winning entries in anthologies.

You will be delighted when an official-looking letter arrives proclaiming you one of the winners. But your heart will sink to your shoes when you realize that in order to *see* your masterpiece in print, you must first buy a copy of the anthology in which it will appear with all the other lucky winners. It's not uncommon for a single copy to cost sixty dollars or more. I've also seen letters from contests that only awarded prizes (cash and/or trophies) to "winning" contestants who paid to attend the awards banquet. Others may offer to send a certificate verifying your winning entry, then offer to mount it "free" on a beautiful plaque that will only cost you fifty dollars to have engraved and shipped to your home.

Here is a portion of an actual award letter sent to an unsuspecting friend of mine. (For legal reasons, references to the organization's identity have been omitted.)

Dear _____ Entrant:

CONGRATULATIONS! The judging has been completed in your category/categories, and one or more of your entries has been selected for a _____ award.

The entries this year were exceptional in all categories, and yours was/were among the best.

The honorarium for each category award is $110. Your total *contribution* [italics mine] is $220. Each category winner is (sic) of beautiful Gold, Silver, or Bronze _____ statuette.

PLEASE REMIT YOUR HONORARIUM ALONG WITH THE PROPER FORM/FORMS BY DECEMBER 31, 1992.

Again, congratulations for being a _____ winner!

Accompanying this "awards" letter was a sheet claiming: "Most recipients of the _____ award wish to order additional

---

Author's Tip:

....

Webster's New World Dictionary defines honorarium as "a payment as to a professional person for services on which no fee is set or legally obtainable."

Honorariums (gifts or money) are often given to speakers as a token of appreciation from the sponsoring organization. Reputable contests *do not* require winners to pay *anything* in order to collect their awards.

---

duplicate statuettes and certificates for other individuals who have contributed to the creative and productive aspects of the winning entry." The price for each duplicate statuette was even *higher* than the first one, plus, they wanted fifteen dollars for a duplicate certificate!

"What turnip truck did they fall off of?" asked my friend incredulously. While she did not bother to collect her award, I doubt the contest sponsors really cared since before declaring her a winner, they had already collected sixty dollars in fees for the two essays she had entered.

Such publication and contest offers, before their true nature is exposed, are particularly enticing to beginning writers anxious to see their names in print or writers frustrated by a continual stream of rejection slips. (Even experienced adults get fooled occasionally. The friend mentioned above is an editor.) There is nothing illegal about such offers. But, to me, they take unfair advantage of writers' dreams of success by getting them to believe that this is how the publishing business traditionally works. Worse, they usually charge writers a lot more than it would cost them to take their manuscripts to local print shops and have them typeset, printed and bound into book form. *That* is known as self-publishing.

THE SELF-PUBLISHING DIFFERENCE

Many poets, writing clubs or other community groups self-publish collections of their work, primarily to share with family and friends. This is similar to students publishing a yearbook, school

---

Author's Note:
....
Young Author Day books, which many elementary students write, illustrate and help bind, are an excellent example of worthwhile self-publishing projects.

---

magazine or classroom anthology. They may sell a few copies; some even make a profit. The difference is that when people self-publish their work, they understand from the beginning what they are responsible for and have control over how much it will cost. For instance, they can choose the number of copies to print, what type of paper to use and how it will be bound. No one is making exaggerated claims of fame and fortune. (I hope!)

EGO ALERT!
The worst thing about subsidy publishers and vanity presses is that they often puff up writers' egos with flattery that has no connection to the truth. Like Grandpa Ingalls, some writers think it's an honest appraisal of their talent or potential as a writer. And, like him, they declare themselves failures when they learn the truth about the circumstances. What they don't realize is that they haven't learned anything objective about their talent or potential at all! After such an experience, some good writers will give up writing entirely thinking they can't ever succeed, while others charge blindly ahead believing they are great writers producing work that could never be improved.

Don't become victims of such misguided assumptions and sales tactics. This is not how reputable publishers and contests operate. Beware of any publisher or contest that asks you to pay to see your work in print or to collect your prize. Read all acceptances, evaluations and award notices carefully. You should *never* have to pay to have accepted manuscripts published or to collect awards from contests. In any case, when in doubt, check it out with someone more experienced.

In compiling this *Guide*, I have taken great care to avoid listing such questionable opportunities. Please write to me immediately if you receive a request for money to collect an award or to guarantee your work will be published from any of the listings included in this book, or any others you become aware of. Send a detailed letter and include photocopies if possible of any correspondence you have received to

Kathy Henderson
c/o Writer's Digest Books
1507 Dana Avenue
Cincinnati OH 45207

ADVICE TO THOSE WHO SELF-PUBLISH

As pointed out earlier, self-publishing can be a fun, inexpensive and worthwhile experience, especially for students or community groups. Unfortunately, too many writers waste time and money self-publishing their work as a way to avoid or ignore the editing process based on the assumption that it would destroy the quality or creativity of their work. As can happen when you work with subsidy publishing and vanity presses, this may lead to questions about the credibility, integrity and quality of your work or your writing ability later on.

If you insist on self-publishing larger works, such as books or newsletters, at least do so in a responsible manner. You may be able to do all the necessary editing on your own, following advice found in many excellent reference books. However, it is much wiser to enlist the help of someone with professional editing experience. Find someone whose judgement you respect but who can also be counted on to bring objectivity and perspective to the task. Rewriting, revising and polishing are key steps to producing quality work. Producing a quality product should be the goal of any publisher.

GAINING A COMPETITIVE EDGE

Unfortunately, no one can guarantee that all writers, regardless of age, will find a willing, reputable market for their work. There are, however, several things you can do to give your material an edge against the competition. These basic principles (covered in chapter three) are the same ones followed by professional writers. Bear in mind that while other people may be available

---

Author's Tip:

....

Draw & Write Your Own Picture Book, by Emily Hearn and Mark Thurman, is an excellent reference book that even younger students can read and follow themselves. Teachers (K-12) and older students will find more detailed advice in David Melton's book, *Written & Illustrated by. . . .*

The Complete Guide to Self-Publishing, by Tom and Marilyn Ross, is an excellent resource for those wanting to know everything about writing, publishing, promoting and selling their own books.

---

to help you, you alone are responsible for the final content and condition of the manuscripts you submit.

GETTING DOWN TO BUSINESS

If your parents have ever paid out good money to give you music lessons, you've heard them say a million times, "Go practice." And off you'd trot to your piano, tuba, drum or violin and try to hammer or blow or rap or stroke out the notes of the scale. All the while, your mom's taken refuge in the garage gratefully out of earshot and your dad is in the kitchen trying in vain to tap his foot to your beat.

But hand your mom or dad a little story or poem you just wrote from the top of your head and out come the "Ohs" and "Ahs" and "Neanderthal is sooooo talented. He's a natural born writer." No one ever tells you, "Go practice your writing."

Until now.

I'm telling you, "Go practice your writing." Give that budding talent a chance to bloom and grow. You'll be amazed at what a little daily stretching of the mind and fingers will do for the quality of your writing. Quality writing gets published. Practice will also help keep the idea mill churning.

FOR YOUR EYES ONLY

Try keeping a notebook handy for writing down special thoughts or feelings. Jot down descriptions of places you visit. What makes

---

Author's Tip:

....

Have trouble thinking up new ideas? Can't tell a good idea from a bad one? Then check out *Where Do You Get Your Ideas?*, by Sandy Asher.

---

them different from other places you've seen? Why do some places, like McDonald's or Kmart, look the same wherever you go? Try to describe your home for someone who is blind or deaf.

Learn to exercise your senses. What does your living room sofa *feel* like? Is it rough or smooth? Can you smell the kind of stuffing it has? Go through each room recording how things feel, smell, sound, look and, sometimes, taste.

Study how people look. What do their expressions say about them? Have you ever been really close to a very old person? Did you ever notice the different medicines that seem to seep from some of their bodies? What does a baby smell and look like while he's in the process of messing a diaper? Don't just wrinkle your nose, *show* what he looks and smells like using word pictures. What comparisons can you make?

Record how people talk. Do they use slang or proper English? Do their clothes reflect the way they talk? Do they slur their words, and if they do, why? Is it a speech impediment or just out of laziness? Are they bashful and shy or boisterous and loud? If you could feel the voice of a big husky man, what would it feel like? Does he pound out his words like a jackhammer? Does his breath smell?

How does your teacher look when you first see her each morning? How does she look at the end of the day? Can you tell if the day has been good or bad?

Read, read, read. But avoid reading only what currently interests you. Read a variety of things—books, magazines, newspapers—even if you don't fully understand them. Sample topics and genres[1] you would normally skip.

---

[1]Pronounced *zhan ra*, genre means kind or type. For instance, romance, western, realistic fiction, science fiction, fantasy, historical and how-to are examples of different genres.

While reading the work of favorite authors can be a great help in learning to write well, you should postpone it while drafting your own stories, especially if you tend to be too critical of your own work. Besides deflating your confidence, it can hamper your originality and make it harder for you to finish the stories you start. In fact, some writers deliberately read a few pages of what they would ordinarily consider boring material in order to motivate themselves to get back to their own work.

A SECRET WEAPON ONLY YOU CAN USE

If I asked one hundred people to write a story based on the same idea, do you know what I'd get? One hundred different stories. That's because each of us is a unique individual; no two are exactly the same.

Exercise your writing mind daily and your writing will grow stronger and more creative. You'll gain the confidence needed to risk writing stories only you can tell. You will get a feel that is natural for you, for the way words can be woven together in interesting, inspiring and informative ways. With practice, your writing will take on a special cadence, a distinct rhythm that flows with the tone of your writing. This is part of what's known as a writer's *style*. It is what helps to make your writing different from all other writing. Your style may vary with each new manuscript you create. What's important, however, is that your style develop from the inside out as you draw on your own emotions, interests and experiences to create something brand new.

Style is what makes our writing special. And *your* style is the secret weapon only you can develop and use in becoming a successful writer.

THE POST POSITION

In horse racing, jockeys like to start from lane one, the post position, because it offers the shortest distance around the track to the finish line.

If there's a shortcut to getting published, it's taking time to first find out what editors and contest judges want. So, before you burst out of the starting gate, set yourself up for the post position by reading chapter three, "The Basics of Getting Pub-

Author's Tip:

To better understand how successful writers draw from their own interests and experiences, read biographies and other thought-provoking works by or about well-known writers. My personal favorite is *Gates of Excellence*, by Katherine Paterson, author of such wonderful books as *The Bridge to Terabithia*, *The Great Gilly Hopkins* and *Jacob Have I Loved*.

For help in developing your own writing style and habits, try *Writing from the Inside Out*, by Charlotte Edwards, and *Becoming a Writer*, by Dorothea Brande. Both these books include stimulating exercises. Brande's book is especially useful for writers who lack self-confidence, have trouble finishing what they start, or sit down to write and suddenly find they can't get started. Don't let some of the big or old-fashioned words and phrases discourage you. Look up or skip over words that confuse you, but read it from cover to cover!

lished," and chapter four, "How to Prepare Your Manuscript." For inspiration and insight, read in chapter seven about the races other young writers have won, plus get a look behind the scenes of several markets and contests in chapter eight.

Chapter Two

Are You Ready to Market?

When most people think *markets*, they mean stores and shopping: buying groceries at A&P, perhaps, or a new pair of jeans at the mall.

But when writers think *markets*, they mean all the places where they can send their manuscripts in the hopes of having them published.

The world is full of people who would like to be published. *Wouldn't it be great*, they think, *to see my name splashed across the cover of a best-selling book?* Or, *I bet people would pay big money to read how my great-grandfather sailed ships across the Atlantic.* Or, *Someday I'm going to write a story about the time I visited Uncle Ned and Aunt Fanny's farm and how I sat on some eggs in the chicken coop and tried to hatch them.*

Their ideas may be good, even great. The problem is they are would-be or wanna-be writers. They want to be published, but they don't want to write. They are not ready to market.

ARE YOU A WRITER?

Well, . . . do you write?

Do you capture your thoughts and imaginings on paper? Yes? Then you are a writer.

Sometimes it's hard. Very hard. Like trying to catch dandelion puffs in a wispy net on a windy day. Or struggling to connect with the baseball for a hit when it's the bottom of the ninth and there's a guy on third and your team is one run down. We get frustrated, angry and impatient forcing words out when they don't want to come. Then we look at what we've written, expecting—

hoping—to see something wonderful for all our hard work. And all that's there is a sorry little jumble of words that doesn't sound at all like the wonderful, perfect story we had planned in our heads.

Sometimes, it's easier. Words seem to jump out of our minds and scamper straight down our fingertips to form tidy black images on paper. The story picture is clear, often better than we had imagined. Correct a misspelling here, cut an adjective there, and poof, we've created something interesting and well written.

Poetry. Short stories. Essays. Plays. Newspaper articles. It doesn't matter what you write. Or how well you write. Or how easy or hard it is for you to pull the words out of your head and have them land creatively on paper. If you write, you are a writer.

BUT, ARE YOU READY TO MARKET?

Some writers write a lot and hope that everything they write will be published. Some writers write only when inspired. They usually don't create as many marketable manuscripts as more active writers who are determined to get published. Just the same, they hope their work will be published.

Then there are people who write just for themselves. They may enter a contest occasionally or send a poem that they wrote to a friend, or they may not want to share their work at all. They don't care if they get published. They may not even *want* to be published. (They may even be afraid to let others read their work. I know. I feel that way sometimes.) And that's okay. It should be their choice to make.

Unfortunately, in school you don't always have a choice about this. Your teacher assigns a writing project. She's going to read what you wrote or you won't get a grade. Reading your essay or book report to the class may be mandatory. You have to do it. It's likely you are a part of a process writing class where students must read and critique each other's work. Then, as the last step in the process, everyone's work gets published in some kind of form, which is usually distributed to parents and other students in the school to read. It might even be printed in the local newspaper.

However, when it comes to work you've written on your own,

just because you wanted to, you have a choice about whether to share it with others. No one should ever force you to enter it in a contest or submit it to a market if you don't want to. It doesn't matter why you don't want to share it. *It's perfectly OK to write just for yourself.* Even though you're not ready to try marketing your work now, you may change your mind later. I suggest you read chapter seven, "Young Writers in Print." You may find just that bit of encouragement and inspiration you need to give marketing a try. And, take time to read through all the how-to market information that follows, just to get an idea of what it's all about.

BEGINNING, YOUNG, NEW, EMERGING—IN WHICH CATEGORY DO YOU BELONG?

Not all young writers are beginners, and not all beginning writers are young.

There are some very accomplished and successfully published young writers. And then there's Dennis Volmer, who is considered to be one of the youngest writers (at age six) to have had a book published under a professional royalty contract. There are many, many others, some with enough experience writing and marketing that they're far beyond the "beginner" stage, even though they still have a lot to learn and many more situations to experience.

Some folks waited to start writing or trying to publish until they were great-grandparents. One woman in our local writer's club was ninety-three when she entered our contest for the first time. She'd been writing her whole life. She was a beginner at marketing.

I never planned on becoming a writer. It happened quite by accident one day when I read an editorial in our rural weekly newspaper. It made me so angry I sat right down and wrote a letter to the editor to complain. After the editor read my letter, he did a most surprising thing: He called and said, "I like the way you write. Would you consider writing 'The Farmer's Wife' column for us?" All of a sudden, not only was I going to be a writer but a published writer. I was a real beginner even though I was already married and had a child. I knew nothing about getting published or how to prepare a manuscript. Plus, the only writing I'd ever really done before was for school assignments or entries in a diary that read like weather reports. You know the kind: It snowed today. The temperature was 32°. Mom drove me to school. Hardly publishable material!

Stephen King, now one of the world's most famous and successful writers, has been writing since he was a child. At one time, he and a friend even published their own "magazine," which they wrote, photocopied, stapled together and then sold to kids at school, charging as much as a quarter. The school eventually made them stop selling their magazine, but King didn't stop writing. Stephen King may have been young and inexperienced, but compared to me, he was hardly a beginner. He wrote regularly and was serious about practicing his writing craft. (Note: Read one of King's early short stories in chapter seven.)

Gordon Korman signed his first book contract when he was thirteen. The book started out as an assignment for English class. By the time he graduated high school, he had published five novels! Gordon, because he was newly successful in the publishing field, was known as a "new and emerging" talent. But he was also young and, compared to most professional writers, still a beginner.

CHECK YOUR WRITING AND MARKETING ATTITUDE

How serious are you about your writing? Do you work at it every day? How do you feel about editing? Do you always review your work with the idea that it could be improved? Are you willing to rewrite, revise, cut and polish your manuscript until every word has a purpose that helps move the piece smoothly from beginning to end?

Do you put yourself—observations, imagination, feelings, emotions, opinions, fears and joys—into your work so that you write pieces that mean something special to you? Do you include in them something of value for the reader, something he or she can relate to?

Robert D. Sutherland, editor and publisher, put it this way in a note he asked me to share with young writers:

Authors of poetry and fictional stories should write to please themselves first; one has to be true to one's vision and express oneself honestly for the work to "live" and for the labor of creating it to be enjoyable and fun. But authors should remember that if they submit their work to be *published* (which means making it available to a broad audience), they have certain responsibilities to their readers, too.

If one says, "Here, read my work," that work had better be worth a reader's time. In other words, it should provide something worthwhile, useful, or valuable (including enjoyment) for the reader to take away. If it does not, if it is too personal to the writer, or too obscure, or too trivial or silly, the readers will feel their time wasted. Therefore, writers had better submit for publication only their *very best*, and that which will have value for others. Writers should *not* indulge themselves at their readers' expense.

That's good advice for writers of nonfiction, too.

SEND ONLY YOUR VERY BEST WORK

Revise and rewrite as many times as necessary to ensure that what you submit is the best you can do.

Revise and rewrite until each paragraph, sentence and word says exactly what you mean it to say. This type of editing plus the drafting of new manuscripts should be a regular part of your practice or training routine. Like a skater repeatedly etching figures onto the ice, or a musician practicing to perfect the way he plays a certain tune, or an athlete working to develop both body and game skills, your writing will improve with practice and fine-tuning.

Consider asking an adult, perhaps a teacher, a parent or a more experienced writer to read your manuscript and offer constructive criticism. Listen carefully to their comments, then decide whether you agree or disagree with their advice. Sometimes hearing someone else's opinion will help you to see your material in a new way, yet always remember that *you* are the creator. You must be the final judge of whether or not your work is ready to submit. In the end, follow the advice you agree with and politely

---

Author's Tip:

For help planning and editing fiction stories, I recommend that young writers read *Wild Words!, How to Train Them to Tell Stories*, by Sandy Asher.

Older students may also enjoy my personal favorites by author Gary Provost: *Make Every Word Count* and *Make Your Words Work*.

---

disregard the rest.

It helps also to hear your material read aloud. You might try reciting into a cassette recorder, then playing back the tape while you follow along with a written version. This often makes it easier to note glitches in construction and awkward words or phrases. If you do the reading, be sure to read what you have *actually written*. Also, read it as if you are seeing it for the first time. Don't add a lot of voice inflections as a dramatic actor might. You're looking for places that may need editing, not auditioning for a part in a play! (Play and script manuscripts benefit from a different form of testing. See page 60 for more details.)

It's easy to read what you *think* you have written or *intended* to write. However, your *actual* words, not your reading of them, must provide all the drama, action and emotion. Readers should be able to visualize your settings, feel and see right along with your characters just as if they were there with them in the story. Show, don't tell, your story. This applies to poetry and nonfiction work as well. If you find yourself having to explain what you meant, then your job as a writer isn't finished.

It's always a good idea to put a piece of writing away, out-of-sight, for a day or two, even a week or more for longer works, before editing it. You'll be amazed at how mistakes you didn't notice before will suddenly jump out at you like they were waving little red flags. Granted, you may not always have time to let writing assignments from school "cool" before turning them in. But take the time before sending a manuscript to an outside market or contest.

MORE ABOUT REWRITING AND REVISING

Rewriting and revising refer to the types of editing you do to improve the *content* of your manuscripts. Many people use the terms interchangeably. To me, however, rewriting refers to the efforts I make to reword a particular sentence or paragraph to make it say exactly what I mean in the best and least words possible. I'm not changing the meaning, only how I'm presenting it. I'll substitute more precise (active) nouns and verbs for weak adjectives and adverbs. I'll fiddle with sentence structure and word placement.

When I revise something, I'm making bigger changes, like taking whole sections of a story or article and putting them in a completely different order. Or I may change my mind about the kind of statement I'm trying to make, start over with a slightly different topic, add a new scene, twist a plot, create a whole new story opening or ending, add or subtract characters, deliberately lengthen or shorten the manuscript. Sometimes you can revise a previously published manuscript and make it suitable to submit again to a different market or contest.

POLISH AND PROOFREAD

Correct all grammar, punctuation and spelling mistakes in your final copy before mailing it out.

If, while evaluating your work, you discover it doesn't seem quite right yet, rewriting and revising are what you do to fix it. Polishing, on the other hand, prompts you to view the work as a whole, checking to make sure all the parts fit snugly together like a completed jigsaw puzzle. You want to make sure there are no missing or misplaced parts. As you read it again, forget that you are its author. Try to be as objective and as truthful as possible. (Often not an easy task when editing our own work!) Here are just a few of the questions you might ask yourself:

- Is there a strong beginning that flows smoothly into the middle section, which in turn stimulates the reader and leads him into the climax and ending?
- Do characters sound and act like real people? Could a reader predict how they might realistically behave in a different

setting?

- Can you imagine a setting that would make your characters uncomfortable? Happy? Excited?
- What is the main conflict or problem the main character faces? What point have you tried to illustrate?
- Have you tied up all loose ends, supported your premise with word illustrations (facts and images) that readers can easily identify with?
- If you have a market or contest already in mind, does the length fall within the word limit set?

Many times the various aspects of the editing process overlap. You might notice and correct problems associated with the above questions during the initial rewriting and revising stage. Or you might get so involved working on small parts of a manuscript during rewriting and revision that you overlook problems that affect the overall presentation. It's like the adage: You can't see the forest for the trees.

The good thing about proofreading is that you don't have to bother doing it until your manuscript is ready for its final presentation. After all, why bother correcting a misspelled word in a first draft when it might get cut in a second or third or fourth. Plus, it isn't wise to stop to fix typographical errors, look up correct spellings and fret over just the right word or phrase to use while you're trying to be creative. It's too easy to lose your creative momentum. The purpose of first drafts is to get the basic idea down on paper, much like painters first sketch in pencil the basic elements of the pictures they plan to paint. You can add the flourishes and details later.

Many manuscripts could be improved if writers put more time and effort into their editing. Yet, be aware that a manuscript can also be ruined by too much editing. Like writing, editing skills improve with practice.

After a thorough polishing, you'll need to go over the material again looking for technical mistakes, such as misspellings or errors in punctuation and grammar, that you may have missed. For instance, you want all your nouns and verb tenses to match correctly. If the manuscript is already in standard format, now is

---

Author's Tip:

....

There are many good how-to-write books on the market that identify and discuss in detail the various parts of a story, poem, article, etc., and how to seamlessly weave them together. Studying these will help you improve both your writing and editing skills. *Writing for Children and Teenagers*, by Lee Wyndham, contains a lot of detailed information suitable for many young writers ages twelve and up, especially those interested in writing fiction. Teen writers working on "adult" topics will also find this book useful.

For honing your nonfiction writing and editing skills, I recommend *Words' Worth*, by Terri Brooks, in addition to the Gary Provost books mentioned earlier.

For final polishing and proofreading, there is no better addition to any writer's personal reference library than *The Elements of Style*, by William Strunk, Jr. and E.B. White.

---

the time to also look for typographical errors. The typographical error most easily overlooked appears as a misspelled word, but you don't notice it because it's also a word you are sure you know how to spell. Our mind assumes it's correct, so our eyes tend to skim over the word rather than see the mistake.

It's a good idea to write or type out a fresh copy of your manuscript after any major editing session. Computers and word processors make this a simple task. Incidently, although computers and word processors make it possible to edit work directly on screen, most writers still think it's easier to work on a printed copy (commonly referred to as a hard copy).

LEARNING TO EDIT

An excellent way to hone your editing skills is to reverse the creation process by rereading favorite books, stories, poems, articles, etc. After enjoying the overall impression the work makes on you, try taking it apart. Why did the author choose *this* way to begin instead of *that* way? Identify where the beginning ends and the middle begins. Look for specific words that evoke one or more of the five senses: seeing, hearing, tasting, smelling, touching. How does what the characters say and do help you imagine them as real people? Try to rewrite a passage using your own words. Is your version as effective as the original work? Can you identify specific things the author placed early in the story that plant certain ideas in the reader's mind and point to things that happen later? What happened during the most crucial point in the story? How did the main character react? What if the main character had acted differently?

This dismantling process works equally well for nonfiction and poetry. For another perspective, try this process on works you *didn't* enjoy. Try to determine exactly what turned you off. For instance, did you have trouble identifying with the main characters? If yes, was it because of the writing (story construction, word choice, directions the plot took, etc.) or just because you aren't interested in this type of story? Was the story too predictable or meaningless or absurd?

BECOMING A SUCCESSFULLY PUBLISHED WRITER

The level at which you are now, as well as your chances for publishing success, depend not so much on your age or experience but on your *attitude*. Writers who are determined to publish usually succeed. They may be serious about pursuing a writing career or just enjoy it as a hobby. Occasionally, getting published occurs by happy accident like it did for me. (But don't count on continued success this way. The odds of it happening again are probably worse than winning the grand prize in the Publisher's Clearing House sweepstakes.) Most often, and especially to get the most rewarding results, getting published takes dedication, persistence, patience, lots of hard work, good writing, plus a willingness to learn *who* is publishing *what*.

MORE ABOUT YOU

Do you believe in yourself? Are you willing to risk rejection? Are you anxious to improve? Will you spend the time it takes to learn what editors want to see in the manuscripts they receive? If you can honestly answer yes to these questions, you are ready to travel the writing and publishing road.

Think about what is in store for you in the future. What writing and publishing goals do you have? How do you plan to reach them? How much time are you willing to devote? From whom can you get help? Five years from now, what will you have written? In ten years? Twenty?

Other questions will help you identify what kinds of writing to pursue. Ask yourself, What am I interested in? What are my hobbies? What types of writing do I like to read? What sort of writing turns me off? What's my opinion of the world today? If I could go anywhere, where would I go? If I could be anything, what would I be? Who do I admire most? What traits do I look for in a friend? What do my enemies have in common? How are they different?

Take time to jot down your answers to these and other questions that make your mind search for answers. Explore them in journal or diary entries. Often we really don't know what we think until we see our thoughts spelled out on paper. Later on you can refer to these answers as you decide what to write about and as you research which markets and contests to enter.

From time to time, reevaluate your responses. Have you reached your short-term goals? Are you closer to your long-term ones? Is it time to set new ones? How has your outlook changed? What experiences have had the most influence on you?

As mentioned in the first "Author's Tip" in chapter one, Janet E. Grant's book, *The Young Person's Guide to Becoming a Writer*, is an excellent book for serious young writers. Through a series of exercises, forms and "food for thought" narratives, Ms. Grant helps young writers develop their talents. She demonstrates how to experiment with different writing techniques, how to develop character sketches and how to work in different genres. More importantly, Ms. Grant (once a young writer herself) shows you how to personally and objectively evaluate your own writing skills, as well as brainstorm and set goals. It's almost like having an accomplished professional writer as a personal mentor.

Writing is exercising the brain and pouring the sweat out on paper. The more thinking you do, the more you'll find to write about. The more you write, the more work you'll have to publish.

Chapter Three

The Basics of Getting Published

Have you ever played Pin the Tail on the Donkey? It can be pretty hard to get that tail to stick in just the right place while wearing a blindfold. Yet, a lot of writers try to get published in much the same way. They sort of grope their way around hoping their manuscript will land in the right place. Writing and marketing can be both fun and challenging, but if you approach it as a professional writer would instead of like a game, your chances of getting published will improve dramatically.

Acting in a professional manner and trying to write like an adult are not the same thing. Trying to write like an adult is one of the worst things a young writer can do. One of the best things you have going for you is your youth. Write to express your feelings and your ideas; don't try to mimic what you think an adult writer might do. Believe in yourself. Tell the stories you need to tell, and tell them in your own way.

Acting professionally also has nothing to do with age. It means behaving in a courteous, responsible way. It's learning what's expected and taking the time to provide it. Your interest in reading this book indicates that you're not only eager to get published but are interested in how to do it right.

This chapter and the next explain the right things to do. If I didn't think you were smart enough and ambitious enough to do them, I wouldn't have bothered spending so much time and trouble to share them with you. And if there weren't a lot of editors and contest sponsors who believed you could do it, and do it well, the last half of this book would be pretty empty. Here, then, are the basics of getting published.

Author's Tip:

Many beginning writers have a hard time understanding both the creative development and the visible changes their manuscripts may go through from draft to polished, properly formatted manuscript to final printed page. In 1992, a marvelous paperback book was published that not only describes in detail how one writer got an idea and transformed it into a book, but includes reproductions of handwritten notes, drafts in various stages, comments from editors requesting changes, and copies of printed pages before and after final editing.

The book is titled *James A. Michener's Writer's Handbook: Explorations in Writing and Publishing.* Even the youngest writers will find it interesting and learn from it.

LOOK SHARP—PREPARE IT LIKE A PRO

Prepare your finished manuscript following the standard formats described in chapter four. Proofread again making any needed corrections before submitting your work.

Occasionally, editors or contests will want, or allow, manuscripts formatted in a slightly different way. For example, while most editors insist that manuscripts be typed, a few will accept handwritten work. Some contests do not want judges to know any personal information about the entrant, so they will want the author's name and address to appear on the entry form but not on the manuscript itself. The preferred format for individual poems, plays or scripts also varies between certain markets and contests. Under most circumstances, editors and contests will expect to see manuscripts prepared using standard formats.

If you have made only one or two small mistakes per page on a final draft, neatly correct them. To make them as inconspicuous as possible, use a lead pencil or black ink pen. (Editors generally will use colored pens or pencils to indicate where corrections or edits are needed.) Acceptable handmade corrections include

- Indicating that two letters or words have been accidentally reversed (transposed). words Two

- Drawing a thin line through a word or short line that should be deleted. [~~word~~]
- Correcting a misspelled word by drawing a line through it and printing it correctly in neat letters directly above or in the nearest margin. [~~ecorect~~] *correct*
- Using a small arrow to indicate a missing word or two and adding the word by printing it neatly as you would when correcting a spelling error. [add ⌢word] *the*
- Using the paragraph symbol (¶) to indicate where a new paragraph should have been started.
- Placing a forward slash (/) between two words that have run together.

If you find more mistakes or if your page has a sloppy appearance, take the time to make a fresh copy. *Then check it again.* This is for your benefit. Since editors cannot meet with you personally and have no idea whether or not you are a good writer, the first impression they get will be from the overall appearance of your manuscript. By sending a neatly prepared and properly formatted manuscript, you will be telling editors and contest judges that you care enough about what you write to give it the best chance of acceptance.

Think of yourself as a busy editor out to buy a new pair of shoes. Where would you expect to find the best quality? In a store where the shoes are soiled, mismatched and thrown in a jumble on a display table for you to sort out? Or in a store where the shoes are neat and clean and paired together for easy selection?

Make it easy for editors and judges to read your material. They will respect the time and effort you have taken. When the choice is between two manuscripts of close or equal merit, the one that looks better will always win.

SIMULTANEOUS SUBMISSIONS

Plan to submit (send) one manuscript at a time to a market or contest. In other words, do not submit the same manuscript for consideration elsewhere until you have received an answer from the one before. Mailing the same manuscript to more than one place at a time is called a "multiple" or "simultaneous" submission. Editors become extremely annoyed when they discover that a manuscript they have spent time and trouble to read is accepted somewhere else before they have had a chance to make their decision. Many guidelines specifically state: *No simultaneous submissions accepted.* Although some adult writers do make simultaneous submissions occasionally, my advice to young writers is to always stick with the one-to-one rule.

Occasionally, writers are encouraged to submit several poems together to a single editor or contest. This is not a violation of the "one manuscript to one market at a time" rule because you are not asking two people to consider the same material at the same time. Again, read individual guidelines for details.

You may, of course, send different manuscripts out to different markets and contests. In fact, writers are encouraged to have several things "in the mail" at the same time. More about that later.

STUDY AND COMPARE OPPORTUNITIES— THE WHY

Sending your very best work will not help you get published if you submit it to the wrong place. But how can you tell for sure which is the *right* place?

The answer, unfortunately, is you can't. Not if the right place means the place where your manuscript is guaranteed to be accepted.

But there are ways to determine which are *appropriate* places for you to try, places where a particular manuscript has a good chance of being seriously considered. Keep in mind that an appropriate market or contest for one manuscript may not be an appropriate place to send the next one. And one that is good for your friend may not be the best place for you.

Studying and comparing market opportunities is a multistep process. It is also a process that needs to be redone from time to time because the publishing field is not like a stone wall that stays the same year after year. It is more like a meadow. New opportunities sprout like wildflowers while others fade and die away. A few markets and contests last, getting bigger and branching out like strong oak trees as the years go by, but even they go through changes. Editors come and go, staffs may move to new locations, editorial policies are changed, regular departments and special columns may be added or deleted, they may decide to publish more fiction or less poetry or—best of all—raise the rates they pay writers for their manuscripts.

—AND THE HOW

First, you need to determine which markets and contests are the most appropriate for you. That means understanding which ones accept submissions from someone of your age, writing ability or experience, location and interests. You also need to decide which of these markets are of most interest to you.

Part of this work has been done for you. Of the many thousands of markets and contests open to freelance writers (that means a writer who does not regularly work for the publisher), only those who are interested in receiving submissions from young people (ages eighteen and under) have been included in this book. However, not all of these opportunities will be appropriate for each reader. As you read through the listings, you may want to make a list or place a mark next to those that sound like they would be appropriate for you to try.

Try not to become overly enthusiastic at this point. Because you are naturally creative, dozens of new ideas for articles, stories and books will suddenly burst like kernels of hot popcorn in your head as you read through the listings. (Tip: Keep paper and pencil handy to jot down ideas so you won't forget them.) Be selective. For now, try to pick from five to fifteen markets and/or contests that seem to want the same types of manuscripts you have already completed or plan to write.

You may want to make two lists, one with opportunities that look good for a specific manuscript and another of markets that pique your interest or seem especially suited to you.

Next, send for the writer's guidelines and/or contest rules from each of the places on your list. If possible, also request a sample copy or borrow one from the library. You don't need to request materials from everyone at once, but you should make requests from at least five. That way you'll have a variety to study and

Author's Tip:

If you have friends or classmates[1] who are also interested in getting published, you can share the chore of collecting sample copies and writer's guidelines. Whether you do it alone or with others, be sure to keep a master list of what you have already sent for and received. Note on it the date you received the guidelines and the issue of the sample copy. Send for updated material every year or so.

compare. Be sure to enclose a self-addressed and stamped business-size (#10) envelope (commonly referred to as SASE), or whatever the listing says to include, with your request.

When the guidelines and samples arrive, read them thoroughly. Study each individually to get a feel for the type of material published in it. Read *everything*: featured pieces, author blurbs, letters to the editor, editor and/or publisher's messages, table of contents, even the advertisements. Watch for announcements of special contests or invitations to send your writing. Just as no two writers are the same, neither are any two markets or contests. There are *always* some differences no matter how similar they may look at first.

Ask yourself some questions:

- Is this what I expected?
- Did I misinterpret the information contained in the listing?
- Do I still think this is an appropriate place to send my work?
- Can I tell how much competition I would have submitting here?
- Would I be proud to have my manuscript published here?
- What new ideas for writing occur to me as I read this?

In addition to all this studying and comparing of opportunities, you need to take a good, objective look at any manuscript you

---

[1]Collecting, studying and comparing publishing opportunities is a valuable experience that helps young people develop both their creative and critical thinking skills. Teachers should make sure students take an active part in the process, rather than compiling the information for them.

are planning to submit. Make a list of its identifying features. For instance:

- Is it a short story, poem, script, essay, etc.?
- What is its genre or subject matter? That might be mystery, adventure, humor, science fiction, etc., but could also be sports-related, outdoorsy, about school or church.
- If there is a main character, how old is he or she? What interests does he or she show in the story? What happens in the story?
- What is the setting for your piece?
- What age reader would it appeal to most? Someone your own age, younger, older?
- Do you have illustrations or photographs that would be appropriate to submit with it?
- How long is it?
- Has it ever been published before?
- How well written is it? Do you think it is one of your very best pieces? Or just pretty good?

Now comes the hard part. Taking into consideration all that you know about your manuscript, of the markets and contests that still seem appropriate places for you to consider, ask yourself two questions:

1. At which one or two places would my manuscript have the *easiest* chance of getting accepted?

2. Which one or two represent the *highest quality or most prestigious places* (could be a well-known publication, one that offers payment or one of particular interest to you) that are appropriate for a manuscript like mine? Be aware that your chances of getting a manuscript accepted in these markets may be lower because the editors receive many submissions, publish only a few pieces like yours in each issue (such as just one short story), say that they are very selective, or have some other reason (perhaps it's an adult market).

If you are very lucky, the answer to these two questions will be the same. Most likely, however, you'll have the names of four different opportunities. Do you submit to the easier one or go for the biggest reward first? That's a choice you will have to make yourself. I know many writers who have almost everything they submit accepted the first or second time out. But they always pick the easiest markets.

Personally, I prefer being rejected by the best and working my way down my list. (Actually, I prefer getting accepted by the best!) You'll have to decide for yourself. The important thing is to pick several solid possibilities so if it isn't accepted by your first choice, you are ready to send it back out right away to the next choice on your list.

If it gets rejected by all four, then start a new list. While you're at it, reevaluate the merits of your manuscript. Could it use a little rewriting or more polishing before you tackle that second list of appropriate opportunities? Did you receive any useful comments on it? (See the section "Some Words About Rejection" on page 47 for some tips on dealing with rejection and evaluating editor's comments.)

LOCAL, REGIONAL AND SPECIAL OPPORTUNITIES

Some of the best, and often the most appropriate, markets and contests for young writers are in your own neighborhoods, cities and states, or relate to a special interest or circumstance. In every edition of the *Market Guide for Young Writers*, I list several opportunities that are representative of what can be found in many areas around the country. The TAWC Spring Writing Contest, for instance, is limited to amateur writers in Michigan, but every state has some type of writer's group that publishes a magazine or newsletter or sponsors either regular or occasional writing contests.

Don't overlook writing "Letters to the Editors," editorials or guest opinion pieces, and feature or filler stories about people and events of interest in your community. Many writers overlook writing nonfiction pieces, yet they are much easier to get published, and usually pay. This is especially true of magazines that may publish only one or two poems or short stories but ten or more columns, tips, articles, how-to's and other types of nonfiction in each issue. Obviously, the more of something they publish, the better the chances of getting that something accepted.

Author's Tip:

....

Writers interested in targeting some of the easier nonfiction markets should read Connie Emerson's book, *The 30-Minute Writer, How to Write and Sell Short Pieces.* It includes dozens of tips and ideas for writing personal essays, humor, opinion pieces, reviews, anecdotes, mini-profiles and more.

Your local newspaper is also a great place to get a job as a stringer reporter or columnist. Newspapers, especially smaller dailies and weeklies, are always short staffed. My local paper (and the one where I was first published) is constantly looking for young writers interested in covering school sports and community events.

Whether you reply to an ad or go in on your own, be prepared to answer any questions the editor might ask you. (You may want to do a practice interview with a parent or friend acting the part of the editor.) Try to anticipate his reaction, any objections that might be raised. What will you answer if you're asked what you want in return? Are you looking for a paid job (most likely a set fee—in 1971, when I started, I got two dollars for each weekly column published—so don't count on getting rich. On an up note, my column did run above Erma Bombeck's), or are you willing to work for just the opportunity to get published and learn more about the business. (Tip: If you apply to a nonprofit organization, be prepared to donate your services. At a regular business, however, try first for a paying position even if it's a tiny amount. Part-time reporters should receive at least minimum wage for time on the job, but you may not be paid for the time it takes you to actually write your article.)

Figure out in advance how you will present yourself: You need to show enthusiasm, dedication, persistence, and that you can be trusted to meet deadlines. You must show that you are willing to accept criticism and to rewrite and polish when necessary. Editors will also want to know that you won't get discouraged or ornery if your section or piece gets moved or cut altogether occasionally because the editor decided something else was more important (you most likely will not be consulted on this).

Have samples of your work with you, or mail a few of your best pieces with a query letter. Be very selective; they won't be as interested in how much you've written as whether you show real promise as a writer. For local interviews, it's acceptable to take along a scrapbook binder with your pieces (published and/or unpublished). Since the editor may not have time to read through them immediately, have a few photocopies of your best pieces handy that you can leave behind.

You might also try local radio and television stations, especially local cable and PBS stations, and the community relations directors at area hospitals or other civic-minded organizations. And, don't forget to get involved at school.

Special interest magazines and other periodicals you may read from time to time also offer young writers excellent opportunities. Always be on the lookout for one-of-a-kind contests or invitations to submit material. A few years ago, for instance, The Learning Company, which makes computer software programs for children, and The Tandy Company, which makes Tandy computers, sponsored a Silly Story Contest for students using one of The Learning Company's software programs. It was a fun, one-time contest that drew thousands of entries from eager young writers.

For special interest magazines, you will often be submitting right alongside adults. But if you target publications that are of high interest to you, such as a hobby, computer or pet market (anything that you read regularly), you will be able to compete on equal footing. Many times, because you have taken the trouble to learn the basics of getting published, you'll have a better chance of getting published than adult readers who don't realize how to prepare a manuscript properly or edit their work to make it the best. *Lifeprints*, which limits submissions to those from writers who are visually impaired, is just one example of a specialty market listed here.

Writer's Digest, *The Writer* and *Byline* offer writers updated market and contest information in each month's issues. If you are *very* interested in writing, you might want to subscribe to one of these magazines. *Byline* is the best one for beginning and young writers. But I know writers as young as ten who regularly read

Writer's Digest.

Writing and marketing are ongoing processes. Try to keep several pieces (to different places, of course) in the mail so if one comes limping home, you can still hope the best for the others.

And don't stop writing while you wait to hear from an editor. Get started on a new project right away.

THE BIG "NO"

Editors will sometimes reject even well-written material. There are a number of reasons. But by far the biggest reason is something editors call *inappropriate submissions.* This means that that particular publication or contest *never* uses the type of material that was submitted. The subject of the manuscript may be of little or no interest to that magazine's readers. It may be a short story when only nonfiction is used. It may be hundreds of words over the preferred length. The wording or topic may be too easy or too hard for the readers. The reasons are many but, in general, they make a manuscript inappropriate for that particular publication.

Editors waste a lot of time and energy each month dealing with inappropriate submissions—time they could have spent reading and replying to *your* submission. In fact, so many inexperienced writers (old and young) submit inappropriate material that some editors will no longer consider unsolicited manuscripts. (Unsolicited means that the editor did not specifically ask to see the material before receiving it from the author. All of the markets and contests listed in this book will consider unsolicited material from young writers if submitted properly.)

The only way to avoid making an inappropriate submission is to take the time to study the market and contest information carefully. Send for and study the guidelines or tip sheets offered. Buy, send for or borrow a sample issue[2] if you are not familiar with the publication. Then read it objectively to determine if your manuscript would fit in.

---

[2]Occasionally, free or low-cost sample issues of a publication are not available. This is the exception, however. If at all possible, make it a point to read one or more issues of a publication before submitting material to it.

Author's Tip:

....

If you've ever had a little brother or sister want to tag after you wherever you're going, then you know how an editor feels to receive inappropriate submissions. He doesn't have any use for them, and after trying to explain this nicely a few times with no result, he gets frustrated and doesn't ever want to be asked again!

Pay close attention to the "Editor's Remarks" and the "Sponsor's Remarks" sections in the listings. Here you will find special advice, from the editor or sponsor of that publication or contest, about submitting material. If your manuscript does not closely match their requirements, look for a market that does. You might consider rewriting a manuscript to meet the guidelines of a specific market. This is often possible when a manuscript meets most of the requirements but is either too long or too short or when the subject and genre are OK but you haven't emphasized the right perspective or angle.

EXPECT TO BE EDITED

Once your work has been accepted by an editor (and even some contests), there is a good chance that it will need further editing before being published. This happens to all writers no matter how carefully they have edited and polished their manuscripts before turning them in.

There are many reasons an editor may edit or make changes to your manuscript. It may have been too long to fit the available space, or the editor may have felt a different word or phrase would make your message easier for readers to understand. This doesn't happen just with books or magazine stories but with all types of work.

Editors have a responsibility (it's a large part of their job) to edit material when they think it is necessary. Thankfully, most editors will only make minor changes on their own. And most of the time you'll discover that the changes an editor has made in your manuscript have made it better.

Occasionally, you may not like the changes an editor makes. If the piece has already been published, there really isn't anything you can do about it except try to forget what happened and go on to your next project. If you absolutely *hate* the changes made, do not submit to that editor again. There are many other markets from which to choose.

Try to view any change from the editor's point of view. If you can't seem to get over it, break a few pencils or kick a few wastebaskets until you calm down. Think long and hard before writing or calling an editor to complain. Consider this message from Dawn Brettschneider Korth, former editor of *Straight*:

> Please tell teens that it's normal to have your work edited. I've had complaints from teen writers when I changed *one word* of a poem—when it was misspelled and used incorrectly! A sixteen-year-old threatened to sue the company over a poem in which I reversed two lines to make his rhyme scheme consistent. Such scathing letters make editors reluctant to deal with inexperienced teen writers. All we want to do is help them.

WORKING WITH AN EDITOR

When editors feel that all or parts of a manuscript need to be rewritten or revised, they will often make suggestions and ask the writer who submitted the manuscript to make them. If this happens, you will have to decide whether you think making the changes will improve your work. (Please note that even if you change a manuscript according to an editor's suggestions, it is not a guarantee that the revised work will be accepted.)

If you don't understand what you are being asked to do, or if you don't agree with all the suggestions, take time to discuss your feelings with the editor by phone (if invited to) or in a letter.

Be prepared to explain why you think some or all of the suggested changes are unnecessary and/or make new suggestions of your own. This give-and-take between writers and editors happens all the time. Don't be afraid of it. It's not very different from the way coaches work with their players. If, by some chance, you and the editor can't come to an agreement about what needs to be done, you can always decide not to have it published there. Most times you will be free to submit the manuscript somewhere else.

All manuscripts get edited, even those by famous authors. It is a necessary, though sometimes uncomfortable, part of the publishing process.

The more you know about writing, editing and publishing, the easier it will be for you to understand and work with an editor throughout the editing and publishing process.

KNOW YOUR RIGHTS AS AN AUTHOR

When you write something, by law you automatically become the copyright holder (owner) of that manuscript. If an editor agrees to publish your manuscript, he will "buy the rights" to it. Often magazines, newspapers and newsletters buy "first serial rights" or "one-time rights," which give them permission to publish your manuscript one time. Then the rights are returned to you, and you may offer the same manuscript to another editor for "second" or "reprint" rights.

A number of publications and some contests buy "all rights," which means that once you agree the publication can publish your manuscript (or artwork, photographs, etc.), the work becomes *their* property (they hold the copyright), and it is no longer yours. You may not send it to another market or contest. Even though you no longer own the copyright, if it is published, you will be credited as the author.

Be aware that for legal reasons (and often to make things simpler for staff members), many markets and contests that accept submissions from young people assume all rights to that material whether or not it is published. You will notice that some markets and contests state that policy in their listings. Even if it is not listed here, it will be spelled out on the guidelines or rules sheet or in a letter or contract sent to you when your work is accepted.

Professional writers and other adults seriously pursuing publication of their material are often advised *not* to sell all rights if at all possible. However, the situation is very different for young writers. Since many of the best opportunities for young writers are also the ones that insist on buying all rights, I personally think young people (and many beginning adult writers) have more to gain from being published by such markets than retaining copyright to their material. It is a decision that you and a trusted adult should make together. Take into consideration the manuscript in question and the reputation of the market or contest with whom you are dealing. Also keep in mind that many markets that buy all rights will reassign them to the writer at a later date upon written request, particularly if the writer is planning to reprint the material in a noncompetitive way.

For example, I once sold all rights to my research and interview notes about farm accidents to a top-quality agricultural magazine. Later, when I wanted to reuse some of the material in a safety article targeted to high school students, I wrote to the editor, explained the situation and asked for reassignment of my rights. He was happy to comply. He had no further use of the material, and the market to which I planned to submit was not in direct competition to his.

On the other hand, especially for teens, it never hurts to try negotiating with an editor. Suggest to him that you prefer to sell only first serial rights. Don't be surprised if he just says, "OK." Buying all rights saves some paperwork, but a publication that doesn't intend to reuse your manuscript in some way will have no objection to buying first or even reprint rights instead.

(Incidentally, I had to ask Matthew Cheney for permission to reprint part of his story that appears as a sample manuscript in the next chapter even though the story had appeared in two separate issues of *Merlyn's Pen: The National Magazine of Student Writing*. However, I needed reprint permission from Landmark Editions to reprint two of Amity Gaige's poems that are included in her book, *We are a Thunderstorm*, even though the book's copyright is registered in her name. I tell you this to illustrate how every situation is different. How did I know from whom to seek permission? I asked!)

Negotiating a book contract is more complicated and confusing than dealing with magazines and newspapers. There are many, many things to take into consideration. Most publishing companies offer writers what is known as a "standard book contract." Unfortunately, what is standard at one company is different at another. All writers (young and old) are advised to have any

Author's Tip:

For young writers (and their parents and teachers) interested in learning more about contracts, I highly recommend *Negotiating a Book Contract, A Guide for Authors, Agents and Lawyers*, by Mark L. Levine. This slim handbook takes you step-by-step through the negotiating process and explores in simple language what the various contract clauses, legal terms and publisher's offers mean.

---

contract offered to them checked by a reputable literary agent[3] or lawyer familiar with the publishing industry. All writer's organizations offer contract information and/or trustworthy advice. (Note: Young writers are welcome to join the National Writer's Association, which offers such services to members.)

A number of questions in chapter six, "Answers to Questions Young Writers Ask Most," deal with these and related issues.

You should also know that the copyright of a message or library file of an online information service, such as GEnie, CompuServe or America Online, is usually held by its author. You must obtain the author's permission to make further use or to distribute any portion of a message or file.

Copyrights can be confusing. More information about current copyright law is available by sending $3.75 with a request for Copyright Office Circular 92, stock number 030-002-00168-3, to
Superintendent of Documents
U.S. Government Printing Office
Washington DC 20401-9371
Forms and instructions for registering your copyright with the U.S. copyright office are available free by writing or calling
Copyright Office
Library of Congress
Washington DC 20559
(202) 707-9100

---

[3]Literary agents seldom represent young writers, and normally, there is nothing a literary agent can or would be willing to do for an amateur writer that he can't do for himself.

It now costs twenty dollars to register a copyright. Remember, however, you *do not* need to register your copyright. As soon as you put your thoughts down in some type of fixed form (on paper, audiotape, film, computer disk, etc.), your work is automatically protected by law. You are the legal copyright holder until you give it away. Neither ideas nor titles, however, are protected by copyright.

CONTEST TIPS

Contests offer young writers some of the best opportunities to get published. And you'll want to pay just as much attention to writing and editing your entry as you do with any manuscript you are planning to submit. But contests also require an extra amount of care so you don't sabotage your chances before you even get started. Keep the following additional guidelines in mind.

When entering writing contests, be sure to follow all the stated rules *exactly*. If a contest says you may submit only *one* poem, don't send *two* of your poems. They *both* may be disqualified. And you'll lose any money you may have sent for an entry fee without any possibility of winning.

If a contest states that entries *must be typed*, be sure to type them. Don't think a judge will overlook the mistakes you make when entering a contest. Chances are the judge will never see your entry. Most contests have a secretary or someone else to open entries and read them to see if the rules have been followed. Only those entries that have followed all the rules will be sent on to the judge or judges.

Don't be a loser before you get started.

Entering a writing contest can be an exciting and rewarding experience. To boost your chances of winning, follow these additional tips and suggestions:

Send for a complete list of the contest rules, regulations and eligibility requirements. Unfortunately, space does not allow for all the rules for every contest to be listed in this book. It is best to send an SASE to receive the rules or guidelines.

Follow all the rules exactly. This includes where your name, address and other information are to be placed; the number of entries you may submit; and how manuscripts are to be prepared. If the rules do not give specific guidelines for this information, follow the standard formats provided in this book for submitting manuscripts to an editor.

Don't forget to include entry fees or required forms with your submission. Some contests for young people request that a parent, guardian or teacher include a *signed* statement verifying that the entry has been written entirely by the young person. Be sure to include this statement if it is required.

Don't limit yourself to contests designed just for young writers. Many talented young writers have placed or won in contests open to adults. However, you have the best chance of winning in contests that (1) are for or have categories open to young people only, especially if they also have age groups; (2) are specifically or exclusively sponsored for young people in your local, regional or statewide community; or (3) focus on a topic of special interest or importance to you.

If possible, try to read the winning entries of an annual contest from the previous year. Just as reading back issues of magazines will help you understand a publication's editorial preferences, so will studying past winners of a contest. Yet, don't let this stop you from entering something that may seem a little different.

For example, Amity Gaige won first place in the 1989 National Written & Illustrated by . . . Awards Contest for her submissions of poems and photographs, *We are a Thunderstorm*. That same year Adam Moore was named a Gold Award winner for his nonfiction book, *Broken Arrow Boy*, which recounted his experience recuperating from a serious accident. Though Adam did most of the writing and illustrating, it also contained some material done by other people. Nearly all past submissions (and winners) of this contest were fiction stories with drawn illustrations, yet Amity and Adam won with entries that met all the contest requirements but were a little different.

Remember, too, that judges often change from year to year.

Don't be discouraged if you don't win. Most contests award prizes for only first, second and third place. Some also name a number of honorable mention winners. A judge, like you, has his personal likes and dislikes. Out of the many entries, a judge must choose only a few, and he will make his selection according to what he likes best. Another judge, or editor, may like your work better.

SOME WORDS ABOUT REJECTION

To become a published young writer takes more than enthusiasm and talent. You must also be aware of opportunities. You must be willing to study and follow the guidelines set by editors and contest sponsors. You must understand that while some manuscripts are rejected for poor writing, others are rejected for reasons not readily apparent to the writer. These include the time needed by a publication to print an issue, the space available for printing manuscripts, how many manuscripts are received for consideration, the number of manuscripts that have already been accepted for publication and the personal preferences of the editors, staff and judges.

Rejection is disappointing. It hurts.

But rejection must be put in perspective. The editor or judge has not rejected *you* personally. He has simply picked someone else's manuscript that better suited his needs at that moment—much like you might consider one pair of shoes over another of equal quality.

You should feel especially honored if an editor or judge sends back any constructive advice, comments or criticism about your manuscript.

Editors are busy people who deal with hundreds of manuscripts each year. They cannot afford either the time or expense to write to you personally about why your manuscript was rejected. Most times you will receive a generic, preprinted note known as the "form rejection slip."

The wording on a form rejection is usually so vague it is difficult to tell exactly why a manuscript was rejected. There is, however, a sort of unofficial code many editors use to signal writers that their manuscript has some merit. It is a busy editor's way of offering encouragement. The code goes something like this:

If an editor *signs* his name himself, then something in your manuscript caught his eye. It may be the flow of your words, your ability to make a point, your characterization within a story or something else. You are on the right track. Keep at it!

If an editor jots a word or two of encouragement, such as "good idea" or "nice try," he means your manuscript was better than most but perhaps lacked that certain spark that would have made it outstanding.

If an editor writes a few words of advice or criticism, such as "your characters are a little weak" or "the plot needs tightening up," he means your manuscript was good enough to be given careful consideration. With a little more effort, you may have a winner.

Of course, there are variations on this code. Some editors try hard to encourage promising young writers and will send a short, personal note rather than a rejection slip. Others simply do not have the time to spare. And sometimes a rejection slip that simply says, "Sorry. This does not fit our needs at this time," means just that. They can't use it whether or not they like it.

Rather than dreading a bit of criticism, look forward to it. It is usually easier to pinpoint minor flaws in a well-written manuscript than in a poorly written one where the trouble is so spread out, it is hard to offer any meaningful help in a short note. An editor who takes the time to offer encouragement, either by praise or constructive criticism, deserves your appeciation. Whether you make use of that advice is up to you.

You may be lucky enough to find yourself a published young writer with your first attempt. Then again, you may need to submit material many times before, finally, one of your manuscripts is selected for publication. If you have a strong desire to write, never be discouraged. With practice, your writing will get better and better, and so will your chances of being published.

SET THE RIGHT GOALS

Be careful not to set the wrong goals for yourself. A writer whose only goal is to be published will likely experience many more disappointments than will a writer who hopes to be published one day but whose goal is to enjoy writing and become a better writer.

It is unrealistic to expect everything you write to win a contest or be accepted for publication. Consider how a musician prepares for a performance.

She may continue to take lessons, trying out new pieces, practicing over and over again the pieces she has learned in the past. For her actual performance, she will not play every piece she has practiced. Instead, she will pick and choose those she plays and enjoys the best. She also considers which pieces she feels the audience will like hearing.

As a writer, your audience is your reader; your performance, your manuscript. Pick and choose manuscripts you feel represent your best work. And when choosing which markets and contests to submit to, consider what you have to offer that would interest the readers of those publications.

Chapter Four

How to Prepare Your Manuscript

Next to the care you put into creating your work and the attention you pay to selecting an appropriate market, nothing is more important than how to present it to an editor or contest judge. You want your manuscript to look crisp, clean and polished so the editor will concentrate on what you have written. This is especially important for teen writers targeting adult markets and contests.

It is extremely important that you follow the specific guidelines requested by a particular market or contest if they differ from the standards, *especially for contests*. Otherwise, your work may be rejected no matter how good it may be. Worse, some markets and contests won't return an inappropriate submission even if accompanied by an SASE. And *no* market or contest will assume responsibility for unsolicited manuscripts or original artwork or photographs.

With so many variations in policy, it's impossible to give specific advice for preparing all types of manuscripts, artwork and photos in this Guide. What follows are the general guidelines and formats that most magazines and contests will accept. They are easy to understand.

Resist all urges to use scented or colored paper, fancy typewriter type or decorative computer fonts, hand-drawn pictures in the margins or special bindings, folders or covers for your manuscripts or mailing envelopes. And, *please*, don't bother concocting any tests for an editor to pass such as turning a few pages upside down, backward or out of order. Many insecure amateur writers (young and old) do this thinking that if a manuscript is rejected and returned to them with the pages still mixed up, it proves that the editor didn't even bother to read their submission.

(These writers also prefer to think that editors are prejudiced against them or not smart enough to see what wonderful writers they are—anything to avoid admitting that their manuscripts could be improved, or that they chose inappropriate markets, or that it just wasn't possible for the editors to use their work.)

What they don't realize is that an annoyed editor will simply return a rejected manuscript in the same condition it arrived. Editors are delighted to discover new talent of any age, but they will shy away from working with writers who obviously do not trust them to do their jobs right.

Remember, there's nothing wrong with being a young, inexperienced writer. But if you are serious about getting published, you don't want to *look* like a young, inexperienced writer. Editors haven't time to be entertained by the way manuscripts are prepared. They have barely enough time to read and select submissions. Give your writing the best possible chance of attracting an editor's eye by following the formats outlined here. If you feel you need to overlook or bypass some of the guidelines, be sure you have a sound reason for doing so. This is one time where it's best to follow the logical side of your mind and not the creative side.

Of course, for very young writers who will be handprinting their material, the guidelines are less strict. In fact, a few markets and contests, such as *Stone Soup* and Written & Illustrated by . . . Awards Contest, want to receive a student's original handmade manuscripts and artwork. The majority of markets and contests, however, prefer to receive typewritten manuscripts. The original text and artwork (or photocopies of it) can be included along with the typed version.

GUIDELINES FOR STANDARD FORMAT

Whether you handwrite or type, there are some specific things to keep in mind.

Write or type on only one side of a page. Leave wide margins of at least one inch on all four sides of each sheet. Use only a standard typewriter pitch, such as pica, or a basic serif computer font that resembles typing, such as Courier or Times Roman, and prints 10 cpi (characters per inch). Always print your final draft using a good, clean black ribbon in your typewriter or printer, or use a laser printer[1]. (For handwritten guidelines, see page 57.)

The text of all manuscripts should be double-spaced. To double-space, set the line spacing on your machine to number two. This will leave a full line of empty space between each line of type. For those using computers, check your software directions for printing double-spaced. Depending on your software, double-spacing may or may not appear on your screen even though it will print correctly.

For typed work, always use regular twenty-pound white bond paper. Never use erasable typing paper for a final manuscript. It smudges and smears too easily and may give an editor's sleeve an unwanted tie-dyed effect. For simple mistakes, use a light film of liquid correction fluid or the newer (and neater looking) liquid correction paper. If you need to correct or delete an entire sentence, try press-on correction tape available at office supply stores.

Pay attention to word length limits on fiction and nonfiction, and to line limits on poetry. If you send a manuscript with both writing and illustrations, try to include a second copy of the manuscript text prepared in the standard format.

Many typewriters and computers can justify (make even) the right margin. However, editors prefer that manuscripts have a "ragged" margin on the right side. (Note: The pages of this book are justified. For examples of ragged right margins see Figures 1 and 2.)

---

[1]Computers and word processors have become so commonplace, at least in the United States and Canada, that *typewritten* manuscripts refer to those created on any typewriter, word processor or computer. Listings that read *no computer printouts* or *no dot matrix* mean (1) they don't want to receive manuscripts printed on green and white striped computer paper and (2) they do not want to receive manuscripts printed with dot matrix printers that do not give a sharp, easily read impression. As long as your dot matrix printer prints out manuscripts with strong, black type, feel free to use it.

PAGE 1

You will use a slightly different format for the first page of your manuscript. (See Figure 1 on page 54.) At the top of your first page, starting at the left margin, use single-spacing to type your name, address, city, state, zip or postal code and telephone number with the area code. (*For contest entries, be sure to check where this information should go.*)

Next type your Social Security number. If you don't have a Social Security number, include your date of birth. Editors must have this information in their files before paying writers for material. On some submissions, it is appropriate to put the exact or approximate word length of your manuscript across from your name, next to the right margin. I also like to include the date I mailed my manuscript. You can easily add this later just before mailing by printing it neatly with a black pen. (Be sure to put the date you are mailing it, not the date you originally wrote it.)

A copyright notice is not really necessary, but it is OK to include it if you choose. Copyright notices are most often placed on poetry submissions, or manuscripts that are being sent to small, literary magazines, newspapers or newsletters that are not copyrighted. This will encourage the editor to include your copyright notice when your poem or other manuscript is published.

With the exception of your first page, plan on twenty-six lines of manuscript type on each page. If you find yourself always typing too close to the bottom of the page, try marking lightly with a pencil where your last line of type should be. Then erase the line later.

Typing the same number of lines on each page will make it easier to estimate the number of words in your finished manuscript. With proper margins and twenty-six lines of type, you will average two hundred and fifty words to a page.

Drop about one-third of the way down the page and using capital letters, type the title of your manuscript. Under the title, center the word "by," then center your name the way you wish it to read in print.

Switch your typewriter (or computer format) to double-space, drop down two lines and begin your story or article. Editors will use the empty space that you have left on the top of your first

---

Matthew Cheney   *word count* → About xxx words
00000 Street   *date* → September 1990
City, ST Zip code
↗ (000) 555-0000
(SS# 000-00-0000
↘*Your name,*
address, phone,
SS# here

THE NAUGA HUNTERS ← *title*

by

Matthew Cheney ← *author*

(*Start your story here*
↳ Hank, a thirteen-year-old boy with wispy brown hair

and spindly legs, spotted his little brother sitting on the

floor of the living room, watching a cartoon.

"Hey, Chucky, wanna go nauga hunting?" asked

Hank.

"What's a nauga?" asked Chucky, turning away from

the television.

"A nauga's a little thing—'bout the size of a cat—

Figure 1. Sample story format, page 1

page to write notes to the typesetter or copyeditor. Remember
to leave at least a one-inch margin at the bottom.

If you wish to include a title page, type it exactly as you would
the first page of your manuscript without including any of the
story. It is not necessary to include a title page with a manuscript
that is less than six to eight pages long.

PAGES 2, 3, 4 . . .

On each additional sheet, put your last name at the top left-hand
corner, followed by a forward slash and key words from your

last name
keyword from title
page number

Cheney ✓   ↳ NAUGA HUNTERS   ↳ 8

Hank stood up and jumped on his brother; they fell
to the damp ground. His eyes were sparkling and his lips
were unfirm. "Would I lie about that, you little . . ." His
voice faded as he pulled his arm up to punch Chucky.
Chucky was crying now. Hank stood up. "Forget it," he
said. "Supper'll be almost ready." Chucky was still on
the ground. "You comin'?"

Chucky pulled himself up and brushed off his rear
end. His face was streaked with tears. "Yup," he said
softly.

"Well, hurry up. Then after supper maybe we can go
hunt some more naugas. They ain't invisible at night."

"Thought you said they ain't real—like dragons."

"You *believed* me? Boy, maybe you are stupider than
you look." He turned around and headed for home, his
little brother trying to keep up.

THE END

Figure 2. Sample story format, second through last pages

title, and place the page number at the far right side of the same
line. The key title words may also be centered on the line. This
is called a "header." (See Figure 2 above.) This will help an
editor put your story back in order if it should get dropped or
shuffled around.

In book manuscripts with multiple chapters, I use both methods. Here's how the header for this page looked in my manuscript:

Author's Tip:

....

Most word processing software allow you to type in the header information once and it will automatically be repeated on each new page as needed. Check to make sure the page numbers are correct and in the right location.

Henderson/MGYW   Chapter 4   96

At the end of your manuscript, drop down two lines and center the words "The End." This may seem a little silly but a busy editor or typesetter will appreciate knowing for certain when he's come to the end of your piece. Journalists sometimes center the number thirty (-30-) instead of typing "The End." However, this symbol is not used very often anymore.

If you use a computer, you may also want to note the filename you use for your manuscript. This is especially useful if you are or expect to submit the manuscript on a floppy disk or via electronic transmission.

Never staple or bind your manuscript together in any way, except if the guidelines for a market or rules for a contest specifically tell you to do so. At the same time, however, use common sense. Short manuscripts, such as a few poems, a short story of up to six pages and articles of smiliar lengths may be held together by a simple, single paper clip to keep pages from getting lost. Consider using a binder style clip on bulkier manuscripts (25-50 pages), such as a longer collection of poems or short stories or in-depth nonfiction articles or book proposals. Larger manuscripts, such as a complete fiction novel, are best held together with two sturdy rubber bands, one going around lengthwise, the other across the width.

Of course, copies of manuscripts for your own files can be held together in whatever way you prefer. I often use a relatively new product called a Paper Gripper. It holds pages together with the ease of a paper clip and sturdiness of a staple, yet can easily be removed and either replaced or reused.

HANDWRITTEN MATERIAL

If possible, type your manuscript or have someone type it for you. However, some editors who are willing to receive material from young people thirteen and under do not mind receiving handwritten or handprinted material as long as it is neat and legible.

Unless you have excellent cursive handwriting, print your manuscript. Check editors' guidelines for their preferences. Use separate sheets of white-lined, loose-leaf paper for handwritten manuscripts. Wide-ruled paper is best if you tend to write big. If you use narrow-ruled paper, be sure to write on *every other line*. It will make it much easier for an editor to read.

Follow the same rules of format for preparing each page of your manuscript that apply to typewritten material.

Write on *only one side of the paper*. Remember to number each sheet.

Never use paper torn from a notebook. The pages tend to stick together and bits of the edges are always falling off, making a mess.

For very young writers, it is okay to use tablet paper with ruled lines. Remember to write on only one side of the sheet. For all writers, put the pages of your manuscript in order but leave them loose. Never bind or staple them together. (If a teacher is submitting several copies of her students' work, a paper clip may be used on each individual manuscript.)

Make corrections on handwritten material by drawing a line neatly through the mistake, then going on. If you make a lot of mistakes on one page, rewrite the whole page.

Use the same guidelines for mailing handwritten manuscripts as with typewritten material. Follow the market tip sheet for submitting art or photographs.

COMPUTER PRINTOUTS

As personal computers and word processors become more popular, editors are agreeing to read manuscripts prepared on a computer if a letter-quality or laser printer is used for the final draft. The print on many older dot matrix printers can be very light and hard to read. Sometimes photocopying the printed sheet will produce a copy dark enough to read easily. Keep the lighter printout as your copy, and send the photocopy to the editor. If you use tractor-fed paper be sure the finished size measures 8½″ × 11″ instead of larger-size computer paper. And as with traditional typed material, use a good, black ribbon for your final draft.

Follow the same guidelines as those for formatting and mailing typed material. Be sure to number your pages at the top right-hand corner (either by hand or through computer commands). Then, if necessary, remove the pinhole strips on each side and separate the printout sheets before mailing.

COMPUTER UPLOADS

Formatting for manuscripts that will be uploaded (that is, sent *from* your computer *to* another computer using a modem) depends on two important factors: (1) the type of communications software that operates your modem and (2) the preferences and requirements of each computer system to which you want to send material. Generally, manuscripts are saved and sent in standard ASCII or binary formats with hard carriage returns and line feeds inserted directly into the text.

By using one of these two forms, almost anyone who has access to the same online system can download manuscripts, usually stored in library files, to his own computer even if it is a different brand than yours. For instance, someone with an IBM-compatible computer system can upload a manuscript that someone with an Apple, Amiga, Commodore or some other brand can download.

(Remember that work uploaded to another computer system is still protected by copyright laws. You can download it to read for your own enjoyment, but you *cannot* sell it to others or use it as if it were your own.)

It is very important that you find out how to format a file in advance of trying to upload a manuscript. You will only waste valuable time and money if you don't. On commercial information services, such as CompuServe, GEnie and Prodigy, complete directions, guidelines, as well as additional tips and advice can be found stored in special library files. To find out what library and file has the information you need, leave a message for the systems operator (SYSOP) in charge of the special interest group (SIG) that you want to participate in. Also watch for special announcements either displayed on screen when you log on or in the printed magazine distributed to subscribers.

Procedures may differ for independent bulletin board systems (BBSs). You'll need to contact the SYSOP at each one by modem, through a regular phone call or by *snail* mail (writing a letter and sending it through the U.S. Postal Service!) to find out individual requirements. Other systems, such as the AT&T Learning Network and Internet World Wide Web sites may have special requirements and procedures. Contact them individually for complete information.

While formatting manuscripts for uploading may differ from traditional markets, you should still make sure to follow the general advice given in chapter one. Take time to rewrite, revise and polish before sending a manuscript. That means checking and correcting grammar, punctuation and spelling, too!

POETRY

Poems may be single- or double-spaced. You may want to type your poem as you wish it to appear, double-spacing between verses if necessary. Which you choose will often depend on how it looks on the page. (See Figures 3 and 4 for examples.)

Type only one poem per page. Include your name, address and other information on *each* page.

Poems should also be centered on the page. Practice typing the longest line of your poem to determine the correct tab position. Here's a tip for those who have trouble centering poems on the page: Using clean white paper, type your poem as you normally would, indenting one or two tab spaces at the beginning of each line. On a second sheet of paper, type your name and other information where it should appear. When you are finished, cut your poem neatly from the first sheet leaving as much white space as you can. Now position your poem where it should be and secure it lightly with one or two small strips of tape. Send clean photocopies of this master.

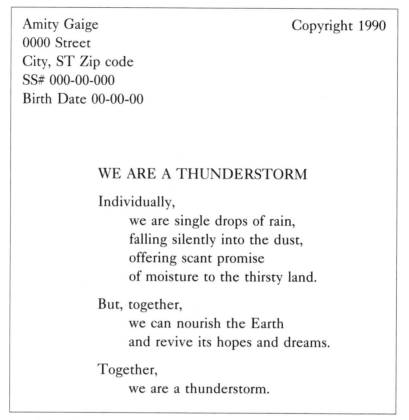

Figure 3. Sample poem

PLAYS AND SCRIPTS

The standard formats for preparing radio and theatre scripts often differ from the written formats for stories, poems, articles and fillers. It would be best to check with your librarian or audio/video teacher for help in locating a sample script. Study it carefully. Notice the differences in typing dialogue, description and sound effects. Use the sample script as a reference when you type your play, radio, film or video script.

Sample scripts may also be found in many language arts books. If you need more help, check with the drama teacher at your school, or ask for advice from someone involved with your community theater. Also check the guidelines provided by the markets and contests.

When submitting a play or script to a magazine, leave the

Vicki Larkin   Copyright 1992
0000 Street
City, ST Zip Code
SS# 000-00-000
Birth Date 00-00-00

OPOSSUM

It would be awesome
  to have a pet opossum.
It would be fun
  to have just one.
"Do you think, Mary Lou,
  that I should get two?"
"It would appeal to me,
  if you would get three."
I'd like to open the door
  and have marching in, four.
The house would sure be alive,
  if I brought home five.
They could help pick up sticks,
  if I decided on six.
It would be heaven,
  if I had seven
It would be cause to celebrate
  if I stopped at eight.
It would be fine,
  with just nine.
I would really like ten
  but then again . . .
It might not be that awesome
  to take care of an opossum.

Figure 4. Sample poem

Author's Tip:

··

Since I know next to nothing about play and script writing, I asked Sandy Asher, writer-in-residence at Drury College and an award-winning children's book writer and playwright, to share some tips and resources. Read her comments in Appendix A. Also see advice from Raymond F. Pape, associate editor for Baker's Plays, on page 180.

In addition, Jerry McGuire, video consultant for the National Writer's Association, recommends that you place your copyright notice on the bottom right-hand corner of the title page of your play or script. He also advises you to protect your script by registering it with the Writers Guild of America. Send a twenty dollar money order and a copy of your script to 555 West Fifty-seventh St., Suite 1230, New York NY 10019. The Guild will send you an official certificate and your property will be protected for ten years.

---

pages unbound, and double-space each line of the text. That's because a magazine plans to publish your work on the printed page, very much like a fiction short would be published.

However, most theater groups and contests prefer scripts that are professionally formatted in proper play, script or audio/video format and submitted in lightweight folders or grip binders. To allow for binding, set your left margin at one and one-half inches.

Older teens interested in submitting plays or scripts to professionally oriented markets and contests should consult a reference book such as *The Writer's Digest Guide to Manuscript Formats*, by Dian Dincin Buchman and Seli Groves. This book contains every single formatting detail you will need to prepare a polished, professional-looking manuscript. Guidelines are also included for writing treatments, synopses, outlines, concepts and story lines. There is even information for pitching ideas to television and movie agents or producers. The following simplified formats are suitable for submissions to many local and regional markets and contests and to several of the listings contained in this Guide.

In Figure 5 (page one of Beth Lewis's 1992 award-winning

play), notice how the set descriptions and actions of the performers are italicized. If you can't italicize type, use all caps.

Figure 6 shows the first page of *Hefty's*, a short (thirty-minute) film produced by Dick Rockwell, who wrote and produced the script (he is also a station manager of WOAK, a cable TV channel at Dondero High School, Royal Oak, Michigan). Notice how (1) the scenes are numbered for reference; (2) camera directions and set location are indicated in capital letters; (3) actions to be performed are typed; and (4) the name of the character who is speaking is centered on the line and typed in all capitals. The dialogue is also indented from both margins. A footer lists the date of the draft, the title and the page number. The wide left margin leaves plenty of room for a binding. The two-column format shown in Figure 7 is standard for audio/visual scripts.

EXCEPTIONS: WHEN AND HOW TO BREAK THE RULES

There may be times when you want to send an editor material prepared in a special way. Just remember to include the *written part* of the manuscript on a separate sheet of paper following the standard formats as best you can. Then if the editor decides to publish your material, he will be able to give this copy to the typesetter to use.

Here are some examples where you might consider breaking the standard formats for submitting material:

Situation: You do beautiful calligraphy work, and your manuscript tells teens how you make extra money by designing and selling personalized stationery.

You might: Prepare your manuscript following the standard formats. Then include as your cover letter a short message written on a sheet of stationery you have designed.

Situation: Your class has put together a special collection of stories written and illustrated by the students. One of the students or your teacher has written an article about the project.

You might: Type the article using the standard formats plus include a free copy of your book for the editor to read.

GENIE OF THE LAMP

NARRATOR: The dictionary defines autism as "detachment from reality together with the relative and absolute predominance of the inner life . . . The reality of the autistic world may seem more valid than that of reality itself; the patients hold their fantasy world for the real, reality for an illusion . . ." In other words, "wishes and fears constitute the contents of autistic thinking . . ."

Lights dim and end scene 1.

ACT 1

Backdrops of buildings and lights in a big city. A man, woman and young teenage boy gather around a trash can from where a small fire is giving them warmth in an alley. They are bundled in ill-fitting clothes, torn and dirt-stained. The woman has a scarf over her head and tied under her chin. She also has on a pair of fingerless mittens and open-toe shoes. The older man has on a ragged khaki army jacket, but no hat or gloves. He keeps his arms pressed to his side and leans close to the fire. The boy is wearing oversized pants and shoes, and a woman's winter coat that has fur on the collar and cuffs. He is seated on the bare ground near the can, is cradling an old metal teapot in his arms and is rocking back and forth. A female narrator stands center stage dressed in black. A spotlight as she speaks.

GRIFFIN: *(angrily)* Boy! How many times do I have to tell you to get up and warm yourself?

(The boy stares out blankly at the man and continues rocking.)

ANNIE: Now Griffin, don't yell! My head can't take it with you always yellin' all the time. Don't you see the boy's busy? Leave him be.

Figure 5. Simplified sample play format

1. FADE IN

2. EXT. JERRY'S BACKYARD—DAY

LEGS pumping across an expansive luxuriously green lawn. JERRY sprints the final fifty yards of his run and stops.

He leans forward, breathing heavily, placing both hands down on the top of an ancient sundial on a carved pedestal. Even his patio is elegant.

3. INT. JERRY'S LIVING ROOM—DAY

LOUIS, the family's lifelong servant, anticipating Jerry's arrival, pushes aside the luminous draperies covering an enormous picture window.

4. EXT. BACKYARD—DAY

Jerry catches his breath. He appears exhausted but purposeful. This is his day. He is preparing for the challenge of his life.

5. INT. LIVING ROOM—DAY

Jerry enters, sweat dripping like champagne from his body. He is thirty-something, wearing a yuppie jogging outfit.

Louis greets him by handing him a towel. This guy is waited on hand and foot. Does Louis wipe him too?!

LOUIS
Good run this morning, sir?
JERRY
Thanks Louis, I'll be ready in a few minutes

6. INT. JERRY'S HOUSE BATHROOM—DAY

JERRY—(VO)
When I think back to that day at Hefty's, I recall that I was in the best shape of my life—physically, mentally, and gastronomically.

| 2/6/91 | HEFTYS | 1 |

Figure 6. Simplified sample film script

VIDEO	AUDIO
A foggy day in London Town.	Fog horns echo through mist-shrouded streets. Carriage wheels clatter on cobblestone.
Sherlock Holmes runs down the steps of his Baker Street home. Watson follows furiously behind.	Footsteps . . . then . . . **WATSON:** HOLMES, WAIT YOU FORGOT YOUR UMBRELLA.
Holmes turns.	**HOLMES:** WHAT IS IT YOU SAY, YOU BLUBBERING IDIOT.
Watson looks embarrassed.	**WATSON:** MY GOOD MAN, YOU'VE STUMBLED OUT WITHOUT SO MUCH AS A RAINCOAT AND GALOSHES. AT LEAST HAVE THE COMMON SENSE TO TAKE A BUMBERSHOOT AND WEAR YOUR RUBBERS.
Watson tosses Holmes his umbrella. Holmes flinches, misses it and it bounces off the porch railing and lands in a puddle.	**HOLMES:** YOU CONTEMPTIBLE OAF. IF I WANTED SAFE-SEX ADVICE FROM YOU I WOULD WAKE YOU IN THE MIDDLE OF THE NIGHT WHEN YOU ARE MOMENTARILY SOBER.

Figure 7. Simplified sample audio/video script

Situation: You have a handicap that makes it difficult to type or write neatly.

You might: Prepare your manuscript the best you can. Include a cover letter telling a bit about yourself. Consider having someone else help you prepare your final copy.

Situation: For a holiday present, you typed some of your poems on special paper, then illustrated or decorated them yourself and hung them in pretty frames.

You might: Retype your poem on a separate sheet of paper using the standard format. Include this with a photograph of your framed poem, or include an extra illustrated poem for the editor.

COVER LETTERS

If you wish to tell the editor something about yourself or give some added information about your story or article, such as how you came to write it, you may do so on a separate sheet of paper called a "cover letter." This letter is written like a regular personal or business letter with your name, address, telephone number and date at the top plus the name and address of the publication to whom you are writing. If possible, locate the name of the editor in a current issue of that publication. Then begin the letter, "Dear Mr." or "Ms." followed by the editor's last name. If you don't know the editor's name, simply write "Dear Editor."

Make your cover letter as short as possible, almost never more than one page. Cover letters should always be typed, using single-spacing. Use a regular business letter format. Unless a listing suggests otherwise, tell the editor only those things that relate directly to the manuscript you are sending. Though editors may be interested in knowing all about you, your family, your friends and your hobbies, they probably do not have time to read about you now. If editors want more information, they will ask you to send another letter. Remember you are trying to interest the editor in your manuscript, not in you personally.

QUERY LETTERS

A writer sends a "query letter" to an editor to find out in advance whether the editor would be interested in receiving a manuscript about a certain topic. Most editors prefer that young writers send a complete manuscript, though older teens attempting to publish in adult publications may send query letters outlining their proposed articles.

Like cover letters, try to keep query letters to one page and no more than two. *Always* type a query letter, and address it to a specific editor if at all possible. (You may need to call the publication for the name of the current editor. A receptionist or secretary can give you the information; do not ask to speak to the editor directly.) Include an SASE with your query letter so the editor may respond. If you have been published before, it's a good idea to send one to three photocopies of your best pieces, especially if the article (or book) is similar in style or genre.

In one or two paragraphs, briefly describe the article (or book) you have written or plan to write. Give a few pertinent details, especially facts about people interviewed or relevance to current topics. In another paragraph, briefly describe why you are interested in this piece and any *pertinent* credentials you have. Many writers find drafting a good query letter harder than writing the finished manuscript. That's another good reason young writers should concentrate on submitting completed manuscripts. Many of the resources mentioned in this book have sections on writing query letters.

It is highly unlikely for young writers to be represented by literary agents[2]. If you are a serious older teen with a full-length book manuscript, play or script, you may send a query letter to an agent asking if he or she would consider you as a new client. Be sure to enclose an SASE. You may send a short sample of previously published work. *Do not send your manuscript or a synopsis or outline with your query.* If an agent finds your project interesting, he will write and tell you *exactly* what you should send.

PACKAGING AND MAILING

If your manuscript is more than four pages long or if you are including artwork or photographs, use a large manila envelope

---

[2]The best method for a serious young writer to find a reputable agent is through the recommendation of an established author. Many writer's organizations maintain lists of agents.

Susie Kaufmann
2151 Hale Rd.
Sandusky MI 48471

Place
Stamp
Here

Gerry Mandel, Editor
Stone Soup
Children's Art Foundation
P.O. Box 83
Santa Cruz CA 95063

Figure 8. Sample mailing envelope

that will hold your material without having to fold it.

When addressing your mailing envelope, use the editor's name whenever possible. Example:

Janet Ihle
Thumbprints
928 Gibbs St.
Caro MI 48723

You can locate the name of the current editor by checking the masthead, usually located near the front of the publication.

Protect artwork or photographs by placing them between pieces of cardboard. *Never* use a staple or paper clip on a photo. It will cause ridges in the photo and make it difficult to reproduce. *Never* write on the back of a photo with a pencil or hard-tipped pen. Put the information on an address label, which can be stuck to the back of the photo. You can also write safely on the back of a photo using a special grease pencil found in art and office supply stores.

Affix the proper amount of postage on both your mailing envelope and the self-addressed stamped envelope or postcard you put *inside* your mailing envelope with your manuscript.

SASE: SELF-ADDRESSED STAMPED ENVELOPE

Use a second manila envelope for your self-addressed stamped envelope (SASE). Fold it in half to fit in the mailing envelope.

Stone Soup
P.O. Box 83
Santa Cruz CA 95063

Place
Stamp
Here

Susie Kaufmann
2151 Hale Rd.
Sandusky MI 48471

Figure 9. Sample SASE

Place
Stamp
Here

YOUR NAME
YOUR ADDRESS
CITY, STATE ZIP CODE

Figure 10. Sample front of self-addressed postcard

Remember to include enough postage to have your material mailed back to you.

An editor will not return your material if you forget to enclose a self-addressed stamped envelope with the right amount of postage. Some editors will not even read a manuscript that is not accompanied by an SASE. This may not seem like a good way to do business, but editors cannot afford to pay for the return of manuscripts from every writer who submits material. It would cost them thousands of dollars each year! They would rather use the money to pay writers for work that is accepted for publication.

A few of the markets listed state they do not return material at all. You do not need to include a self-addressed stamped envelope with your material when submitting manuscripts to

(Title of your story) _____

(Date you mailed it) _____

(Who you mailed it to)

_____

_____

Received by

_____

Date

Figure 11. Sample message side of postcard

Author's Tip:

....

Don't guess. It is important to have your package—manuscript, plus letters, artwork, photographs and self-addressed stamped envelope—weighed at the post office or on a reliable postal scale so you will use the proper amount of postage.

Do not seal your package until it has been weighed and the correct postage determined. This way you can take out your self-addressed envelope and put on the correct amount of return postage. *Do not use postal meter strips on SASEs.*

If you frequently send the same size packages, make a chart that will remind you how much postage you'll need.

---

these markets and contests.

If you are worried that your package may not reach an editor, or if you want to make sure your manuscript did arrive at a market that will not send it back, you may enclose a special self-addressed stamped postcard. (See Figures 10 and 11.) Most editors will take the time to mark a postcard and return it to you.

MODEL RELEASE FORMS

Occasionally a publication or contest will ask that the author, artist or photographer provide a statement signed by the person granting an interview or photograph to prove that he or she agreed to the project and understood how the material might be used (such as in a magazine). When the person signs the form, it means that he or she is saying that it's OK to publish the material. Such a form is known as a "model release." Sometimes a market will supply a copy of the model release form it prefers, or you can find examples of them in reference books. However, if only a simple form is needed you can make one up yourself. Here's how:

Using a clean sheet of paper, write your name, address, phone number, and the name, address and phone number of the person being interviewed, photographed or used as a model. Have that person write a sentence or two that clearly shows he or she understands that the information, photograph, etc., may be published or used for publicity purposes. (You could write up this statement ahead of time.) Then have the person sign his or her name, and that day's date. Sign your name, too. If possible, have another person sign it as a witness.

If you are dealing with someone eighteen or younger, have a parent or guardian also sign the model release form.

You do not need to provide this form unless the market or contest requests it. But because you may not always know when you'll need one, it's a good idea to have a model release form signed by anyone readily identifiable in a photograph you hope to have published.

ARTWORK

While some larger, flexible pieces of artwork, such as posters and illustrations, may be sent rolled up in a special cardboard mailing tube, most markets and contests prefer that artwork be mailed *flat*. You especially don't want to fold or crease it in any way.

Protect the surface of your art with a sheet of paper so it

doesn't become smudged or dirtied. To mail it, put your artwork between two pieces of sturdy cardboard cut slightly larger than the artwork itself. Secure with at least two rubber bands. Ordinary manila folders, large enough to hold your work, cardboard and extra papers, such as entry forms or a manuscript, may be used. For pieces larger than 9″ × 12″, it's best to use a shipping envelope that has a special lining made of plastic bubbles or other filling. These may be found at art and office supply stores. They may also be carried in your local grocery or department store. For overly large artwork, you may need to make your own mailing "envelope" by measuring and cutting sheets of sturdy cardboard from a box (such as the ones televisions, bikes or other things come in). Be sure to use strong, waterproof shipping tape on every exposed seam, as well as around the entire package, to ensure that it does not come open in transit.

Be sure to include your name, address and phone number somewhere on your artwork. (You'd be surprised at the number of artists and writers who forget!) Check the market or contest guidelines sheets for the specific location to put this information. Some like it on the back as long as it doesn't "bleed" through or otherwise damage the front of the picture. Often there is a small corner where you can put the information so it doesn't interfere with the subject of the piece. Understand that this information is in addition to any personal signature you include directly in your illustration or painting.

Some contests do not want personal information to appear on the artwork itself. In this case, be sure you have included the proper entry form with all the necessary information.

PHOTOGRAPHS

Some markets and contests insist, and most prefer, that you shoot with 35mm film at the lowest shutter speed that will still give you a clean, unblurred image. According to a survey done by professional photographer Lawrence F. Abrams, editors with a preference like photographers to use Kodak film. However, the majority did not indicate a preference. What was most important was the quality of the photo.

In the same survey, 95 percent of the editors said they preferred that unmounted (or unmatted) photos be submitted. However, you should always protect your photos by putting them between two pieces of sturdy cardboard, then wrapping the cardboard with two rubber bands. If you are sending more than one photograph, separate them with tissue paper or other paper that won't scratch the surface of the print. Except in rare instances, you would *never* send a negative. Do *not* clip a photo (or any artwork) to a sheet of paper or thin sheet of cardboard because the paper clip will almost always bend or dent the picture.

Slides, sometimes called transparencies, should be inserted in the pockets of a clear plastic slide holder sheet available where most camera and film supplies are sold. Use this method to also protect slides you keep for yourself if they are important to you. However, avoid sheets made with plastic containing polyvinyl-chloride (PVC) if you expect your slides to be stored for a long time.

Be sure to identify every photo and slide you send. Most of the time you'll want to do this directly on the back of photos or on the sides of slides. A grease pencil, available at art or office supply stores, works well for writing on the back of photos without damaging them. Self-sticking name or address labels also work well. To avoid damaging the photo, *do not* write directly on the back with a pen or lead pencil.

You can safely write on the cardboard sides of slides, though some photographers type up small strips of self-sticking paper with their names and addresses. Many professionals have inexpensive rubber stamps made with their names, addresses and copyright notices on them plus blank lines to write other identifying information about the slides.

Unless you are just sending a portrait-type photograph of yourself or someone else (often called a "head shot"), you should always provide a caption for your photo that identifies the people in it and what is taking place. Sometimes you'll have room for this information to be placed directly on the back of each photo. However, it's best to also include a sheet with your submission that lists all the captions in one place. Be sure to number or code each photo or slide so it's easy to tell which caption goes with which photo.

Many times, photos and slides may be submitted directly with a manuscript. There are some markets, however, that only want you to send these after the editor has requested them.

To help ensure that they get at least one good photograph or slide, many photographers "bracket" their pictures by taking several shots at different settings. This is a good practice for any photographer. However, don't send a whole batch of photographs to an editor or contest expecting someone to select the best ones. That's *your* job. When selecting which ones to send, look for clear, clean pictures with good contrast and interesting content. An "action" shot is preferred to a photograph where everyone is staring into the camera. Make sure the subject of your photo takes up most of the frame; that is, don't send a photo of someone riding a bicycle where the rider and bike are just specks in the distance. And try to avoid chopping people's arms, legs, wrists and ankles off at their joints. As with writing and art, a good photographer improves with practice.

KEEP A COPY FOR YOURSELF

Always make a copy of any manuscript you submit, *especially* to those that won't return your work. It is insurance against a manuscript that gets damaged or lost in the mail. Occasionally, an editor will want to discuss your manuscript with you over the phone. It is much easier when you both have a copy to look at.

Copies can be made using carbon paper, by retyping a piece, using a photocopying machine or by storing a copy on a computer disk.

KEEPING TRACK OF SUBMISSIONS

Once you decide to submit material to an editor or contest, you must also devise a system of keeping track of your manuscripts. This is especially important if you are anxious to get published and will be sending more than one manuscript out at the same time.

One way to keep track is with $3'' \times 5''$ index cards kept in a file box. Prepare a new index card for each manuscript you send out. (See figure 12 for a sample format.)

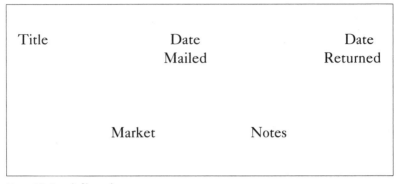

Title	Date Mailed	Date Returned
	Market	Notes

Figure 12. Sample file card

Record the title of your manuscript or contest entry, the date you mailed it (not the date you wrote it) and the name of the market or contest you sent the manuscript to. Under "Notes" you may want to write down the amount of postage the manuscript needed. Include the cost of the self-addressed stamped envelope or postcard, too.

When you receive an answer from the editor or contest, write the date under the "Date Returned" heading. Under "Notes" or on the back of the card, mark whether the manuscript was accepted or rejected and any other information, such as how much you were (or will be) paid for the piece and when the editor plans to publish it.

If the manuscript was rejected, select another market from the lists. Mark the new information on the same card if there is room.

If students will be submitting material as part of a class project, one file box may be used to keep an accurate record of all student submissions and editors' remarks.

Similar records may also be kept in an extra notebook or in a file on a computer disk.

ADDITIONAL TIPS

Think ahead! If you're really anxious to submit material, don't wait until you have a manuscript in final draft form before sending away for market guidelines, sample copies and detailed contest information. But don't send away for all of them at once either.

Author's Tip:

The standard formats and advice featured in this guide will suit the needs of most young writers. For more information about manuscript formats and the marketing process, read *The Writer's Digest Guide to Manuscript Formats,* by Dian Dincin Buchman and Seli Groves. The detailed checklists and submissions logs are particularly helpful for anyone planning to do a lot of writing and marketing.

Choose a few markets and contests that are looking for material similar to what you are most interested in writing. Consider also markets and contests directed toward people your age.

You'll need an easy way to store your market and contest information so when you have a manuscript ready to submit, you can consult your files and choose where you would like to send it first.

All this information can be kept in a desk drawer, file cabinet or even a shoe box. An even better method is to make your own personal marketing guide. You'll need a large three-ring binder and a box of vinyl sheet protectors. Top-loading sheet protectors work best. You might also want a package of tab dividers to separate various types of markets and contests or to file information alphabetically.

When a sample copy and guideline sheet arrive, slip them into a sheet protector for safekeeping. Some sample copies won't fit into the sheet protector. You'll have to store these somewhere else. Put a note on the corresponding guideline sheet to remind yourself where the sample copy is. Insert a reference sheet at the front of your binder to record which market and contest information you have. Also include the date you received the information and the date of the sample copy so you'll know when you need to send for more current information.

Your personal marketing guide is also an excellent place to keep additional notes about writing, the names and addresses of new markets and contests, samples of published material you think is well written and even your record of submissions. If you attend young author conferences or writing workshops, or if published authors speak to your class, store your notes or any handout material in your marketing guide for easy reference.

Chapter Five

Opportunities Online

Imagine writing and getting published without using a single sheet of paper, stuffing one envelope or licking one stamp. Impossible, you say?

Not if you are one of a growing group of writers, publishers and readers using personal computers and telephone lines to communicate with one another. We may still be light years away from becoming a paperless society, but modern technology has launched a new generation of communication opportunities. Sometimes I wonder what Johann Gutenberg[1] would think of all this.

This chapter introduces you to just a few of the opportunities that have developed in recent years for writers online, such as

- Markets and contests where you can submit your writing
- Bulletin board systems (BBSs) where writers who share interests gather to chat, offer each other help and encouragement
- Electronic libraries bursting with informational and recreational resources; electronic versions of magazines, books and newsletters; samples of works-in-progress
- Ongoing workshops and critique sessions covering all types of writing and genres
- Real-time conferences (RTCs) that allow writers from all over the country—all over the world, in fact—to gather at the same time to chat informally or pose questions to guest speakers

---

[1]Gutenberg is often credited with printing the first book, a Bible, using a machine with moveable type during the mid-fifteenth century. This innovation made it possible to publish multiple copies of books, which previously had to be copied by hand.

Once you become involved, perhaps you'll become a pioneer in this rapidly expanding field.

WHAT IS ONLINE COMPUTING?

Online computing is communicating with others by using a personal computer and modem, rather than talking face to face, corresponding by regular mail or speaking on the telephone. Modems, one attached to each computer and programmed with special communications software, interpret computer messages and files, then transmit the data over regular touch-tone telephone lines using electronic signals. Standard transmission formats have been developed that allow different kinds of computers to read and use the same files, even if they were created on noncompatible machines. For instance, someone using a Macintosh will have no trouble reading my message that I created on my IBM-compatible machine.

ASCII, which stands for American Standard Code for Information Interchange, is the format most commonly used to transmit data electronically. Letters and numbers, simple punctuation (such as spaces, periods, question marks), basic typing commands (such as a tab to indent text, paragraph or hard return) and special control codes (to let the other computer know the transfer of data is completed, for instance) are each represented by a special ASCII code.

Facsimile (or fax) machines work in a similar way, but the information sent is printed out by the receiving fax machine. With a modem, however, files can be sent to a host system, such as CompuServe Information Service or the Internet, where they will be stored until someone retrieves them. Modems also allow two or more people to interact with each other at the same time. For instance, during a real-time conference (RTC), when one person types a message and presses the "enter" or "return" key on her keyboard, the host system (that's the one to which everyone is connected) receives the message and then passes it on so it will appear on the computer screen of all the other people who are participating.

Author's Tip:

If you are interested in learning more about how computers and modems access online services, an excellent resource is Peter Norton's book, *Outside the IBM PC and PS/2*. Mr. Norton has a talent for explaining the often complex and confusing world of computer technology in an easy to understand way. Chapter three, "Communications Technologies," and chapter four, "Modems," provide particularly useful background information.

Dozens of reference books are available explaining what can be found on the many electronic host systems.

WHO'S ONLINE?

As mentioned above, an online information system, such as CompuServe or GEnie, can serve as a host. These systems offer many more services than the few described so far. There are bulletin board areas (called forums on CompuServe and roundtables on GEnie) for almost any area of interest imaginable. They also serve as gateways to huge databases of information that you can search from your own computer. This is particularly helpful when writing nonfiction or researching papers for school. Host systems also offer electronic mail (e-mail) delivery. A letter sent e-mail will usually appear in the other person's online mailbox within a few minutes instead of the days it takes regular mail to be delivered.

Many schools and libraries offer free or low-cost access to the thousands of "web" sites along the Internet "superhighway." Some, especially colleges and universities, set up their own web locations. Many computer stores will maintain a BBS so customers can contact them by modem to order new software or equipment, report problems or meet other people with similar interests. Several writer's groups maintain private BBSs that allow members to post messages and hold RTCs.

Even schools are setting up BBSs so students in one area can communicate with students in other areas. Besides a suitable computer system, modem and communications software, and available phone line, all that's needed is for the two (or more) schools to decide which one will act as host for the upcoming session.

For our purposes, we're going to concentrate on some of the online writing and publishing opportunities available on CompuServe and GEnie. While CompuServe was the first online information service to offer access to the general consumer (in 1979), the Writers' Ink RoundTable (WINK) on GEnie has established itself as the leading electronic community for writers, according to its founder, Jack D. Smith.

ADVANTAGES AND DISADVANTAGES

There are two major disadvantages to becoming a member of an online service. The first is cost. Fees vary depending on which service you belong to, which areas you access, how long you stay online, what time of day you log on (evenings, weekends and holidays are least expensive) and what you do while online. However, there are several special software programs that can help automate your online session. Basically, they allow you to write messages offline (when you are not connected), log you on, retrieve any e-mail or messages to you, post your new messages, download any special files you have selected, then log you off automatically. Then you can read your messages, etc., whenever it's convenient for you.

CompuServe recommends its communications program called CompuServe Information Manager (CIM) for beginners. Aladdin is used most by IBM and IBM-compatible users on GEnie. Information on these and other programs is available from the individual services.

A second cost consideration is whether or not you must dial long-distance to log on. Telephone charges are billed like any other long-distance call you make (another reason to log on in the evenings or on weekends). They are in addition to the connect charges you pay for the service itself.

The second major disadvantage to becoming a member of an online service is that it can be addictive. You've got to watch your time to keep phone and connect charges within reason and so you don't neglect your writing, school or family.

Still, most online writers think there are more advantages than disadvantages. The biggest, perhaps, is being able to communicate with other people who understand what it's like being, or wanting to be, a writer. Sheri Sinykin[2], a writer who is an active member of WINK in the children's and young adult books category put it this way:

> On GEnie, you never know which children's book writers and illustrators might pop in to say hello and share their experiences, problems and excitement about the writing life. Many well-known writers, as well as authors like me who are just beginning their publishing careers, enjoy chatting online almost daily about the ups and downs of our lives and our manuscripts-in-progress. When one of us has a question, someone else is likely to stop by with an answer or two. Some people even upload and critique manscripts online. My real life friendships with writers have deepened through speedy e-mail letters—and I've made wonderful new friendships with writers—both struggling and published—who I never would have met otherwise.

REAL-TIME CONFERENCES

Perhaps the biggest advantage of participating online is the opportunity to attend a wide variety of workshops and conferences that would normally be out of reach to young people because of cost, location or other restrictions. But online, almost every area of the system is open to young people, no matter how young they might be. Just like in the real world, you will be expected to mind your manners. But no one will know how old you are unless you want to tell them.

That means that you can attend both regular and special RTCs sitting at a computer and participating by asking questions, posting replies, etc., if they aren't happening too late for your time

---

[2]Sheri Cooper Sinykin is the author of several children's books, including *Shrimpboat and Gym Bags*, *The Buddy Trap*, *Sirens* and *The Shorty Society* (summer 1994).

zone. Or you can do what many members do, download the transcript of the RTC at a later date.

You'll want to check your special interest areas for regularly scheduled RTCs. The Literary Forum, for example, holds a regularly scheduled conference for both adults and young writers interested in writing for children every Wednesday beginning at 9 P.M. eastern time. On WINK, screenwriters meet regularly at 10:30 EST every Monday night.[3]

Is there an author or publisher in particular you would like to have at an RTC? Then make a suggestion. Forums and roundtables are a lot like local writer's clubs; they depend on active member participation.

ONLINE MARKETS AND CONTESTS

A small sampling of online markets and contests is included alphabetically in the regular listings sections in chapters nine and ten. Like all the listings in this *Guide*, they have expressed an interest in hearing from young writers.

Some opportunities, such as *Kopper Bear Press* (page 220), *The Write News* (page 244) and *Texas Young Writers' Newsletter* (page 237) are actually traditional publishers who allow writers to contact them using an electronic mail (e-mail) service such as GEnie, CompuServe or America Online. Others, such as Writers' Ink Round Table, offer access to online magazines, newsletters, short stories, poetry and other types of writing that you can download to your computer to later read on your monitor or print out. However, many new electronic-only markets and contests are being founded. For example, see the profile of Greg Sanders on page 189.

In the listings for GEnie and CompuServe, you'll find other more general areas where opportunities readily exist. Again, these forums and roundtables (commonly referred to as SIGs, or special interest groups) have each said they welcome submissions and participation by young writers. It was not possible for me to contact each and every one of the various SIGs individually. If you have

---

[3]This was accurate as of June 1995. Be sure to check for current dates and times.

Author's Note: Proceed With Caution

Just as you should do with any market or contest before submitting material, study and compare online opportunities. In addition to traditional publishing offers, there are vanity publishers and subsidy presses you'll want to avoid.

Also, know that there are a large number of self-publishing opportunities available online. Some, like uploading your stories or poems to forum libraries, provide benefits similar to contributing to school anthologies or Young Author Day projects. Others, however, more closely resemble the self-publishing ventures described in chapter one under "Ego Alert!" Enjoy yourself, but don't get so caught up in sharing your work with the world (either on paper or electronically) that you forget the long-term goals you have set for yourself as a writer.

---

a special hobby or interest (virtually anything from aquariums to zoology, casual or technically oriented), be sure to check in the information service directory that comes with your membership for additional forums, roundtables and SIGs in which to participate. Similar groups might also be found on other information services, such as America Online, Prodigy or the Internet.

To locate appropriate markets for your work, it's best to check the descriptions of the various sections (or categories) and libraries within individual SIGs. For instance, in the Writers' Ink RoundTable on GEnie, there is a special category (5) just for young writers where topics include "Round Robin Stories" and a "Humorous Short Story Exchange." Young poets may be more comfortable, or find more expert help, participating in Category 30, the "Poet's Retreat."

On CompuServe, the primary forum for creative writers is the Literary Forum. But other forums offer a variety of opportunities as well. For instance, SYSOPs (that stands for system operators, the people who manage each area) in the Outdoor Forum, Motor Sports Forum, Computer Graphics Forums (there are several) and the Comic Book Forum all say that young people are more than welcome to join in. Even the Legal Forum has a library file written by a young student. Dann Marvin, the nine-year-old son of attorney William Marvin, wrote about his experiences visiting some court proceedings.

Contest opportunities can pop up unexpectedly. In February 1993, for instance, the Student Forum offered members a chance to win a twenty-five dollar CompuServe usage credit in a new creative writing contest. The idea was sparked by a then upcoming book *What Do We Mean When We Say Love?* Members were asked to submit short compositions of 300 words, which could be serious or humorous but had to be as creative and original as possible, explaining what love means to them.

Joshua Hauser even started an online publishing opportunity himself by suggesting interested members write a community story. He started things off by writing

> It was a dark and dreary day in the big city, but since I was in a totally different city, it didn't affect me. I was making breakfast when the phone rang.

News about online writing, art and photography contests is often featured in special messages (called banners), which scroll by whenever you log on to a service or SIG. To access the specific rules and regulations of each contest, you need to go into the SIG that is sponsoring the contest and download the special library file containing the information. If you don't know where to look, post a message to a SYSOP and one will reply within a day or two.

ONLINE GUIDELINES

Basically, the guidelines for preparing traditional manuscripts and art apply equally well to the more traditional online markets and contests. That means spending time writing, rewriting, revising and polishing your stories; checking for grammar, spelling and punctuation mistakes; and making sure you are submitting an appropriate manuscript in an appropriate place.

Many markets that accept electronic submissions have posted their guidelines in various libraries. The best place to check is in the libraries of writing-related areas, such as the Writers' Ink

---

Author's Note:

Useful information abounds online. And nowhere does it collect more swiftly than on the Internet. One of the most popular (and fastest-growing) ways to access what's available is by exploring World Wide Web "pages."

One great place to visit is "Resources for Young Writers," a special linked page from *INKSPOT: Resource for Children's Writers*. INKSPOT began in 1995 and is overseen by Debbie Ridpath Ohi of Toronto. The direct Web page address (URL) to get you there is

http://www.interlog.com/~ohi/dmo-pages/youngbk.html

To access INKSPOT, use

hhtp:/www.interlog.com/~ohi/dmo-pages/writers.html

RoundTable on GEnie and the Literary Forum on CompuServe.

In addition, remember that most library files must be sent (uploaded) in standard ASCII format. You won't have to worry about margins and headers and page numbers. But you should understand that ASCII does not recognize special features (called attributes), such as boldface type or underlining. If you want to emphasize a word or short phrase, TYPE IT IN CAPS or *place it between asterisks*. To indicate that something should be underlined, as when typing the name of a book or something that should appear in italics if the manuscript is printed by traditional methods (on paper), place it between two underline characters:__ Market Guide for Young Writers__.

Don't forget to include your name and e-mail address on all files you upload. It is also recommended that you add the standard copyright notice at the beginning or end of every file you upload. (This applies to library files or special text sent as a manuscript but not to ordinary chitchat type messages.) To indicate your copyright notice type the word "Copyright," the year the manuscript was created (put in fixed form, such as when you typed it) and your name. Here's an example:

Copyright 1996 Kathy Henderson

Check your word processing software manual to find how to save your text in ASCII format. Sometimes this is called generic DOS. By the way, graphic files are usually quite large compared to straight text. They should be uploaded separately, using an acceptable graphic format.

Don't be shy about asking questions. SYSOPs agree that the only dumb questions are the ones that aren't asked!

ETIQUETTE ONLINE

Because time *is* money online, the messages members post are usually brief and informal. Unlike the care you should take polishing a final draft or writing a cover or query letter to an editor, don't worry about minor misspellings or typos and lapses in punctuation and grammar.

On the other hand, messages also tend to be clearer and more concise. It's a fact that even a Pulitzer-Prize-winning writer like Roger Ebert[4] has noticed. During a visit to the Journalism Forum on CompuServe, he said, "For some reason, most of the people on CompuServe in the forums I visit are very good writers. Maybe electronic mail helps you become concise because of the cost and memorable because of the competition."

If you have a reason to post a long message (perhaps you are sharing what you learned at a workshop you attended), preface it by giving readers fair warning. Here's an example:

To ALL

Kathy Henderson recently did a writing and publishing workshop at my school. I thought you might enjoy hearing some of the advice she gave us.

* *

WARNING – LONG MESSAGE

* *

---

[4]Readers may know Ebert, an internationally known film critic, as half of the Siskel and Ebert team. He is also a former teacher and magazine editor. A complete transcript of his seminar visit is available in Library 3 "Free-lancers," of the Journalism Forum on CompuServe. The file name is EBERT.TXT.

Then continue with what you want to share.

Fellow online members will appreciate the courtesy you've shown. They can download the message if they are interested or send a break command to bypass it. (They can capture it again later if they want.)

COPYRIGHT PROTECTION AND UPLOADING

Bear in mind that copyright law applies to the messages and other files you download from online sources just as it does to printed, taped and other fixed methods of creative work. Chapter six contains some additional information regarding copyright.

Answers to Questions Young Writers Ask Most

QUESTIONS ABOUT GETTING PUBLISHED

Why should I include an SASE?

SASE is the abbreviation for self-addressed stamped envelope. All editors and most contests insist that writers include an SASE with their manuscripts. The editor will use it to send you an answer or to return your manuscript if it is rejected. To prepare an SASE, write your name and address on the front of an envelope as if you were mailing it to yourself. Put the same amount of postage on your SASE that you put on your mailing envelope. Example: If it costs you fifty-two cents to mail your manuscript, you must also put fifty-two cents on your SASE. Put your SASE inside the mailing envelope with your manuscript when you mail it.

Special note about the U.S. Postal Service: Always use regular postage stamps on your SASEs. Do not use metered postage tape or the post office may not return the envelope to you. This is because the metered postage tape will show the date you originally mailed the manuscript or letter rather than the correct date when the SASE was mailed back to you.

A friend told me she used to always include SASEs with her submissions, but now she only includes one sometimes. Aren't you always supposed to include an SASE?

Yes, you should always include some type of SASE with every submission. Most of the time your SASE will consist of an envelope large enough to easily hold your manuscript plus with enough postage on it so an editor or contest can mail it back to you if needed. Sometimes manuscripts are sent back so you can edit them following an editor's advice and then resubmit them.

Some writers, mostly those with computers, feel it is easier and cheaper to simply print out new copies of manuscripts when needed rather than have editors return them. Under these conditions, writers should *still* include a #10 self-addressed and stamped envelope or a self-addressed and stamped postcard for a reply when submitting to editors or contests that expect SASEs. Explain in a cover letter or a short note what the editor should do with your submission if it's rejected, such as suggesting that the paper be recycled.

Some writers are afraid to suggest to an editor that their manuscripts be destroyed rather than returned if not accepted. They worry that it might give an editor the wrong impression about the quality of the manuscript or the writer's talent or self-confidence. If this method makes you uncomfortable, then stick with enclosing a traditional SASE when appropriate. I personally do not share this fear. Today's editors are too busy to question a writer's preference. In addition, many will appreciate and respect the writer's effort to make the unpleasant process of a possible rejection as quick and inexpensive as possible. What is more important is that an editor recognize the writer as someone who has taken the trouble to learn what is expected when submitting a manuscript.

Enclose a regular SASE, however, any time you feel an editor may offer suggestions and comments on your manuscript even if it is rejected for publication.

An exception to the rule: You do not need to enclose an SASE when submitting to markets or contests that *specifically* state in their guidelines or rules that manuscripts are not returned. Sometimes, but not always, they will return a self-addressed postcard (if you enclosed one) so you will at least know they received your submission.

I sent a self-addressed stamped envelope with my manuscript but never received a reply. What should I do?

It often takes an editor four to eight weeks to respond. If you have waited this long, send a polite letter to the editor asking if she received your manuscript and if a decision has been made.

Be sure to include an SASE or self-addressed stamped postcard for a reply. Remember that some markets receive so much mail that they have a policy not to respond at all unless a manuscript is accepted for publication or wins an award. Check the market's listing or guidelines. If a market says "Does not respond" or "Does not return submissions," you do not have to enclose a self-addressed stamped envelope. If you want to make sure an editor or contest has received your manuscript, enclose a postage-paid *postcard* addressed to you. (See Figure 10, page 70.)

If you still receive no answer from a market that normally responds and returns manuscripts, I suggest you write one more time saying that you are withdrawing your manuscript from consideration and would like it returned to you immediately. Some professionals feel that if an editor hasn't responded within a reasonable time (normally about two or three months), writers should feel free to simply submit their manuscripts elsewhere without bothering to notify the first editor.

Most editors try to be as prompt as possible.

Can I send a manuscript to a publication that is not listed in *Market Guide for Young Writers*?

For various reasons, not all publications that consider material written by young people are listed in this *Guide*. Some editors have asked not to be listed because they prefer that only their readers submit material. If you have read a notice in a publication asking for submissions, you are considered a reader and may send them your submission whether or not they are listed in this *Guide*. Be careful to follow their guidelines.

Editors who currently receive more submissions than they can handle or use also sometimes ask not to be listed in a particular edition.

There may be other publications of which I was not aware, or that were too new at the time this edition was printed, that may also consider your manuscript. (If you discover a market not listed, please send me its name and address so I can see if it would like to be included in future editions.) Send your suggestions to Kathy Henderson MGYW, c/o Writer's Digest Books, 1507 Dana Avenue, Cincinnati, OH 45207.

Feel free to check other resources, such as *Writer's Market* or *Literary Market Place*, for additional market and contest opportunities. Several writer's organizations, such as the National Writer's Association, and many trade magazines for writers, such as *Byline*, *The Writer* and *Writer's Digest*, are also useful sources of current market and contest information. Note, however, that it will be harder to tell in these resources which opportunities are practical for young writers to target.

Why don't you include the editor's name and phone number with all the listings?

Phone numbers are only listed when the editor includes the information on the survey sheet that is returned to me *and* indicates he wants it included with the listing. (For examples, see the listings for *Stone Soup* and *Merlyn's Pen.*) Most editors do not want their phone numbers included because they fear having to answer too many phone calls from people who should be sending their questions by mail. If you have a legitimate reason to call, you can usually locate the phone number on the guidelines sheet or masthead in your sample copy.

The same criteria applies to including the name of an editor or contest coordinator. If you send for guidelines and/or a sample copy *before* submitting material, as advised, you will have access to the names of editors and contests coordinators.

Can I send the same manuscript to more than one magazine at the same time?

Sending the same manuscript to more than one market at the same time is called a multiple or "simultaneous" submission. It is not recommended for either adult or young writers. However, you may send different manuscripts to separate publications at the same time. Be sure to keep a record of which manuscript you sent to which market.

Most contests want only new material that has not been published or submitted to another contest or market before. A few contests (for example, see NWA Novel Contest) state in their guidelines that you may also submit entries to a publisher. The only way to know for sure is to read the directions.

Why does a listing say "send holiday or seasonal material six months in advance"?

It takes the entire publication staff several months to collect, edit and print a single issue. Therefore, they must consider material several months in advance of the issue's scheduled appearance. Often editors are reading Christmas stories in July and surfing stories in December. This is called the "lead time" (pronounced like "reed"). Different publications have different lead times. Generally, a magazine's lead time is much longer than the lead time for a newspaper.

What is an International Reply Coupon?

International Reply Coupons (IRCs) are redeemed at post offices for postage, similar to how subway or bus tokens substitute for coins. The *value* has been paid for in advance. Writers need to send IRCs instead of putting postage stamps on their self-addressed envelopes (or postcards) when submitting manuscripts to foreign markets. For instance, U.S. postage cannot be used by people in other countries, including Canada, to mail a letter or package back to you. You also couldn't mail a letter *from* the U.S. *to* Canada with a Canadian stamp. Sending IRCs instead of stamps allows an editor in one country to purchase the appropriate stamps to respond to a writer in another country.

If you wish to submit to a foreign market, ask a postal clerk for the appropriate amount of International Reply Coupons to enclose with your self-addressed envelope instead of a regular stamp.

If I submit a manuscript to a Canadian magazine, do I need to spell words like color "colour"? I live in the U.S.

It's usually best to spell words the way you normally would, provided that you spell them correctly, of course. That is, if you normally speak and write American English, then spell words like color and favorite the way you usually do. There's no sense trying to fool an editor into thinking you're Canadian. There are more differences between Canadian English and American English than just the spelling of some words. The same advice applies for Canadians sending manuscripts to the U.S. The words you choose to express yourself, and even the traditional way you spell them, are part of the overall style you bring to your manuscripts. Editors in Canada and the U.S. will edit such spellings if they think it's necessary. Otherwise, they will leave the spellings as they are.

Can my friend and I send in a story we wrote together?

Usually, this isn't a problem, especially when submitting manuscripts to markets. Some contests, however, insist that an entry be the original work of one writer. Again, it's important to check the guidelines sheet.

Why doesn't my favorite magazine publish more poems by young people?

A publication is limited in how much material it can print in each issue. This is usually determined by the amount of advertising used or, in the case of publications that carry no advertising, a predetermined number of pages. You might try writing to the editor and explaining that you would like to see more poems (or short stories, or whatever) by young people. Also, look for more opportunities to publish your work in your local area. You may even want to consider starting a newsletter of your own.

My story won first place in a writing contest. Can I send it to a magazine to be published, too?

Some contests retain the copyright to entries and some do not. It should state in the rules when and if you may submit your manuscript elsewhere. For instance, NWA contests say that you *may* submit contest entries to a market. However, The American Beekeeping Federation Essay Contest competition guidelines state "All national entries become the property of The ABF and may be published. No essays will be returned." An entry submitted here, whether or not it wins, *cannot* be submitted anywhere else. That's because the manuscript would no longer be *your* property. By entering it, you agreed to relinquish (that means to give up) your rights to it. Be sure to consider this when deciding where to submit your work.

Do I have to subscribe to a magazine before I can send them a manuscript?

It depends. Some magazines want material only from their current subscribers. One of these is *Poets at Work*. Subscribers can usually find submission guidelines in current issues. Some magazines prefer submissions from readers, though not specifically subscribers. If you don't have this type of magazine delivered to your home but read it in your school, library or church, etc., you are still considered a reader and may submit material. For most magazines, newsletters and newspapers, you do not need to subscribe before you submit material.

I don't own a typewriter or computer. What can I do?

Some editors will accept handwritten manuscripts if they are legible, which means neat and easy to read. Almost all markets for teens and adults, however, require manuscripts to be typed. You might try borrowing or renting a typewriter (perhaps at school), or find someone who will type your manuscript for you. Consider saving your money to buy a used typewriter, or no-frills word processor or computer system if you can't afford a new one. The point is, if you are serious about getting published, you will find a way to get your work typed. Don't bother complaining that such policies are unreasonable to writers who don't own typewriters or don't want to find other ways to get their manuscripts typed, as some frustrated beginning adult writers do. Expecting manuscripts to be typed is no more unreasonable than expecting someone who wants to play hockey to get a pair of ice skates.

Remember that nowadays "typed" means it can be produced with either a typewriter or computer as long as the final printout is legible. When using a typewriter or dot matrix printer, make sure to use a good ribbon that produces solid black type. Light print is not only very hard to read, it does not fax or photocopy well.

My story is 1,927 words long, but the magazine I want to send it to only accepts stories 800 words long. Should I send it anyway?

You have three choices: (1) Cut, revise and polish your story until you get it down to the 800-word limit or close to it. A little over, say 50 words, is usually acceptable. This type of editing usually produces an even better manuscript. (Stories may always be under the word limit.) (2) Look for a different publication that accepts longer stories. (3) Send it as is and take your chances. Obviously, the first two suggestions are the best to follow.

Remember, do *not* go over the maximum word limit when entering a contest. Your entry will be disqualified.

When the magazine published my story, they changed some of the words and left some parts out. I liked it better my way. Why did they do that?

There are several reasons an editor may change your story. It may have been too long to fit the available space, or the editor may have felt a different word or phrase would make your message clearer for readers to understand. This doesn't happen just with magazine stories but with all types of work. Editors have a responsibility (it's a large part of their job) to edit material when they think it is necessary. Thoughtful editing can make a good manuscript even better. Thankfully, most editors will only make minor editing changes on their own. If they think more changes are needed, they will make suggestions and ask the writer to make them.

Unfortunately, if a piece an editor changes has already been published, there really isn't anything you can do about it except go on to your next project. However, when an editor requests that you make some changes in your manuscript before she will consider publishing it, you will have to decide whether making them will help your work or not. If you don't understand what you are being asked to do, or if you don't agree with all the suggestions, take time to discuss your feelings with the editor by phone or in a letter. Be prepared to explain why you think some or all of the suggested changes are unnecessary and/or make new suggestions of your own. This give and take between writers and editors happens all the time. Don't be afraid of it. If you and the editor can't agree on what to do, either she will decide not to publish it or you can decide that you would prefer to submit the manuscript somewhere else.

All manuscripts get edited, even those by famous authors. It is a necessary part of the publishing process.

Note: If you self-publish your work, it should still be edited first. Rewriting, revising and polishing are key steps to producing quality work. You may be able to do all the necessary editing on your own, but it is much wiser to enlist the help of someone with editing experience.

A story I sent to a magazine was rejected. But the next issue had a story almost like mine. I think they stole my idea. What can I do?

First, because of a publication's lead time (see page 94), it is unlikely that someone stole your story. Second, many writers have the same idea for a story, although they do not write the story in the same way. Your story was probably rejected because the editor had already accepted the other one before your manuscript arrived. Try sending your story to a different market. And get busy writing new ones. Ideas, by the way, like titles, are not protected by copyright. Many of us have similar ideas, but we write them in different ways.

I'm afraid someone will steal my story and publish it if I send it to an editor. Is there some way to keep people from stealing it?

It is unlikely anyone will steal your story, especially if it is unpublished. When a story is stolen and someone pretends that he wrote it and then gets it published or entered into a contest, it is called "plagiarism." Plagiarists are usually found out and can be taken to court.

There is a poem I really like but it has no author name on it. Can I submit it?

No, especially if you hope someone will think you wrote it. That would be plagiarism. *Someone* wrote that poem. It wasn't you. If you do submit it, make sure you note where you found the poem (what book, magazine, etc.), and identify the author as unknown or "anonymous."

Author's Tip:

....

Plagiarism is a serious offense. It means to use or submit someone else's work as your own original work. Plagiarism often hurts innocent writers in ways that are not always apparent.

For example:

Several years ago I was one of fifty judges who evaluated entries in a large student writing competition sponsored by the Detroit Free Press. Many of the entries were so well written that some judges (many were public school teachers) were genuinely surprised yet pleased at the level of talent displayed by the young entrants. Then, halfway through the first day of judging, I read an entry that I knew without doubt was plagiarized material. The student had copied two entire chapters out of a juvenile novel by Dorothy Haas. Not even the name of the characters had been changed.

Immediately, the judging atmosphere changed. Judges who moments before had been surprised and delighted to discover well-written manuscripts among the hundreds of entries were suddenly wary and suspicious. Whether consciously or unconsciously, we all feared the same thing: Was this another plagiarized entry? Can such a young student really write this well?

If the student who submitted this plagiarized entry thought no one would be hurt by the deception, he or she was wrong. True, no harm was done to Mrs. Haas, the original author. But consider the harm done to all the young writers whose work was judged after the plagiarized entry was discovered. Hurt most were the most talented young writers because their entries drew the most suspicion and thus may have been given lower marks than they would have been given the day before.

Are there any other exceptions to the plagiarism rule?

Yes, there is a situation when you *may* submit something you saw published in one publication to another. A good example is found in *Reader's Digest*, which publishes many short, usually funny, items published in other magazines and newspapers. The difference is that the person submitting the material, called a "clipping," does not pretend that he created it himself if he did not. If you submit this type of item, always give credit to the person who wrote it and/or the publication where it was originally published.

I've never even heard of some of the magazines listed in your book. Where can I find them?

Many of the publications listed are available only by subscription, although some can be found at libraries, bookstores or magazine and newspaper stands. If you are interested in submitting to a magazine you have never read, it is always best to send for a sample copy and its writer's guidelines. The cost to receive a sample copy varies among publications. Occasionally, a sample is free upon request or free if you send an appropriately sized self-addressed envelope with your request. However, it is becoming more common to charge the price of a single issue to receive a sample copy. Check the market listing for that information.

My dad says that charging for sample copies is just a way for magazines to make money by selling extra copies. Shouldn't they be willing to send them to writers free so we can see what type of material they publish?

A few do. They are more likely to be ones hoping that once you see a copy, you'll want to subscribe to it. But most publications simply can't afford to send a free copy to every writer who wants one. Saving money to send for sample copies is not always easy. However, if you are serious about writing *and* publishing, it's money well spent. In some ways, it's almost like paying for lessons to learn how to play the piano better.

It's not necessary to send away for every sample copy that's available. Concentrate on the publications to which you really feel you can sell your work. Remember, you can read issues of many magazines for free at the library. You may also be able to get samples of old magazines from waiting rooms at some businesses. For instance, since my kids are now too old to want a subscription to *Highlights for Children*, I take home old copies from my chiropractor's office, with permission of course.

Is there any benefit to entering a contest if I don't really think I have a chance of winning?

That depends. If you just write and write and never bother to stop to consider how revising and rewriting and polishing your work might make it better, or if you just pick any contest to enter with no more attention than if you'd stuck all the contest names in a hat and drew one, you might not think you had a real chance of winning. And you'd be right. There wouldn't be any real benefit for you to enter in the first place.

On the other hand, if you lack self-confidence, you may think you don't have a real chance of winning, even if you've taken the time to write and edit until it's the best work you can do and gone to the trouble to find a contest that is appropriate for the type of manuscript you've written. It's true, you might not win, but you'd be wrong to think that you didn't have a chance. If you don't enter, you'll miss the benefit of the experience and a chance at placing. And for some contests, such as the Michigan Student Film & Video Festival, you'd miss out on receiving a free detailed professional evaluation that could help you become a better writer.

Do I have to submit to magazines only for kids, or can I send material to the ones my parents read, too?

There are a number of magazines for adults that regularly publish material from young people. Some are listed in this *Guide*. You'll need to judge for yourself whether a publication not listed would consider publishing a submission by you. Review the section on "the how" of studying a market, which begins on page 33. Incidentally, there are *no* circumstances I can think of where it would be wrong for you to express your opinion on a certain topic and address it to Letter to the Editor.

Why should I bother sending my material to a publication that doesn't pay for it?

As a young writer, you should be more interested in gaining writing and submission experience rather than making a lot of money for having your work published. In fact, very few writers of any age get rich by selling their manuscripts. You will gain valuable experience with every "sale" you make to a publication whether or not you are paid in cash for your efforts. It is hard for poets, in particular, to find paying markets for their work. Of course, you can choose not to send material to a publication that does not pay young writers. It is entirely up to you. (Beware, however, of markets and contests that want *you* to pay to have your work published!)

If this advice still doesn't make sense to you, pretend for a moment that you want to become a major league baseball player earning a million dollars a year when you grow up. How much do you expect to be paid displaying your baseball skills while playing Little League?

Why do some magazines pay a lot for manuscripts, some just a little and some not at all?

How much a publication pays for a manuscript varies greatly according to the publication's operating budget and editorial policy. In general, the markets listed in this *Guide*, which normally pay for material, pay the same rates to young people as they do to adults. Note that publications that include advertisements often, though not always, pay at least a little for accepted manuscripts. People and companies selling products and services pay for advertising space. This money increases a publication's operating budget and makes it more likely that it will have money to pay for accepted manuscripts.

On some guidelines, I've read "pays on acceptance" and on others, "pays on publication." What's the difference?

A publication that "pays on acceptance" will send you your check soon after your manuscript is accepted, without waiting for it to be actually published. Markets that "pay on publication" wait until they have actually printed your manuscript in the scheduled issue before sending you a check. Waiting for a "pays on publication" market to pay you is sometimes very frustrating. It may take up to a year or longer before your manuscript is published. When you need to decide between two markets with similar guidelines, it makes sense to submit first to the one that "pays on acceptance."

Do I have to cash the check I got from a magazine? I want to frame it.

By all means, cash it. Consider framing your printed piece or a photocopy of the check instead to signify your first "for pay" sale.

What does it mean to get a "$500 advance against royalties"?

Normally, when a writer sells a manuscript to a book publisher, she receives a contract, which, among other things, tells how much money she will earn for every book the publisher sells. This is usually based on a percentage of the book's selling price. For example, if the writer's contract says she will earn 10 percent for each of her books the publisher sells at retail for ten dollars, the writer will receive one dollar for each book sold. (When you go into a store and purchase something, the price you pay is the *retail* cost.) This percentage of sales is known as the "royalties."

Sometimes, instead of retail cost, royalties are based on the publisher's *net* price, in other words, the price the publisher actually sells the book for rather than the price listed on the cover. For instance, bookstores buy books from publishers at less than the cover price listed. (Bookstores pay the *net* price rather than the *retail* price.) This allows the bookstore to make money (for profit and to cover expenses, such as salaries and rent) by selling the books to customers at the retail price. In the example above, if the publisher sells the ten dollar book at net for five dollars, a writer earning a 10 percent royalty based on net would only earn fifty cents for each book sold.

Royalties are normally paid out to writers twice a year.

Question: How much money would a writer make on a book earning 10 percent royalties based on the retail price for a book that sells for $6.95 if 1,000 books are sold?

Answer: $6.95 × 1,000 × 10% = $695.00

Question: What if the 10 percent royalties was based on a percentage of *net*, and the publisher sells each $6.95 book for $3.00?

Answer: $3.00 × 1,000 × 10% = $300.00

Since it often takes a year or more between the time a writer sells a manuscript and when copies of the book begin selling, publishers often offer writers an *advance against royalties*. An advance is a certain sum of money that the publisher gives to the writer when the contract terms are agreed upon but before the book is actually published. This is not free or extra money that the writer gets. When the book is finally published and copies are sold, the publisher will deduct the amount of the advance from the total royalties due to the author.

Therefore, a five hundred dollar advance against royalties means that a writer will not receive any money earned from royalties until her royalties exceed five hundred dollars. That's the ugh side of advances. However, writers always try to get as big an advance from their publishers as they can against royalties (preferably based on retail) because the good part is you get to keep all of the advance money even if your book doesn't sell well enough to earn you any royalties.

Winners of the Publish-A-Book Contest receive a five hundred dollar advance against royalties. Prism Awards winners, however, receive a five hundred dollar cash award plus royalties (if published). National Written & Illustrated By . . . Awards Contest winners receive royalty contracts.

An article I submitted was rejected because the magazine had printed a similar piece a few months before. How can I know what subjects have been covered without reading every back issue of every magazine to which I'd like to submit?

This happens most with information or how-to articles. For magazines to which you, your friends or neighborhood libraries subscribe, take time to scan at least the table of contents of several back issues. For other publications, have your school or public librarian show you how to use two reference collections called *Reader's Guide to Periodic Literature* and the *Children's Maga-*

zine Guide. Both list by subject, title and author the articles published in many publications. These same or similar resources are often available on the library's computer system or through an online information source, such as CompuServe or GEnie. Finding information is much easier and quicker by computer. Be sure to check with an adult before using an online information source because access fees will be charged to the user's account.

However, don't worry too much if your subject has been covered recently if you've written an essay or opinion piece. Editors often repeat certain subjects if the writer presents a different or interesting viewpoint.

What is a "theme list"?

Some magazines and contests plan issues around a certain topic or theme, such as medicine, sports, dating, Colonial America, holidays, etc. Most listings will specify if a publication or contest follows a theme list. The deadline dates for submitting material will be included to help you meet their lead time. (For examples, see the market listing for *Cobblestone* or the Publish-A-Book Contest listing.)

I'm confused. Do I send my original manuscript and keep the copy, or do I send the copy and keep my original?

Generally, you would send your original manuscript and keep a copy. Note that "original" here means both something new you created on your own *and* the actual final draft you made of it. Markets and contests that accept handwritten work by young people, like *Stone Soup*, are more likely to want the actual work you created and not a photocopy or a copy retyped in standard format. Markets and contests that only accept work in standard typewritten format don't really care if they receive the original or a copy as long as what they receive is clear and easy to read.

The most important point to remember is to *never* send the only manuscript you have. *Always* keep a carbon copy, photocopy, disk copy, extra handmade or typed copy, computer printout or the original just in case something happens.

Note that some contests specify to send originals; others say send a copy.

What should I do with material that is rejected?

First of all, try hard not to take it personally. There are many reasons a manuscript may be rejected, and some have nothing to do with how well, or poorly, it is written. Reread your work and see if you can improve it. If you like it the way it is, look for another market. Make certain you have followed all of the guidelines and any theme or deadline requirements. Remember that even famous writers have material rejected. Some manuscripts are not bought until the fifth or even thirtieth different submission. The key is to keep trying. And to keep writing new material.

What does "copyright" mean?

For writers, "copy" means their written work. (Don't confuse this with making a copy of something.) "Right" refers to the person who has the authority to sell or offer a certain piece of written, drawn, photographed or computer-created work for possible publication. When you write something, you automatically become the copyright owner by law. If an editor agrees to publish your manuscript, he will "buy the rights" to it. Sometimes, magazines buy "one-time rights" or "first North American serial rights," which give them permission to print your manuscript one time. Then the rights are returned to you, and you may offer the same manuscript to another editor for "second" or "reprint" rights. A number of publications and some contests buy "all rights," which means that once you agree the publication can print your manuscript (or you submit to that particular contest), the work becomes *their* property (they hold the "copyright"), and it is no longer yours. You may not send it to another market or contest. Even though you no longer own the copyright to it, if it is published, your name as author will be included.

You should also know that the copyright of a message or library file on an online information service, such as CompuServe, is held by its author. You must obtain the author's permission to make further distribution of any portion of a message or file.

Copyrights can be very confusing. See page 42 for more information.

What is a model release form?

Occasionally a publication will ask the writer to provide a statement signed by the person granting an interview or photograph to prove that he or she agreed to being interviewed or photographed. Some editors can supply you with a model release form. You can make your own model release form using a clean sheet of paper containing your name, address and phone number, and the name, address and phone number of the person being interviewed or photographed. Have that person write a sentence or two that shows he or she understands that the information or photograph may be published. Then that person signs his or her name and the date. Most people don't mind providing this information. If you are writing something about someone eighteen or younger or will be taking their picture, have a parent or guardian also sign the model release form. You do not need to provide this form unless the publication's guidelines specifically request it or if there is any doubt that you received permission to use information or photographs in a manuscript you intend to submit to a market or contest.

Should I include a letter with my manuscript when I mail it?

If there is special information you would like to tell the editor and it is not included in your manuscript, you may send a short, one-page letter. This is called a "cover letter." Often this is not necessary. When an editor receives a manuscript prepared in standard typewritten format, he assumes you are hoping it will be accepted for publication. Note that some markets and contests want you to include a cover letter, particularly if you are under eighteen years of age. For more information, see page 67.

Is a cover sheet the same thing as a cover letter?

Not exactly. While a cover *letter* may also serve as a cover *sheet*, many contests use the term *cover letter* to mean the form that should accompany an entry.

What is a query letter?

Writers send a "query letter" to editors when they want to

know in advance whether the editor would be interested in receiving a manuscript about a certain topic. Most editors prefer that young writers send a complete manuscript, though older teens attempting to publish in adult publications may send query letters outlining their proposed articles.

Someday, if you've sold several manuscripts to the same editor, you may be surprised to receive a query letter yourself from that editor asking you to write on a certain subject. The editor will feel confident doing this because he is already familiar with your previous work and knows you can be depended upon to complete a writing project. Of course, it will be up to you whether or not you accept the assignment. Most of the editors, contest sponsors and young writers profiled in the *Guide* received queries from me asking them if they would be interested in contributing.

What does "solicit" mean?

To solicit means to ask for something. A publication that *solicits* poetry is indicating that it wants to receive poetry submissions to consider for publication.

A *solicited* submission means that an editor has either specifically asked a writer to submit a particular manuscript or agreed in advance to consider a manuscript when it is submitted. For example: If you query (ask) an editor if she would be interested in seeing your manuscript about "What Kids Can Do to Protect the Environment," your manuscript becomes a *solicited submission*.

The opposite, or *unsolicited submission*, refers to a manuscript that is just mailed to an editor without her prior knowledge and approval. In other words, the editor hasn't asked to see it. Unsolicited submissions waiting to be read and answered are often referred to as the "slush pile."

What does "in-house" publication mean?

When a company or organization publishes something, such as a newsletter, intended primarily for its employees or members, it is often referred to as an in-house publication. In other words, it is not meant for the general public. A student school newsletter is a good example of an in-house publication.

Some people also use the term "in-house" to mean that all

the work done creating a publication is done without assistance from outside sources. You may hear for example: "We did it all in-house."

What's a press pass, and how do I get one?

A press pass is a type of identification card or badge. Writers, especially journalists, TV or radio reporters, use press passes to gain entry into special events, especially when they want to gather behind-the-scenes information or interview someone special. Staff members and writers on assignment (meaning an editor has already given an OK to pursue a specific topic because he is potentially interested in publishing the proposed article) can request press passes from their editors. For example, members of your school yearbook staff get a type of press pass so they can attend sports and other activities free in order to get information and photographs.

Read about Michael LaFontaine in chapter seven. He used a press pass to attend a political rally for President George Bush during the 1992 presidential campaign.

An article I read in a writer's magazine gave tips on being polite and treating editors right. One tip was to compliment the editor who will read your manuscript. On what should I compliment her?

First of all, the article you mentioned referred to complimenting an editor *after* she has contacted you and, unfortunately, rejected the manuscript or idea you submitted. Many rejection notes and letters will contain the editor's name. The author of this article was suggesting that writers might want to send the editor who rejected your material a short note that basically says, Thank you for taking the time to read my manuscript and consider it for publication.

Sometimes writers who get rejection notices write very nasty letters back to the editor no matter how kind the editor tried to be. So I'm sure many editors would prefer receiving a nice thank you note once in a while instead. However, I don't think this is necessary unless an editor has sent you a very personal letter that perhaps offers some words of encouragement or advice for improving your manuscript.

What is the "Genre's Trade Journal"?

The word "genre" means a specific type or kind of writing. Science fiction is one type of genre. So are picture books, cookbooks, romances, biographies, even comic books. Every different type of writing can be considered a different genre.

Many professions have magazines (also called journals) devoted specifically to that profession. For instance, doctors have magazines about medicine. Mechanics have magazines about fixing cars. Teachers have publications about teaching. Writers and editors have special magazines for their professions, too. You're a writer and you read *Writer's Digest*. The "Markets" section of *Writer's Digest* often lists the names of editors. Editors and publishers also have special magazines, such as *Publisher's Weekly*. So, one example of a writer's "genre trade journal" would be *Writer's Digest*.

How do I find a publisher to send my novel to? There are only a couple markets and contests listed that want book-length manuscripts.

Unfortunately, there just aren't many publishers who want book-length manuscripts specifically from young writers. However, there *are* hundreds of markets that publish novels and nonfiction books. It won't be easy, because the competition is tough. Your manuscript will be competing for attention with thousands of other manuscripts written by older and often more experienced writers. Make it the best it can be, in content and presentation.

Make sure you've really written a novel and not just drawn out the events of what should have been a short story. Understand that novels aren't novels just because they are longer than what you are used to writing. Read some of the many good how-to-write-a-novel books if you aren't sure of the differences, or see if a novel writing course is offered in your area.

Author's Tip:

A good book on novel writing is *Get That Novel Started! And Keep It Going 'Til You Finish*, by Donna Levin. Published by Writer's Digest Books, it helps you write a novel with step-by-step directions.

When you're sure you've got a marketable book-length manuscript, it's time to check out one of the many other market reference books available, for example, *Writer's Market* or *Novel & Short Story Writer's Market*, both published by Writer's Digest Books.

Be market savvy. For example, beware of "fad" topics. Book publishers often plan their lists as much as two years in advance. "So," as one Atheneum editor says, "if a topic is 'hot' right now, it may be 'old' hat by the time we could bring it out."

DO YOUR HOMEWORK! Everything you've learned here about preparing your manuscript and studying the markets still applies. Once you find a few potential markets, take time to read some of the *recent* books they've published. You may want to "market" test your manuscript by entering it first in a novel contest, such as the one sponsored by the National Writer's Association.

As a young writer, your chances of getting a novel published are slim. But it *can* and *does* happen. Gordon Korman did it (and his weren't even long books). So have others. One is Jessica Carroll, whose *Billy the Punk* was published by Random House in Australia in 1993. She was seventeen at the time.

I wish you the best of luck! Let me know how you do.

I'm afraid I won't know what to do if my book manuscript gets accepted and the publisher sends me a contract. What should I do? Will the publisher decide not to publish it when they find out I'm just a kid?

Publishers are interested in publishing good books. They really don't care what age the author is as long as they feel the author will act in a responsible, professional manner (reread the beginning of chapter three.) Contracts can be confusing, but don't be afraid of them. If there is something you don't understand (and there probably will be), talk it over with your editor. Also get some outside help from a trusted adult. The main things to look for in a contract are: What rights does the publisher want to buy? How much will you be paid and when? What is the deadline for you to turn in a final, polished manuscript? What other responsibilities does the publisher expect from you (for instance, if your book will have photographs or illustrations, who pays for them, you or the publisher)? What happens if the editor does not like your final manuscript? How will the copyright be registered? Must you give this editor first choice for accepting your next book?

COMPUTER-RELATED QUESTIONS

I write on a computer at school that has a special software program that helps me make up stories. Can I send my story to a market or contest?

There are many computer software programs that help students learn how stories are put together by showing part of a story on screen and asking the student to fill in missing parts. They encourage creativity and help students learn new words but really do not help students create original stories. These types of stories are not suitable for submitting to regular markets and contests because the work is not entirely your own.

Occasionally, someone will sponsor a special writing contest based on one of these programs. In 1988, for instance, The Learning Company and Tandy (the company that makes the computers sold by Radio Shack) sponsored a Silly-Story writing contest. Every student used the same story "shell" that came with one of The Learning Company's software programs. They filled in the story blanks with as many creative nouns, verbs, adjectives and adverbs as they could.

My teacher has tried to upload some of our stories in the Literary Forum on CompuServe, but we can never find them listed in the library section. Where are they?

Literary Forum SYSOP Janet McConnaughey says that people

uploading files often forget to include line feeds or carriage returns at the end of *each* line of text. That means you need to press "enter" or "return" as *each* line of type gets to the edge of the screen. Most word processors automatically wrap words that go beyond the screen to the next line. However, you'll need to do this manually for manuscripts you want to upload. Just remember to type as if you were using an older style typewriter, the kind with a handle that sticks out the right side that you push to make the platen advance one line and return to the left margin.

(Check individual online systems for the maximum number of characters that can be included in one line of type. This is sometimes referred to as "number of columns." A typical width is eighty columns.)

For additional help, check both your word processing software manual and the manual that explains how to use your modem communications software. Also, it's a good idea to post a message to SYSOP on any bulletin board before uploading your first few files to obtain advice about which library to use and other uploading information. State in a few words what your file contains, such as the topic or genre, to help the SYSOP give you the most appropriate answers.

Do I need my own user ID number and password to log onto a computer system like CompuServe or GEnie?

Generally, students within a classroom or school, as well as family members, may share one user ID number and password. (For instance, one student who requested submissions from Student Forum members on CompuServe for use in her electronic newspaper project logs on using her teacher's account. Note, however, that the subscription will only be registered under one name. If you spend a lot of time online, your parents may want you to have your own account for tracking purposes. Like any other hobby, consider paying all or a part of the expense involved.

Regardless of whose account you are using, *make sure you have received permission before logging on.*

How can I use my own name online if I'm using my dad's or teacher's account?

On GEnie, users may use nicknames to sign messages. (Tanya Beaty uses Oracle as her nickname on the Writers' Ink RoundTable.) After you log on to a bulletin board area or real-time conference (RTC), use the /NAM command. You will be prompted for the new name. This nickname will appear (along with your normal GE Mail address) in each message you leave in that board. If, for instance, you are the only one using that account to access the Writers' Ink area, the nickname you have chosen will remain the same. If your dad accesses other areas, he can use a different nickname there. Once you choose your nickname, you won't have to go through the process again unless you want to.

CompuServe prefers that users always use their regular names, first and last, rather than nicknames. (Actually, they insist a first and last name be used, but they are nice about it.) But instead of your dad's name being listed, you can change it to show your name instead for a particular forum. How you do this depends on which software you are using. CompuServe recommends that new users use CIM (CompuServe Information Manager). With CIM, select the "SPECIAL" menu and then choose "OPTIONS." Backspace over the present name and type in yours. If you don't want to bother changing the name (or someone, like your dad, doesn't want you to), consider this method instead: Sign messages and identify files with your own name, then add the name of the person who has the subscription since this is the name that will appear next to the user ID number that you're using. Example: John (Joe Smith's son).

Though the how-to may differ slightly, most online information services or bulletin board systems have an option to change the name used during that session. This is especially useful when participating in online conferences. Most special communication software packages also have an option to automatically change the name used online.

How can I tell what stories are written by kids?

Sometimes you can't, unless the manuscript was uploaded as part of a contest that had special categories for different ages.

That's one of the advantages to communicating online! You won't be subjected to discrimination because of your age, sex or background because they won't know (unless you tell them). Young writers who want their ages known can add the information to the uploaded file, in the file description or in the keywords area.

If you're looking for files written by kids, look for addresses within the files or descriptions that indicate a school or class. Example: Written by students at Perry Middle School.

You can also post messages on the bulletin board stating your age and interests and inviting other members to contact you. Finding pen pals online is a popular feature on BBS these days.

I'm having trouble uploading and downloading files. Where do I get help?

First make sure you've read your user's manuals. If a parent or teacher can't help you, leave a message to the SYSOP in the special interest group (SIG) you're trying to access. You might also try asking for help at your local computer store. Many software manufacturers and online information systems have toll-free numbers you can call to talk to a real person.

Is there any way to save on connect charges when I want to log onto a computer information service?

There are several software packages that can help you "automate" your sessions by allowing you to log on, go straight to the SIG you want, automatically up or download a file, then log off—all with the push of one or two keys. These are often referred to as "navigation" programs.

Several are available for CompuServe users, including AUTOSIG and TAPCIS for MS-DOS users (IBM and compatible systems), CompuServe's Information Manager, Navigator for the Macintosh, ST/FORUM for the Atari ST and WHAP! for Amiga users. GEnie users with IBM or IBM-compatible systems can use Aladdin. (A version for Apples and the Macintosh systems is under development.) Most of these software programs can be downloaded and tried free on a trial basis directly from the computer service. Note, you pay connect charges while downloading the file. (Normally, you can upload to any service free of connect charges.)

You can also save money by not logging on during prime time hours, which are usually weekdays between 8:30 A.M. to 6:30 or 8:30 P.M. That means logging on late at night or on weekends or holidays. You can program most communication software to log on and off automatically during off-peak times and when phone rates are the lowest. Check with your local adult computer advisor for help.

I have to dial long-distance to log on to a computer information system. Is there any way I can save money on my mom's phone bills?

Remember, it usually costs less to call anywhere long-distance in the evening, on weekends or during holidays. Call your long-distance service for advice about special rates and services. For instance, if you have AT&T's Reach-Out America plan, it's cheaper to dial an out-of-state access number instead of a long-distance in-state one.

QUESTIONS ABOUT WRITERS AND WRITING

What's the difference between a writer and an author?

If you write, that is, creatively arrange words in some fixed form (usually on paper) to create a poem, story, article, etc., then you are a writer. But you are also the author of the piece you have written. The term *author* is most often used when referring to the writer of a particular piece of published work. Example: Kathy Henderson, author of the *Market Guide for Young Writers*, will be our featured speaker.

How can I tell a good idea from a bad one?

Often you can't. William Saroyan once said, "You write a hit play the same way you write a flop." You've got to have faith in yourself and follow your instincts. Sometimes, it's not the idea that's bad but the way the writer used it. For some tips about getting and recognizing good ideas, refer to chapters two and three.

I love your book but still have lots of questions. Can I write to you?

Yes, you may write to me. I always look forward to hearing from readers. Send your letters to me % Writer's Digest Books, 1507 Dana Avenue, Cincinnati, OH 45207. You may also contact me electronically via CompuServe. My e-mail address is 71660,3100.

Could you help me choose the best place to send my work? I'm afraid of picking the wrong place.

Of all the mail I get, this is the question I'm asked most often. (The second most asked question is "Where can I send my novel?") As much as I'd like to help, I prefer not to choose the places where young writers should send their work. For one thing, I'd never have time to write and market my own work! Second, I can't because most times I've never seen the letter writer's manuscripts so I have no way of evaluating them to know which markets or contests might be most appropriate. Third, marketing your own manuscripts is kind of like homework; if you're going to learn anything, you've got to do it yourself.

Some writers, myself included, find marketing much easier than writing. I like researching the possibilities, analyzing and comparing the differences, weighing the benefits of submitting first to one market instead of another—all essential elements of choosing where to send a manuscript. For me, the process is inspiring. New ideas for articles and stories and books pop into my mind as I read what editors are looking for. Turning those ideas into finished manuscripts, though, is a constant struggle. I have a hard time letting go of a project until I feel it's the best I can make it. (And I'm a tough judge of my own work!) Sometimes, I have so many ideas I don't know which one to work on first. It's too easy to stop working on one thing when the writing gets tough and start another. (If you have this problem, too, reading *Becoming a Writer*, by Dorothea Brande, may help.)

Most writers, however, are more comfortable with the writing process. They really don't like worrying about how to market their work. They balk at learning which editors want the kind of manuscripts they have to offer. In fact, they would prefer to skip the marketing process all together if they could.[1] But, like me, they want to be a published writer. So, no matter whether we enjoy the process or not, we do each step because it's got to be done. If you accept the challenge and learn to enjoy the process, you'll have a much better chance of getting published.

Of course, studying and comparing opportunities doesn't do any good if you're afraid of picking one because your manuscript might not get accepted. This is a fear with which *all* writers struggle. It's no different than a baseball player worrying that he might strike out at the plate. If you simply *cannot* decide, put the names of your best choices (see "Study and Compare Opportunities," beginning on page 32) into a hat and draw one out after another, keeping a list as you go along. Then start submitting.

This all seems too much like work. I thought writing was about inspiration and being creative. Isn't that more important?

For many people, that is what writing is all about. They enjoy being creative and whenever inspired, write. If that's how you want writing to be for you, that's fine. But serious writers can't rely on inspiration alone. They need to approach their craft like anyone serious about improving, using and promoting their skills. Writing when inspired might get you a nice seat on the players bench, but it won't put you in the starting lineup. How many top athletes do you know who only practice or show up for games when inspired?

If I sent you my manuscript, would you tell me if it is good or not?

Well . . . this is a really hard one for me to answer. I love to read the work of young writers, and I don't want to discourage anyone from writing to me. When I have time, I do read manuscripts and make a few encouraging comments if asked to do so. Occasionally, I'll work with one or two young writers on a more

---

[1]Some writers, after they have gained some success, *do* skip the marketing process by paying a literary agent to do it for them. Unfortunately, that's an arrangement out of reach for many writers, especially young ones.

detailed level each year. These are usually students I've met during workshop presentations. Unfortunately, it's simply not possible to give a detailed critique to everyone who writes. Bear in mind that I am primarily a nonfiction writer, although I do write and have published some fiction. Like a maid who doesn't do windows, I'm a writer who doesn't do poetry. So, while I love to read poetry, I am not a good person to ask for help writing or publishing it.

Here are some guidelines for those who would like to write to me:

1. Please include a self-addressed stamped envelope (SASE) with your letter when you write. You will likely get a quicker response.

Note: I receive many letters each year from students and teachers that I cannot respond to because there are no SASEs, and no return addresses on either their letters or envelopes. So, even though I want to respond, I can't because I don't know where the writers live.

2. Tell me a little about yourself, such as your age, school and the kind of writing you like to do.

3. Feel free to ask me *specific* questions. Here, for example, are what three students at Warrensburg Elementary in Warrensburg, Illinois, recently wrote to ask me:

Where do you get your ideas from?

What made you become an author?

What is your favorite animal?

Did you write any books about your childhood?

What is your favorite book you wrote?

(By the way, my favorite animals are my calico cat Page and my horse Spanky. My favorite book that I wrote is this one.)

4. Please ask me questions that you, personally, are interested in knowing. Don't, for example, ask the same thing everyone else in your class is asking. If everyone wants to know something, send one letter like the Warrensburg students above did.

5. Please do not ask me to give you answers to things you can

easily find in my book. That's why I wrote *Market Guide for Young Writers* in the first place—so you would have the basic answers. It is very bothersome to receive six letters (especially all from the same class) that say:

Dear Ms. Henderson: (or TO WHOM IT MAY CONCERN)
"I am in the 5th grade, and am planning to send some things for publication. I need to know the requirements—handwriting, paper size, etc.
Thank you.
Sincerely,
So and so young writer

Unfortunately, I receive several packets of such letters every school semester.

6. If you include a sample of your work, please limit it to five pages. I especially enjoy receiving photocopies of things young writers have had published. *However, I do not publish writers' work myself.*

7. Please be patient while you wait for me to respond. I try to answer within two weeks, but sometimes it's longer. In addition to writing, I also have a full-time job and sometimes travel to speak at schools and conferences.

8. Occasionally, things get lost in the mail, so if you don't hear from me after a while, feel free to write me again. Don't forget to include your address on *both* your letter and envelope in case they get separated. Please include an SASE if at all possible.

Send letters to me c/o Writer's Digest Books, 1507 Dana Ave., Cincinnati, OH 45207. You may also contact me via CompuServe. My e-mail address is 71660,3100.

May I write to other writers?

I can't speak directly for other writers, but generally, yes, you may write to other writers. It's always a pleasure hearing from readers who have enjoyed our work. If you don't know where a writer lives, send your letter to the company that published his or her book or to the magazine where you read his work. Your letter will be forwarded if possible. Note that it may take several weeks for a writer to receive a letter forwarded from the publisher. I once received mail *two years* after it was sent to a publisher with whom I used to work. So, please be patient.

Does it make you happy to get published?

I don't believe having things makes one happy. Once you get it, you always think having more or getting something else will make you happier. Having my work published makes me feel good and excited and proud. But I get happiness from being me and pursuing my goals. I think Margaret Lee Runbeck said it best:

Happiness is not a state to arrive at,

but a manner of traveling.

I wish you all good luck and much happiness as you travel the path to getting published.

PART TWO

Chapter Seven

Young Writers in Print

You've come to my favorite part of this *Guide*, where I get to introduce a new group of young writers who have found from a little to a lot of publishing success.

Even before I finish working on one edition of *Market Guide for Young Writers*, I've already begun to collect information and references for the next. I never grow tired of meeting young writers or of reading and hearing about their experiences. Many people have asked how I learn about young writers in so many different parts of the country and with such different backgrounds. (Each new edition features a different group of young writers; a total of forty-two so far. One young writer, Mike Snyder, was profiled twice because he was the one who gave me the idea for the *Guide* in the first place. I wanted readers to see how well he'd done after following the marketing advice in the first edition [1986]. Another nine successful creative young people are featured in *Market Guide for Young Artists and Photographers*.)

Finding young writers is the easy part. Many write to me each year and not only from the U.S. Letters have come from young writers and teachers in Canada, England, Australia, France, Belgium, the Netherlands, Germany, Puerto Rico and the U.S. Virgin Islands, Malaysia, Japan, China, Spain and India. They send samples of their work, share good and bad experiences they've had marketing and entering contests, want to know more about me personally or ask for more information about writing and marketing. Some I "chat" with online. Many of their questions find their way into new editions.

I also learn about talented young writers by asking for recommendations from the editors and contest sponsors I'm interested in featuring. It's not always possible, but I prefer to feature both an editor or contest sponsor and a young writer with ties to the same market or contest. This gives you, the reader, a unique two-sided look behind the scenes.

The hard part comes when I must decide on the few I can invite to contribute to each new edition. I try to have different parts of the country represented, as well as writers from different backgrounds, writing and publishing experiences and ages. Because I encourage young writers to take advantage of opportunities in their own areas, I also look for young writers who can highlight a small, local or specialty market or contest.

But most importantly, each young writer essay must have three things: (1) something of value to share with readers; (2) some words of inspiration or encouragement, advice about becoming a better writer or marketing tips; and (3) a different style and way of expressing themselves. I always ask them to share at least one good and one not-so-good experience. And, of course, I have to get their submissions in time to meet my book deadline. But if you asked them, they would tell you that I give very few guidelines about how to write their essays. What I give them is a skeleton. They must construct a strong body.

The most fun, however, is when I receive everyone's photo, because I rarely know what anyone looks like in advance! And, of course, it's also fun right now, when I get to introduce them to you. I know you'll enjoy meeting them as much as I have. Plus, this edition features not one, but two, guest celebrity "young writers." I know you'll enjoy reading about the early writing and publishing experiences of Gordon Korman, whose first five novels were published while he was in high school. And then, there's Stephen King. I'm sure you'll recognize the style he's now internationally known for in the special reprint of one of his earliest short stories.

GORDON KORMAN
Former Young Writer
New York, New York

Twenty years after the publication of the first Bruno & Boots book (written when he was a seventh grader), Gordon Korman continues to write books about the two lovable troublemakers as well as many other popular books. His trademark humor makes him a favorite with young readers from middle graders to young adults. When he's not "on the road" visiting schools, Gordon Korman divides his time between Pompano Beach, Florida, and New York City, making his living as a full-time writer of fiction books for middle graders and teens.

Gordon had no interest in writing before his English teacher, who had more experience in his role as the school's track and field coach, gave him an assignment to write a book. It's hard to believe Gordon's first five novels were published before graduating high school!

I was born in Montreal, and I grew up in and around Toronto, Canada. My family couldn't have been more basic: You had my folks and you had me. No brothers or sisters. Not even dogs or cats to shake things up a little. I think one of the reasons I got into writing was that, as an only child, I needed to be creative to keep myself entertained.

I owe my whole career to my seventh grade English teacher. He was actually the track and field coach. I think the main reason he gave us the assignment to write a book was that he didn't have much prior experience teaching English, and so he had no file of assignments from which to draw ideas to keep us busy. He gave us four months, forty-five minutes a day to work on the story of our choice. The average kid wrote about twenty-five pages total. My finished manuscript was eighty-five!

My project was *This Can't Be Happening at Macdonald Hall*, which became my first published book. (It was published with very little editing, except that my original chapter twelve was split into two chapters.) I happened to be the class monitor for the Scholastic TAB Book Club, so I figured I was practically a Scholastic employee already! I sent my novel to the address on the TAB flyer, and a few days after my thirteenth birthday, I had a book contract with Scholastic (Canadian division).

In the beginning, I even had a negative attitude about the project. And I only ended up with a *B* + on the assignment. Well, actually, I earned an *A*, but got marked down for penmanship. Surprisingly, I didn't do any writing in eighth grade. When I did, it was another book featuring Bruno and Boots, the same two main characters as in my first book. Twenty years later, I'm still writing about them and Macdonald Hall, the boys' boarding school. The story's location made it easier to cut down on the number of adult characters, like parents, I had to deal with.

After graduating high school, I went to New York University to study film. I was a total washout as a film major, so I switched to the Dramatic Writing Program. I did get some use out of my moviemaking education, though, when I wrote *Macdonald Hall Goes Hollywood*, which is about a Hollywood film crew shooting on location at Macdonald Hall. That's a big advantage of being a writer: Anything you learn, no matter how useless it may seem at the time, might just fit into a story one day.

Another great thing about my job is that I'm my own boss. I can sleep late and take long vacations, but that can also be a problem. Because nobody is standing over me making me work, I have to make myself work, which isn't easy.

There's no set formula for where I get my ideas for books. Sometimes an idea can take months to develop; the process can be as enjoyable as having teeth pulled. I'll add a character here, a plot point there, and I'll finally be ready to start writing. On the other hand, there are times that the whole story just sort of whooshes into my head in a split second. *The Zucchini Warriors* is a perfect example of that. I was nuts for football, I despised fried zucchini sticks and I wanted to write another Bruno and Boots book. Bang! A football team at Macdonald Hall sponsored by Mr. Zucchini. A few months later, the finished manuscript was on my editor's desk.

In the end, it doesn't matter how quickly ideas come or from where, so long as my readers keep laughing. And I include myself in the audience. I realize it's impolite to laugh at your own jokes, but I really crack myself up when I'm writing.

One of the things I'm most grateful to the track and field coach/English teacher for is that he was aware enough to insist we start with an outline of what we planned to write. In fact, writing an outline was the first week's assignment. I think outlining is the key to writing a book-length manuscript. They don't need to be the formal kind you learn to do for reports and research projects in school. Actually, it's probably best if they aren't. My outlines are basically random notes that I write as ideas for plot twists; characters and scenes come to me. Eventually, I decide I've got enough of a book fleshed out and move the notes around until I get a basic outline that seems right. Then it's a matter of sitting down and writing the book itself.

I don't know if you can learn to write, especially fiction, and how to connect real life with imagination. You just do it over and over and eventually you'll come up with something worthwhile.

Longtime roommates Bruno and Boots have been separated. Now they're trying to get back together by framing their new roommates.

—From *This Can't Be Happening at Mcdonald Hall*, Scholastic, 1978.

• • •

When his roommate was sound asleep, Boots went into operation. Fifteen minutes later the window opened and out he went—along with a monogrammed money clip, a personalized teletype machine key and a gold pen and pencil set, all clearly the property of George Wexford-Smyth III.

• • •

Elmer had not gone to the dance either. "I don't see how everyone can go and dance with *girls*," he said with disgust. "Girls are so icky! I'm glad you didn't go, Bruno. At least one person in this school besides me has some sense."

"Yes, Elmer," Bruno sighed, ready to make his move as soon as his roommate went to sleep. He watched in dismay as Elmer set up an elaborate tripod supporting a high-powered telescope. "Aren't you going to bed?" he asked.

"On a clear night?" Elmer replied, as if Bruno had suggested the impossible. "On a clear night I can scan the whole sky."

"Why in the world would you want to do that?"

"I'm an astronomer," Elmer explained. "My world is the heavens, the universe, the vastness of intergalactic space . . . Now if you'll excuse me, my telescope is a little out of focus."

"*You* are a little out of focus," said Bruno sourly.

"Ah," said Elmer, squinting into the eyepiece and turning two knobs on the side, "it's coming clearer. Yes, I see it— the horsehead nebula!"

"Mmm-hmm," grunted Bruno. Instead of contemplating the universe, he was concentrating on the problem of getting out through the window with Elmer so firmly established there.

Elmer was providing a running commentary. "Look! Can it be? Yes—the crab nebula! Caused by an exploding star millions of years ago!"

"Mmm-hmm," Bruno repeated. He tiptoed through the room gathering up some of Elmer's more recognizable possessions—the skull of a rodent, a signed membership in the Toronto Horticultural Society and a corked test tube bearing the label: *Drimsdale, Test 3-A, Sept. 15/80.* Now how am I going to get out of here? Bruno thought. I'll never get past the house master at the main doors.

Elmer was still raving about the crab nebula and was even starting to sketch it when Bruno opened the door. "Bruno, this is fabulous! I've never seen such a clear night!" The door shut silently. In a second Bruno was knocking on the door of 205.

"Who is it?" demanded Perry Elbert.

"Me. Bruno."

"You! Go away," groaned Perry. "I refuse to open the door."

"No trouble," Bruno promised. "Honest. I just have to borrow your window."

Reluctantly Perry opened the door and let him in. "So long as you're passing through," he said.

"Thanks, Perry, you're a pal. I'll be back in an hour." Bruno swung his legs over the sill and dropped down onto the grass.

At the old cannon, Boots was waiting for him. "What took you so long?" he asked indignantly.

"You won't believe this," Bruno said, "but Elmer is an astronomer. His world is *out of this world!* Tonight is a clear night, the crab nebula looks sharp—and I had to find another window. Now, where are we going?"

"Miss Scrimmage's." Boots grinned in the darkness. "Elmer Drimsdale and George Wexford-Smyth III are going to stage a shameful panty raid on the young ladies."

In no time they were across the road, over the wrought-iron fence and under Diane Grant's window. Again pebbles were thrown and the familiar blonde head leaned out.

"Go away, Bruno," grumbled the girl. "I'm already grounded for a month. Haven't you done enough?"

Bruno ignored her question. "I've got Boots with me," Bruno whispered. "Can we come up?"

"Are you crazy?" Diane exclaimed. "I'll be shot!"

But Bruno was already climbing the drainpipe to the window ledge. Diane and Cathy, her roommate, reached out and pulled him inside. Boots followed right behind him.

"If we're caught . . ." Diane threatened.

"Don't be silly," interrupted Bruno. "I *never* get caught. Can you cut the legs off an old pair of panty hose for us?" Then he turned to Boots. "Go ahead. It's your show."

"Get the girls together for a briefing," Boots ordered, "and tell them to bring their panties—this is a raid!"

Without a word or a question, Cathy and Diane grinned and set off to gather their friends. As each girl slipped into the room, she deposited a pair of panties in a pillowcase that Boots held out. They showed no surprise at the boys' presence. Miss Scrimmage's young ladies were always ready for some excitement.

Boots cleared his throat. "Girls, this is a panty raid. We are the raiders, *but it isn't us*. We are *really* Elmer Drimsdale and George Wexford-Smyth III. Got it?"

"You've got to be kidding!" one girl protested. "George? That pill? He wouldn't raid anything if it wasn't for money. Give me my panties back."

"Quiet! Quiet!" Cathy hissed as the girls started to scream with laughter. "Do you want old Scrimmage down here dropping her bloomers in the bag?"

"Who was the other guy?" another girl asked, shaking with laughter. "Elmer Drysdale?"

"Drimsdale," replied Bruno. "You wouldn't know him. He doesn't like girls—ants are more his type."

Boots held up his hands for order, then passed around George's and Elmer's belongings. The girls fell silent. "Now, here's what I want you to do," he explained. "Plant these things around your rooms and mess up your drawers. Then wait. When Bruno and I start yelling up and down the halls, I want to hear screaming. *Real* screaming—*blood-curdling* screaming. I want chaos and disorder. In short I want a riot—a full-fledged riot. Can you handle it?"

"Certainly," said Cathy. "Riots are our speciality."

"All right," Boots nodded. "Everybody to battle stations. You've got two minutes to get ready."

When the girls were gone, Bruno and Boots pulled the nylons over their heads and tiptoed into the hall. "Boy, this is going to be fun," whispered Bruno.

"*If* we get away with it," said Boots. "Okay, now!"

The two galloped up and down the hallways like wild horses, shouting in the deepest voices they could manage and banging on the walls. Right on cue, the girls began to scream. They were extremely good at it—adding howling and screeching and slamming of doors for effect.

"Boys! There are boys in the dormitory!"

"Help! They're in my room!"

"Miss Scrimmage! Miss Scrimmage! Help!"

Satisfied that the riot was progressing nicely, Bruno and

Boots slipped back into Diane and Cathy's room and shin-
nied down the drainpipe. Just as they reached the ground
Cathy had a great flash of inspiration. She raced down the
hall and yanked on the fire-alarm lever. At the deafening
clang of the fire bell Bruno and Boots shot over Miss Scrimmage's fence, across the road and onto their own campus.
At Macdonald Hall a crowd was already beginning to gather.

Boots grabbed Bruno from behind. "The stocking, you
idiot! You're still wearing the stocking!" He snatched it
from Bruno's head. "Now's our chance to head for our own
dorms and get back into our rooms unnoticed."

Bruno nodded. "Give me some panties first. If Elmer's
going to get blamed for all this, he might as well have
something to show for it." The two separated. Boots slipped
in with the boys from Dormitory 1 and tried to look sleepy
in spite of the fact that he was fully dressed. "Hey, where's
everybody going?" he demanded.

"Are you deaf?" someone replied. "Miss Scrimmage's is
on fire!"

The boys from Dormitory 2 were also outside milling
around in confusion. Bruno suddenly found himself standing
beside Perry Elbert, who stared at him accusingly.

"You promised," Perry wailed. "You said no trouble. You
lied!"

"No way," Bruno answered. "I didn't pull that fire
alarm." Then he turned to the noisy crowd and bellowed,
"Miss Scrimmage and the girls are in danger! Who can save
them?"

"We can!" roared the crowd.

"Follow me, men!" Bruno screamed in delight. "On to
Scrimmage's to save the girls!"

With Bruno bellowing at the head of his army, the brave
men of Macdonald Hall poured across the road and stormed
Miss Scrimmage's campus. Their cries of "Don't worry,
girls!" and "Hang in there, girls!" were met by Cathy's ear-
splitting scream, "The boys are here! We're saved!"

Suddenly Miss Scrimmage appeared on the front balcony
of the residence, wrapped in a bathrobe, her hair in pincurls,

her glasses askew on her nose. She was waving a shotgun and shouting hysterically. "Where's the lion?" she screeched. "Hang on, girls, I'll save you!"

BOOM! The shotgun went off by mistake, blasting a large hole in the sign over the main gate. All screaming stopped abruptly. The girls, who had been carried across the highway to safety by the courageous Macdonald Hall army, began to straggle back.

Finally Mr. Sturgeon and several members of his staff arrived on the scene. They entered the residence and investigated until they could assure Miss Scrimmage that there was no fire—and no lion. A few minutes later Mr. Sturgeon came out on the balcony and addressed his boys. "Return to your rooms at once," he ordered. "There is no fire. I repeat, return to your rooms at once."

• • •

When he got back to his room, Boots discovered that George had not yet returned from the scene of the commotion. Whistling cheerfully, he extracted a pair of pink panties from the pillowcase and stuffed them into the pocket of George's tan jacket. The rest of the panties he pushed under George's pillow. Then he climbed into bed and promptly fell asleep.

• • •

Bruno beat the crowd back to Dormitory 2. As he quietly opened the door to his room, Elmer's voice floated out: "Did you know, Bruno, that some scientists think the crab nebula was formed before our solar system? Do you realize that means I'm looking at it as it actually was hundreds of millions of years ago?"

"Mmm-hmm," said Bruno. Unbelievably, Elmer had never missed him, nor had he noticed the commotion on the two campuses. He had been glued to his telescope all this time—gazing and drawing and theorizing.

"Elmer, old buddy, you're one in a million," marvelled Bruno.

Elmer took this as a compliment. "Thank you, Bruno," he said.

• • •

The battlefield was deserted. A light breeze whispered through the evergreens on both campuses. In front of Miss Scrimmage's, soft moonlight illuminated tattered bushes and trampled flower beds—and a sign which read: *Miss Scrimmage's Fishing School for Young Ladies.*

STEPHEN KING

Former Young Writer

Bangor, Maine

Stephen King (one of today's most famous and prolific writers) started writing in his youth. The following is a reprint of a story that was self-published in the "magazine" written and published (photocopied and stapled!) by Mr. King and a boyhood friend. They produced several, but to his knowledge, only one copy of each still exists. When they sold them for ten cents to twenty-five cents to the kids in school, Mr. King realized for the first time that one could write something and get paid for it. School officials eventually made them stop.

In a 1986 letter to Carol Fenner, managing editor of Flip, *a student literary magazine no longer published, he had this to say about his story:*

This has been very painful for me but I have managed to dig up the rotting body of one of my stories written as a teen of about thirteen. I think your readers will see what a really dreadful story it is, but I think they will also see maybe the first delicate sprouts of what has become the world's bestselling Venus flytrap. If you don't want to use this story, I'd be delighted. But for what it's worth, you have my permission.

Unfortunately, the issue of Flip *that was to have featured Mr. King's story was never published. I'm grateful to Ms. Fenner for her cooperation in helping me access this story and to Mr. King for allowing me to reprint it.*

THE HOTEL AT THE END OF THE ROAD

"Faster!" Tommy Riviera said. "Faster!"

"I'm hitting 85 now," Kelso Black said.

"The cops are right behind us," Riviera said. "Put it up to 90." He leaned out the window. Behind the fleeing car was a police car, with siren wailing and red light flashing.

"I'm hitting the side road ahead," Black grunted. He turned the wheel and the car turned into the winding road-spraying gravel.

The uniformed policeman scratched his head. "Where did they go?"

His partner frowned. "I don't know. They just—disappeared."

"Look," Black said. "Lights ahead."

"It's a hotel," Riviera said wonderingly. "Out on this wagon track, a hotel! If that don't beat all! The police'll never look for us there."

Black, unheeding of the car's tires, stamped on the brake. Riviera reached into the back seat and got a black bag. They walked in.

The hotel looked just like a scene out of the early 1900s. Riviera rang the bell impatiently. An old man shuffled out. "We want a room," Black said.

The man stared at them silently.

"A room," Black repeated.

The man turned around to go back into his office.

"Look, old man," Tommy Riviera said. "I don't take that from anybody." He pulled out his thirty-eight. "Now you give us a room."

The man looked ready to keep on going, but at last he said: "Room five. End of the hall."

He gave them no register to sign, so they went up. The room was barren except for an iron double bed, a cracked mirror, and soiled wallpaper.

"Aah, what a crummy joint," Black said in disgust. "I'll bet there's enough cockroaches here to fill a five-gallon can."

The next morning when Riviera woke up, he couldn't get out of bed. He couldn't move a muscle. He was paralyzed. Just then the old man came into view. He had a needle which he put into Black's arms.

"So you're awake," he said. "My, my, you two are the first additions to my museum in twenty-five years. But you'll be well preserved. And you won't die.

"You'll go with the rest of my collection of living mummies. Nice specimens."

Tommy Riviera couldn't even express his horror.

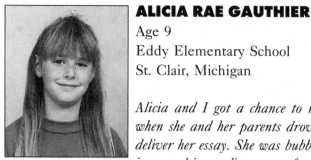

ALICIA RAE GAUTHIER

Age 9
Eddy Elementary School
St. Clair, Michigan

Alicia and I got a chance to meet in person when she and her parents drove up to hand-deliver her essay. She was bubbly, excited and interested in reading some of my books within minutes of her arrival.

We "clicked" right away. Perhaps it's because of the "I hate to write" syndrome we share. Alicia says it's because her hand cramps up from all that handwriting she does for her stories. For me, it's my brain *that seems to get cramped up the most. Where* do *all those wonderful ideas and words go just when I'm about to snag them and trap them on paper?*

Alicia's first experience getting published, although exciting, isn't unique. All across the country, more and more newspapers and other organizations are sponsoring contests similar to the one in which Alicia's mom entered her story. For insight into why the Port Huron Times Herald *first got interested in offering opportunities for local young writers, read the profile of Michael Eckert, Projects Editor for the* Times Herald. *Then look for similar opportunities in your area. If you don't find any, perhaps you can persuade an editor to start one.*

Like Alicia, many young writers are lucky enough to have a supportive parent or teacher who can help them submit their writings. However, I urge young writers not to let an adult do all the planning, preparing, deciding and mailing work for you. It is, after all, your *work. By taking an active role in the marketing of your work, you will develop a better feel for the types of manuscripts specific markets and contests are looking for.*

This might sound weird, but I hate to write. What I mean is the act of actually writing it down. I love to type and use the computer. When I do write stuff it is usually six pages long, so my hand gets tired. Someday I hope to get a computer so I can write even longer stories.

My first published work was in the *Times Herald*, the area's local daily paper. Each Wednesday the paper has a young people's page. I wrote a story called "The Cow Patch." It is a story about me falling off the stage when I was a cow in our school play. My mom thought the story was *so* good, but I just thought it was OK. She sent it in without telling me so I wouldn't be disappointed if it wasn't printed. Well, it was! To my surprise, when I opened the paper, I saw my story! I was so overcome with happiness and joy that I screamed and ran outside! It was reading month at school, and the principal read my story over the loud speaker. I was supposed to read it, but I was stuck home with the chicken pox. Everyone made a big deal over it, and I was so proud.

Even though "The Cow Patch" was just an assignment I wasn't that interested in, I always put in my best effort. Just think, a normal everyday assignment—to "fame"!

My earliest experience with writing that I can remember is when I was two years old. I wrote a three-page story about a dog named Sprinkle Jack. My mom wrote the words for me because I couldn't write or spell. And, I like to make up or change songs.

This was my first contest I ever entered, but it won't be my last. I'm considering sending something into *Highlights for Children* magazine. You never know until you try.

The reason I'm a good writer is because I read. Not every once in a while, but all the time. I won't go for more than a fifteen-minute ride without bringing a book to read. People say that I sound like a book when they read my stories. I talk like one, too. I guess that's because I love reading.

One of the hints I can give is not to make yourself work too hard at writing. Things like names of people or places may take weeks to come to you. Just never give up. Just because one thing isn't exactly what someone wants, maybe they'll want something else. Besides, almost everything can be improved. The best advice I can give is this . . . the best way to get an idea for a story is from past experience. Embarrassing, happy, terrible— just about any [emotion] will work. Just remember to add some detail and action. These things can change a simple, boring sentence like, "The dog ran across the road to see his owner. He was happy." to "He was so happy, he ran right in front of a car, nearly getting hit. When he got to his owner, he jumped up on her and licked her face with his little wet tongue." This makes your work much more detailed and fun to read.

Just keep writing, use your imagination and have fun. Enter your work because you never know who will print it. It's great seeing your writing in print, and every successful writer has to start somewhere.

ALISON TURTLEDOVE
Age 10
Woodcrest School
Canoga Park, California

Imagine sitting in the audience at the awards ceremonies for one of the world's most famous writing awards—The Hugo. The Hugo is the "Oscar" of science fiction. Imagine sitting there and hearing your name called as a winner! That's the situation Alison Turtledove found herself in at the 1993 WorldCon convention in San Francisco. She was just eight years old and the winner of a special short story contest the convention organizers sponsored for young writers.

I learned about Alison's triumph when her mother, Laura Frankos Turtledove, posted the news in the children's writer's category on GEnie's Writers' Ink RoundTable. We were all so pleased for Alison, and what a fun time we had ribbing her father, Harry Turtledove, also a science fiction writer, who had been nominated for the Hugo himself. Imagine his surprise (and delight), tucking an award-winner into bed that night.

In the following essay, Alison mentions two writing contests especially for kids. While they were wonderful opportunities, you won't find information about either in the listings in this edition. I wasn't aware of the American First Day Cover Society writing contests in time to contact them for updated information. (I didn't even know there was such an organization!) But, I'll be sure to check for the next edition. The World-Con is held in different locations around the world every year. The special writing contest that Alison won is not a regular event, so there was no new information to list. However, both were connected to personal interests shared by Alison and her family. As you read through the rest of these profiles, watch for other opportunites that aren't listed.

My name is Alison Turtledove. I'm ten years old, and I would like to be a writer when I grow up. My parents are both writers. My dad writes science fiction and fantasy, and my mom does, too, but she also writes mysteries. I have two sisters, ages nine and six. We like to play games that we write down when we're done. I like to write fantasy, and I love to read.

Because my parents write science fiction, every year we go to a Science Fiction WorldCon. A Science Fiction WorldCon is a convention of science fiction fans and authors from all over the world. The WorldCon is held every year in a different city. Because so many of the writers and fans have children, there is often a separate day care and KidCon. In the 1993 San Francisco WorldCon, there was a children's story contest. The categories were science fiction, fantasy or horror. I sent in a fantasy called "The Elf in the Keyhole." It was about a little girl elf called Eleta. She was very small so she lived in someone's keyhole and built passages in his door. When the man went on vacation, Eleta saved his home from a burglar by making the tip of the screwdriver he was sticking in the keyhole turn invisible, causing him to yell and alert the neighbors. I won for my age division. The stories were judged by science-fiction writer S.P. Somtow. The prize was a ribbon, a T-shirt, a book called *Alien Secrets*, autographed by the author, Annette Curtis Klause, and twelve dollars—six two-dollar bills!

Another writing contest I entered was the Every Cover has a Story contest, sponsored by the American First Day Cover Society, a stamp-collecting organization. (By the way, I collect stamps.) You had to choose a stamp cover, which is an envelope with stamps on it, and write a 100-words-or-less essay about it: either a nonfiction piece about the stamp itself or a fiction story about what was going on in the stamp. I chose the second. My cover's stamp showed a lot of little seagulls watching fishermen at a beach scene. My story involved three of those seagulls trying to fish the way the fishermen did, using a stick, a string, and bubblegum for a worm. In the end they realize swiping fish from the fishermen's baskets is a lot easier. The story got Grand Prize for the 8-13 division. All the contest entries were put on display at the Society's annual convention. I received stamp pins, stamp puzzles, stamp books, real stamps and all sorts of stamp stuff.

If you really want to be a writer, I think you should try to write as much as possible and on as many different things as possible so you can find the ones you like best. Also, try to read a lot. It will let you see how different authors use different styles and how their stories go. Have fun!

SARAH FELDMAN
Age 13
Orchard Park Public School
London, Ontario, Canada

Sarah wrote to me just as I was in the last stages of pulling this edition together. I sighed a big "Ugh" when I first started reading her letter. It said:

Dear Ms. Henderson,
I am in the 5th grade and am planning to send some things for publication. I need to know the requirements—handwriting, paper size, etc.
Thank you.

If you read chapter six, "Answers to Questions Young Writers Ask Most," you know that's the kind of letter I specifically asked young people not *to send me! But then I continued reading. "JUST KID-DING!" Sarah wrote. She went on to detail the success she'd had getting published by following the advice in this book. I enjoyed the joke Sarah played on me and her enthusiasm for writing and publishing. I wrote back immediately, asking her to submit an essay.*

Sarah's first publishing credits came as a result of sharing her opinions in the "Letters to the Editor" section of her local paper. It was a while before she had any more acceptances, but she kept writing and submitting. Soon she had acceptances for several poems, a book review, a letter in the "Afterwords" section of Merlyn's Pen *and then her first place win in the Grand Theater Stage Presence Young Playwrights Contests. Her writing also earned her a third-place win in the* Youth Magazine's *Fiction Contest.*

In addition to writing, Sarah enjoys drawing, singing and acting. She's involved with the All-City Choir and a member of the Original Kids Theatre Company.

I always dreamed of getting published, of having my name printed in huge letters above a story or poem. The allure of publication occasionally brought me to pen and paper but never for long because I generally found the writing process long and tedious. For a long time, writing remained just a dream, and a distant one at that. Then in grades five and six, I had a teacher, Howard Isaacs, who encouraged me to see writing in a different way and to enjoy expressing my thoughts on paper. It wasn't until grade six, however, that I began to write regularly.

I wrote obsessively. Every spare moment was devoted to the creation of some new piece. By the end of grade six, I had filled up more than seventy two hundred-page notebooks. About this time, I received the *Market Guide for Young Writers* and began to submit to some of the publications it described. At first, all I got were rejections, but finally, my local paper, the *London Free Press*, accepted a piece I had written. It was only an opinion letter, but I felt as though I had just sold my first novel. I received more acceptances after that, mainly for poems. Though each one brought euphoria, I don't think anything can really compare to the first time one sees her words in print.

My most exciting experience as a young writer was winning the Grand Theater Stage Presence Award for Young Playwrights. Having an actor perform your words, hearing your script being treated professionally and with respect by actors and directors is an inspiring experience.

Success in literature comes from one thing really. Writing. Every day. It's inevitable that you'll have writer's block at some time or other, but that shouldn't stop you. Write regularly until it becomes an obsession, something you can't do without . . . because writing is the only thing that makes you a writer.

MOLLIE McDOUGALL

Age 15
West Genesee High School
Camillus, New York

The following, originally part of a letter, has been sitting patiently in my files since February 1993. Mollie's now fifteen and a freshman at West Genesee High School. Reading, music and writing are still primary interests. She's had more than sixty poems and stories published. When asked what else she's been up to since then, here's what she had to say:

"I write a column for Young Voices Magazine *in Olympia, Washington, am student representative for a magazine distributed at my school, work on my school's literary magazine and am editor for the yearbook. Last summer I attended Interlochen Arts Camp and will be spending this summer there also, studying French horn.*

"Having a busy life teaches me to be organized. There is never a dull moment! It has also helped me set priorities. Sometimes, it's been hard to see what really comes first in life. When lulls come, there is always music to write, songs to sing, and something to laugh about. My current motto is: Each day is a memory. Some may be fond, sad or bleak, but a memory just the same."

Hello! My name is Mollie McDougall. I am thirteen years old and a seventh grader at Camillus Middle School. I started "really" writing when I was ten. I had written poems and stories before then, but they started getting noticed at ten. I had been writing poems for birthday presents and writing short stories for extra credit in English.

The first "good" poem I wrote was in February about three years ago. It was called "The Peace Child." I was in a singing group called Peace Child. A woman who helped direct the group read my poem and started to cry. I ended up reading it on television and at many of the concerts. My poem was published on greeting cards and also in an anthology called *A View From the Edge.* Since then, I've been writing stories, poems and essays. Our local newspaper has published many of my poems. Also,

I've been published in about ten different magazines and have won a few writing awards. A few months ago, one of my pieces earned me a five-hundred-dollar savings bond. In addition to writing, I enjoy music. I play two instruments.

The best thing, I think, about writing is getting published. I love seeing something I've written in a magazine. Of course, acceptance slips are few and far between, but the sense of success in being published forces me to continue. Rejection slips aren't that bad. Usually, they contain a few words of encouragement. The worst thing about mailing away poems to magazines is the waiting. I always race home to the mailbox and feel rather disappointed when it's empty. Luckily, I'm used to it. I know that some reply will come eventually.

I'd like to say that rejection slips won't hurt, but they will. Eventually, they become as common as bills, but until then, just wait and see. I've gotten published, but I've been rejected many times.

Always follow directions with contests. I once mailed an entry to a national contest but got it back a few weeks later. My entry was too long. Also, the contest was for children fourteen and older. I was eleven.

The best I can tell you is to have fun with your writing and don't be discouraged. Sometimes people can be pretty harsh. Don't quit writing. Someday, you could become famous because you stuck to what you liked doing and ignored what other kids said. Teasing can be pretty rough, but doing your best and ignoring the mean words is your best bet. Remember, you can do anything you set your mind to.

KRISTIN THURSTON

Age 14
Kingswood Regional Middle School
Wolfeboro, New Hampshire

Kristin claims that her family lives in the "Old-est Summer Resort in America." Set along Lake Winnepesaukee, Wolfeboro's summer popula-tion triples during the summer tourist season. She's been fortunate enough to travel to places like Walt Disney World and Six Flags, New Jersey, where she's performed on stage with other members of her dance school. But it's fall at home that she likes best, "when everything is so colorful and mountains are beautiful."

In addition to dance, Kristin is a member of the United States Humane Society and also active in several sports (soccer, basketball, softball and tennis) and the Student Council at school.

At the time of this writing, her most recent accomplishment was winning the title of Miss New Hampshire Junior National Teenager on April 1, 1995. While Kristin had received several English awards at school for her writing, her first published manuscript came as a result of her involvement in the 1994 National Pre-Teen Pageant. (She finished as second runner-up in the pageant.) But let's let Kristin tell the story:

There I was standing on stage with sixty-eight other girls at the 1994 Miss National Pre-Teen Pageant in Orlando, Florida, over Thanksgiving weekend. I was waiting anxiously to hear the winner of the Young Writers' International Open Forum, a new award added to that year's program. Not knowing how many girls had entered the short story competition, my heart was pounding. I had worked for more than three months with my mother (who encouraged me to do this) and a former English teacher (who worked with my mom) to develop and perfect my entry "Hailey's Choice." As Brandon Troutman, that year's master of ceremonies, explained the competition, he also announced that the winner could have her story published. When I heard my name, I knew that my hard work had paid off. I proudly accepted my trophy and gave my mom a huge smile. She knew, too, all the hard work that went into making "Hailey's Choice" a success.

Over the years, I have received several English awards at school, but I had never imagined one of my stories would be published. I guess I would say my writing began at a young age. It was encouraged by my mother, who always read me stories each night. While attending elementary school, I would write short stories. Each was one-page long and usually about my pets. Now, as a more complete writer, I realize how creativity on the content of the story is the most important part, no matter what the length of the story is.

I enjoy writing because it gives me a sense of comfort, and helps me to express certain feelings. Although it can become very frustrating at times, it makes me feel really good about myself when I have finished my story. Writing has also helped me in everyday life. Whether it's writing to friends, submitting articles to newspapers and contests or writing to different organizations to express my views on certain subjects, there is always a sense of self-accomplishment.

I would encourage all people to write because completion of a story or publication is very gratifying. It also helps you sort out different emotions about various things (although don't get too involved in your emotions). Usually, I write about things I enjoy; this helps me think of creative ideas to spice up my story. When it's a challenge for me to write a story, I list ideas to go by. Then I pick one of these ideas and list elements that I feel would fit in well with the story. This helps my mind trigger the writing process of the story. For "Hailey's Choice," I had worked with six rough drafts prior to submitting it for competition. It was then that I realized that perfection was only in the eyes of the author.

I believe wrting has to come from your own ideas and not anybody else's. I feel writing about a subject with which you feel comfortable is a good start to a great story. If you discover that your writing needs some work, go to your English teacher or parents for help. For motivation, I usually go to my mom when trying to create a story. She is really supportive of me, and I know I can count on her to give constructive criticism. I believe anyone can accomplish what they set their mind to do.

Although I am only fourteen years old, I hope to continue

with my writing and grow with the experience. I feel the only way you can become an established author is to write more. Not only has my mom encouraged me to write, but also to expand my reading. As I read material from new young writers, there always seems to be an influential author in their lives. I enjoy John Saul. Horror has always been my reading choice, although, I also find realistic fiction fascinating. "Hailey's Choice," my only published piece to date, is realistic fiction.

If writing is something you enjoy, keep trying, and continue to submit some of your work to your local newspaper or magazines you read. If you haven't yet submitted your work, you may be surprised at how creative you really are. I would encourage everyone to write because I feel writing helps you to develop personal growth and insight into who you are. I also believe it is a very rewarding experience whether you become a published author or not.

MONA WEINER

Age 13
Homeschooled
New York, New York

Susanna Sheffer, editor of Growing Without Schooling, *called to recommend Mona for a young writer profile. She was impressed with the submission Mona had made to* Growing Without Schooling. *I liked the fact that Mona's educational background differed from other young writers I had already selected. Many readers will wonder why Mona would consider herself lucky not to own a television. But, if you find yourself complaining that you don't have as much time as you'd like to write, you may want to think about how much time you waste watching television.*

Other than that, Mona's writing interests and experiences aren't all that different from thousands of other young writers. She's considering a career in a writing-related field and says that "if she really got desperate, she'd get into media." She thinks she'd be good at it.

What do you share in common with her? How do you feel about the images you create on paper? What writing trouble spots do you sometimes wrestle with? How do you try to solve them?

Here's what Mona has to say about her experiences:

I think the main reason I began writing was because everything was there. I've always had a very creative imagination, ever since I was little and playing games with my brother, in my dollhouse or with Legos. My mom would encourage me to dictate stories to her, which she would make into little books.

When I was ten, I began writing on my own because my family bought a computer. I was taught how to use the word processing program. I'd just turn on the computer and write. I'd write stories that would never get finished, mostly about girls and their families. I think the reason why I never finished them was that I had the drive but not the endurance, and I never had a real plot.

I also read constantly. I'm homeschooled, which means that my parents teach me and my brother at home. He and I are free to choose whatever topics we're interested in learning about in each subject (except math) and we report four times a year to our school district on our progress. We are evaluated yearly. Therefore, he and I have a lot of free time. Luckily, my family doesn't own a TV. When I tell people that, they always ask me what I do if I'm homeschooled and don't have a TV. My answer is that I write and I read. If I had a TV, I know I would be distracted by it, and I wouldn't have written half the pieces I have. Reading is something that helped me a lot with grammar and with the way writers lay out their words and present their ideas to the reader.

When I was eleven and a half or so, I wrote one of my first poems. It was basically just playing with words. I remember just fooling around with the words *sliver* and *silver*. I started writing more "professional" poetry when I was twelve. My friends were all very encouraging, and my mom would give me positive criticism. Actually, it got to be kind of weird after a while. I got kind of suspicious of all the positive criticism. Then I met a new friend, and he was really good with criticism; he would tell me the truth. If my poems were not so great (in his opinion, that is), he'd say so. The good point of that is when he said something of mine was good, I knew it was true. I find that very efficient and satisfactory. Of course, there would be times when I'd write something I really, really liked and he would say, "Well . . . you've written better, Mona," and I wouldn't feel so great. But it taught me that even if everyone you show a piece of work to doesn't like it, it's really the way you feel about it that matters.

I've been writing poetry up to this point. I really possess a love for words, and, therefore, poetry is a really good way for me to express myself. More often than not, people to whom I've shown my work turn to me afterward and say, "What?!" But I suppose that's to be expected. Ninety-nine percent of my poetry has something behind it. Most people only catch 5 percent of it. And 100 percent is weaving words. It's the effect of the words twined together. Words are so amazingly powerful, and the way they're interpreted is different with everyone. I like to create images with my poetry—sculpt them into fractured stories, films, a series of pictures that leave you with an image of . . . well . . . whatever I'm seeing. Unfortunately, most people don't see them the way I do. But that's OK. I try to write for myself.

Lately, I've found my poetry is repeating itself. For instance, I have about eight different lines I've written, really concrete, powerful lines that I love. But I haven't found a good set of lines to go with them, so I've been writing all of this so-so stuff, and then I put the great line in and it's so imbalanced. Now, I've got five poems with the same line in it. I also tend to use the same images a lot—like fire, burning, etc.

In the beginning of 1995, I fell into a writing slump. I've written over seventy poems in five months; I like about six of them. It's kind of pathetic. It could be that I just now have higher standards. Or, maybe, I'm being too critical. Or, perhaps, I need to enhance my poetry skills. I'm just being patient, and I think that it is curing itself.

Aside from poetry, I enjoy writing plays. I've won a Scholastic National Gold Award for a play that was the outcome of a play-writing class. Incidentally, the class itself didn't seem very helpful because of my teacher. But I did learn technical things about writing plays. It resulted in making my plays look more professional. I've been entering the young playwright's contest yearly. I also write articles and essays. I've been writing for my younger brother's newspaper, which is published bimonthly for our friends and relatives and members of a homeschooling group we belong to. In addition, I've had articles accepted by Susannah Sheffer, editor of *Growing Without Schooling*, a monthly magazine for homeschoolers. Her advice has been very helpful.

Recently, *New Moon*, a magazine for girls, invited me to write an article for them. Rejections have come from *Stone Soup*, *Merlyn's Pen* and *Cricket*. Before, I got mad and fed up and refused to send things in anymore. I was wrong, though, and their judgments were not unreasonable. I'd spend more time on submitting things, but it's not high on my list of priorities. I'd rather concentrate on the writing now and I want to take college courses on writing and literature as soon as possible.

Writing has more or less been easy for me. I just do it. I've been writing in a diary since I was eight and lately developed a new habit of keeping a notebook with me. I like to decorate it with collages and song lyrics. Plus, I find that there's a lot of material I wouldn't have remembered if I hadn't written it down. It's a really good idea to get a notebook. Write down *everything*, even if you think it sounds disgusting. When this happens to me, most of the time, I later decide I was wrong.

One of the best things about writing is that you can't outgrow it. With writing, as long as you can pick up a pen, you can write.

MICHAEL S. LaFONTAINE

Age 16
Memorial High School
Eau Claire, Wisconsin

Sixteen and a student at Memorial High School, Michael LaFontaine will be graduating in June of 1996, having completed a four-year program in three years. After high school, he plans to pursue a medical career.

Michael enjoys a wide variety of interests. At Memorial, he is actively involved in Spanish Club, the sciences and coaching Special Olympics. As a violinist, he is involved in the school orchestra as well as the Chippewa Valley Symphony, a local volunteer adult symphony. Prior to the past national election, he was instrumental in the formation of the Young Republicans of Eau Claire and currently serves as president.

In his spare time, he enjoys mountain biking, reading and writing. He says, "I like to write various things, however, the style that I enjoy most is the editorial. I feel that this type of writing has given me a chance to have my thoughts and feelings heard."

Michael's writing has been published in many newspapers and national magazines, including It's Your Choice *and* Fellowship. *The editor of* It's Your Choice *enthusiastically recommended I contact Michael for this edition.*

I've been writing for years now, but it was only a few years ago when I started writing with the intention of getting published. For a while, I dabbled around in poetry and prose. I even wrote a few essays, but then I found my calling. I love to write editorials and news or investigative articles. With this in mind, I started writing for my middle school newspaper. I wrote on everything from school policy to interviews with the administration. However, nothing compares to a freezing Halloween night in 1991.

I'll start right at the beginning. The 1992 election was in full swing; George Bush and Bill Clinton were just months away from the final vote. Just a couple weeks before Halloween, Dan Quayle came to our town of 56,000 people. I attended his rally at one of the local high schools and got myself a press pass. Little did

I know that after he was finished talking we would be ushered up to the platform by a few secret service agents. There was no way I was expecting to meet him and have a chance to ask a couple of questions, but I did. Incidentally, I was one of only three reporters out of about thirty that got to speak to him.

Well, anyway, back to that freezing Halloween night. I was notified that President Bush would be traveling through Eau Claire on his Whistle Stop Train Tour of the Midwest in about three days. Immediately, I got myself a ticket to attend the rally with the remote hope of getting close to him. I was astounded when my teacher and school paper adviser handed me a press pass that allowed me to stand on the press platform with the President's traveling press corp.

It looked perfect pinned to my jacket as I crossed the rope boundary and was escorted to the platform by a secret service agent. As I made my way up the stairs, I suddenly realized how close I was actually going to be to the President of the United States. Little name tags were attached on the platform, and I began to look anxiously for mine. My jaw dropped as I started reading off the names on the little white cards: NBC, ABC, New York Times, CNN, South Middle School Tale Feather, CBS, Financial Times . . . now wait a second, what's wrong with that picture? That's what I was asking myself as I stood on this platform between CNN and CBS on that bitterly cold night. I just about swallowed my tongue as the cameraman from CNN leaned over and asked me, an eighth grader, who I was affiliated with. I have to tell you though, I didn't even think twice when I raised my chin and proudly said, "The South Middle School Tale Feather, sir, and who might you be affiliated with?"

So here I am now, going into my senior year in high school, reminiscing about my early writing days. I didn't start freelance writing until about two years ago, and believe me, for every acceptance I've received, I can show you at least twenty rejection notices. Even in all of that rejection, it sure makes it worth it to receive just one letter of acceptance, and that I have. More recently, I have leaned away from writing articles. Instead, I've been doing quite a few editorials. My topics have included things like hunger in America, crime, honesty in politics and humanitarian rights. I find that this genre best suits my personality because I am very opinionated, and I like to express myself in a fashion that makes people really understand the idea I'm trying to convey.

Through many of my experiences, I have gained what I feel to be valuable knowledge about writing and getting published, so here are a few tips for you young writers:

- Write whatever form you feel comfortable writing. That means, if you hate writing poetry, prose or essays, *don't!*
- Always try to include a bit of yourself in your manuscript. For example, in one piece I did entitled "Hunger in America," I included phrases like, "I don't know about you but I have a hard time seeing Americans starving like this" and other lead-ins like, "What I find even more interesting . . ." Sure, you may say that the preceding is just for op-ed style writing, but hey, that's what I'm good at!
- Try to identify with your reader. If the person reading your work can, in some way or another, take a vested interest in your manuscript, the piece is a success.
- Most of all, tell people what they want to hear. In my style of writing, meaning op-ed, this is very applicable. I write about current events, problems and social dilemmas. Sure, my writing is usually slanted toward the way I feel, but I always include both sides of the argument—*I just make mine stronger!!!*

AMANDA LANG

Age 17
Columbine High School
Littleton, Colorado

Currently a high school senior, Amanda is already looking forward to pursing a career as a novelist. But, being realistic, she says, "It'd be nice to make a living off it, but I'm not counting on it." Still, she's already at work on her goal. By the time you read this, Amanda will probably have completed her first novel. Helping her along that path have been writing classes taught by Sandy Whelchel, executive director of the National Writer's Association. (See the profile of Ms. Whelchel in chapter eight). Neither class (Creative Writing nor Advanced Creative Writing and Publishing) was designed specifically for young writers. They were adult *classes.*

Finishing a book-length manuscript can be a daunting task. Without some basic planning (simple outline, nothing formal), it's often hard plugging along chapter after chapter.

Amanda has had a variety of modest publishing successes so far. Several of her poems have found homes, and she occasionally writes articles for her church newspaper. She's currently working on a children's column featuring short stories for that newspaper.

I enjoyed the "tongue-in-cheek" tone, especially in the beginning of her essay. Being able to identify and laugh at some of the mistakes we make as writers is one way to avoid making them in the future.

My philosophy in life once was, "The bigger the word, the better the writing." During my dreary midnight composing sessions, it seemed my best friend was the five-hundred-page, leather-bound thesaurus. It spent its greater existence open on my lap. A psychologist might have attributed this 'large word fixation' to the pretoddler era of my life when my mother refused to talk 'babytalk' to me. Soon, I grew and blossomed into the young writer I was destined to become.

It was my fancy to say, "an overabundance of nourishment preparers seriously impairs the liquid stock," when I could have simply said, "too many cooks spoil the soup." Fortunately, experience—

courtesy of classmates always asking, "Huh?"—helped teach me that lengthy words often obscured the true meaning of my writing. It was a start. I'm currently still huffing and puffing, but what I finally saw underneath was the beginning of my writing talent.

But I'm ahead of myself. Before we can examine the present, we must first refer to the past. Surprisingly enough—more so to my own amazement—I didn't always want to be a writer, nor did I always love to write. In elementary school, writing was simply something we had to do or it was the big *F* on the report card. I had no time for writing. I, like every other eight-year-old female in America, was going to be a famous actress. My name never did show up in limelight. Six years later I discovered that I had a passion for telling stories. I started simple. A poem here, an essay there. The little things that everyone oohed and ahhed over kept me going. It seemed that for the first time in all of my fourteen years, I had actually accomplished something outstanding. I could write better than most people my age. There was no way I was going to give it up.

So, I started my very first novel. How hard could it be? I laugh now at my overgrown ego. Oh no, it's not hard at all. At least not until the Old Fairy of Writer's Block shows up to laugh in your face. Now, I have never been one of great persistence. (Really, it's a miracle I've made it this far.) My first instinct was to give up. I didn't need that aggravation. I ended up setting my first novel aside. Then one night something extraordinary happened.

I was baby-sitting at my church—it's a very old church— chewing my nails, my eyes darting around at every little creak and moan. The building seemed to be taunting me, and I was definitely not amused. But that old saying that an artist must suffer for his work became undeniably true for me that night. Through the minor heart attacks and cold sweats of that terrifying night, my mind put together the most brilliant story idea. I went home and began a new novel, one I feel is the best story of my life. I call it *Letters From Willow*. I'm ridiculously proud of it. When finished—I'm halfway done now—I plan to try painstakingly to get it published. I can only cross my fingers and pray. Publishing anything, let alone a book, is no small feat. To new writers, it can seem impossible.

Having had a few poems published as the result of poetry contests, I know the exhilaration of getting an acceptance note. But I also, unfortunately, know the disappointment when the publishing company sponsoring the contest offers to "send you a book with your poem in it for the low, low price of $50. (Shipping and handling not included.)" I can only say that at least someone in the world, besides my close friends, will be reading my writing, which is essentially all I wanted anyway.

As far as getting my book published, I guess I'll refer to the famed words of my writing teacher, "With a little persistence, every writer will get his or her book published before they die." I only hope that I don't get struck dead by a runaway train before that day comes.

I wanted to end with some words of encouragement. But, in all honesty, I couldn't think of anything to say that hasn't been said a million times before. So, I decided to finish with a poem instead. It's one that I wrote when I felt my writing was going nowhere. Now I read it when I'm struggling to remember that someday I *will* succeed.

> I have known a passion,
> Whose hands reach out to touch the infinite.
> It is the star beyond clear sight.
> It's light blurred only by the hollow tears,
> Of time and life.
> My own outstretched fingers reach and,
> Struggle to be entwined with a hazy destiny.
> If my soul can travel beyond and over the wall
> That stands between me and my destiny;
> If my heart, encrusted by doubt,
> Can forsake the darkness, and discover the dawn;
> If my courage can shine,
> A pin point of diamond realization,
> Upon the ebony backdrop that shadows my inspiration,
> I have known a passion.
> I reach, travel, forsake, and shine.
> I shall be fulfilled.

GREG MILLER

Age 17
Centennial High School
Ellicott City, Maryland

Greg Miller, a senior at Centennial High School, proves that dedication, diligence and persistence do pay off. Already, he has amassed an impressive list of writing credits, including a short story in Paths of Imagination, *an anthology published by Majestic Books, plus another story to be included in a future anthology. He has also won second place in an essay contest sponsored by* Hi Piers, *Pier's Anthony's newsletter, and first place honors in the Balticon's Young Adult Writing Contest, sponsored by the Baltimore Science Fiction Society. A short story, "Jeffrey's Ghost," was published in the December/January 1995 issue of* Merlyn's Pen: The National Magazine of Student Writing, Senior Edition.

More than anything else, Greg wants to pursue an active writing career after school. In the meantime, he plans to continue writing short stories and also start writing novels. He's at work on his first novel now. Greg enjoys writing science fiction and speculative fiction. "However," he says, "I realize that most writers don't support themselves on their writing alone, so I would also like to work in the field as an editor or work in some aspect of the writing and publishing business while I continue writing. Getting published while young gives me a firm stepping stone for what I hope will follow as I grow older, and the writing I'm doing now is a great way to start honing my style."

I wrote my first story when I was in the eighth grade. It was only seven pages long, had taken a week to write, but I'd finished a story! Even after it was rejected five times, I didn't mind because at least I'd taken the first step: I had finished a story, edited it and sent it out to the magazines. The next year it was published in my high school's literary magazine, and I saw my work in print for the first time.

Once it was published, I reread it and noticed to my dismay that it sounded awful. The setting descriptions were weak, the dialogue was too stiff and mechanical and the plot stunk. One of the most important things a new writer has to learn is that in order to improve your writing ability, you have to learn to pinpoint past mistakes, and then try not to make them again. By the time that first story was published, I had written seven others. Each, in my opinion, sounded better than the first. I was learning and was careful not to include past mistakes in the new stories I was working on.

Sometimes, showing your stories to people you trust, and who you can trust to give you an unbiased opinion, also helps. Ask someone to critique your story. Once that person has read it, try to pinpoint how he felt about the story overall and what he liked and disliked about the story. Then ask for advice on how you might go about improving it. I'm a member of the Writers' Ink RoundTable (WINK) on GEnie, the computer online service. I can post a page or so of a story or poem I'm working on and get lots of useful advice from the many different (and very helpful) people there.

You also need to read stories by other authors in order to improve. It's not enough simply to know your grammar, sit down and write. Read everything you can that falls under the category of fiction you enjoy writing. (I read a great deal before I started writing, and I think most other writers did, too. It's often what sparks an interest in writing in the first place.) Notice how plots are constructed. Notice how good dialogue is achieved, but don't copy what you see. Use what you observe as a backbone while honing your own style. Keep what you see in the back of your mind so you know what to avoid and what works.

I think the universal advice for aspiring writers is simply "Write!" That is, you need to experience actually writing in order to get good at it. I've heard many people say that if you want to improve your writing skills, you have to write every day, rain or shine, homework or no homework, school or no school. That's sound advice to an extent. I've given it several times myself. But, I have to admit, the work load that comes with high school doesn't always give me the free time I need to write. A long Wednesday can really leave you exhausted, especially when you have a test in math and a presentation in history due the next day. However, even on that odd day when you can't concentrate to write, there are other aspects of writing that you can work on instead. When one of those days gets you down, spend some time that doesn't require as much "brain work." Take an hour or so and write different magazines for guidelines. Write a cover letter or two, get some stories ready to mail, proofread a story that's already finished in rough form. Maybe you could just sit quietly and brainstorm, jot some loose ideas on paper. Those are necessary steps, too. They're all essential to the writing process. Even so, *write* as much as you can. Don't let that one day you don't write become a regular occurrence.

Another thing: Don't give up. Don't let rejections discourage you. The process of learning to write takes time, and unless you're willing to roll with the punches, you're bound to fail. When you send something to a publisher, hope it gets accepted, but don't expect it to be. I've accumulated close to seventy rejections since I started. Of the thirty stories and three articles I've written, only seven have been accepted. Still, even one acceptance makes the rejections seem insignificant. My first "major" acceptance came on March 8, 1994, when *Merlyn's Pen, Senior Edition* accepted my story, "Jeffrey's Ghost." That was a full two years after I started my first story. When you finally get that acceptance letter, you realize all that sweat and toil was well worth it.

Why write? It doesn't often pay well. It's hard work, and, often, it's constant work.

Only *you* know what it is that attracts you to writing. I write because stories are an excellent way of communicating my thoughts and ideas to other people. I try to convey a message in my stories that most people can find if they look hard enough. It's my main way of expressing myself. Even so, the beauty of the mind rests in the fact that thoughts can never be expressed in totality. I realize this, but still I keep trying to find that ultimate expression. All writers do the same.

CHRISTY ANTHONY

Age 17
Linganore High School
Frederick, Maryland

Christy says that her interest in writing should probably be accredited to the many fine teachers (particularly her journalism advisor, her mother, her English teacher and a close family friend) she's had that inspired her to read. "Someone said that in order to write well one must read well," Christy told me. "And I must thank these people for exposing me to literature of all types."

She knows the goals she has in mind when she writes. Often it's to express her frustration with the current environment and perhaps be a catalyst for change. At the very least, Christy hopes to encourage people to think. To accomplish this, she spends time writing editorials and sending them to her local paper. Then, Christy says, "I wait for the angry responses to come in. That is a favorite part, and they've all been saved. If people respond, I must have made them think."

Another goal is to "capture a moment in 1,000 words when she doesn't have a camera." To this end, she writes prose essays about her personal revelations and hopes others find them as interesting as she does.

She'd like a career in writing but doesn't see it as her only career. "It seems to be too introspective. Ideally, I'd like to write a syndicated column and freelance as a features writer. To pay the bills, I plan to major in English and minor in French education." With that educational background, she plans to teach secondary French and English.

You'll note in the following essay that Christy gives a lot of credit to luck for her writing success. But she's smart enough to know that luck doesn't just happen. It's most often the result of deliberately putting oneself in a position to take advantage of any "lucky" opportunities that break through.

I can also relate to Christy's "need" for the pressure of deadlines to avoid getting lazy about her writing. Serious writers, whether professionals like myself or student freelancers like Christy, don't have the luxury of being able to wait for inspiration to strike.

I became involved with *Kids' Byline* through my journalism class at school. It's a very writing-intensive class and is (in the words of my advisor) "marvelous." That class led to a variety of experiences, in terms of developing my writing and publishing. That is the first advice I would give about getting published: Take advantage of opportunities. They may never come again, and one opportunity leads to many others.

Working on *The Lance* (my school paper) led to being published in the local paper, working for *Kids' Byline*, meeting professional writers and writing for *Writer's Market*. I'm thankful for my writing skills, but they won't get me everywhere. I credit most of my publishing to luck—being in the right place, with the right people, at the right time.

The more work-intensive aspect of getting published is perseverance, hard work and revision. Working for *The Lance* and *Kids' Byline* forces me to discipline my writing. I can't wait for the creative mood to strike me. There is a deadline, and it is my job to meet it. I need pressure. Otherwise, I'll get lazy. Writing is never an easy process. It takes practice to make improvements.

For me, taking criticism is difficult. No matter how much talent I may have, I don't know it all. I've had one piece published with no outside editing, and I hate it. I know how rotten it feels to come to an editor, hand over your latest brilliant work (so you thought) and have it returned looking like it just went through battle with The Red Pen. I hate rewrites more than anything else about writing, but all I have to do is haul out that piece I hate. Then I'm ready for anything my editors throw at me.

I don't always take their advice. When I'm writing for me, not on assignment, I decide what is good advice. After rereading, I may agree with all the comments. If they write some advice I disagree with, I read it, remember it and ignore it for that piece. A lot of advice is useful for later projects.

Writing on assignment is another story, and one I'll have to get used to because I want writing to be a career. That's another way *Kids' Byline* and *The Lance* are marvelous. Most of my pieces are assigned. I love writing but hate some assigned pieces. I hated the thought of writing them, I hated doing them and I hated the final product. I regret none of them. I am learning how to write in styles other than what I might prefer. This improves my preferred writing style. It also makes me a more well-rounded writer and, therefore, more capable of publishing a variety of pieces, which gets me noticed by more readers, which brings me more opportunities.

It can be so hard, especially if you truly love writing, to sit down at a computer, type in your thoughts and not enjoy it. If I'm writing a piece I don't want to do, I'll usually put it off and dread it more. I called a friend, also a writer, and complained, "There's nothing I can do. This piece is just going to be boring." He said, "Then just enjoy it being incredibily boring. Get into it." I started laughing at myself and my own stubborn desire to *not* enjoy writing. That story turned out well and is among my favorites.

My first assigned piece was an interview. My editor called and told me about this man who had worked his way up from the bottom of the corporation and was now president. She said he was great to talk to, and would I interview him? I was so excited. It was the first time I was asked to work as a writer outside of class. However, it was also the first time I had to ask questions of a total stranger. I felt terrified. What if he hated me? Reporters aren't known for their popularity. The best advice I ever had about that was from a professional interviewer: "Say you're a writer. Never say you're a reporter. They'll trust you more."

Funny thing, though, most people like to be interviewed. It makes sense. Here is a captive audience who wants nothing more than to hear them talk. A great ego trip. The only thing a writer can do to ruin an interview is to appear uninterested. Again, it makes sense. If you've come to interview someone, they expect to be the center of attention. They took time out of their day to talk to *you* at *your* request. And here you are, not even listening. That professional interviewer also said, "Never think you're more important than the person you're interviewing."

I love doing in-depth interviews. The only terrible kind are those where I'm not prepared. Then I must ask a question like, "What exactly does your program involve?" *Always* do background research, whether it's talking to other people or finding it in the library. Know something about the person you are to interview. At *absolute minimum*, I go in with ten questions. I rely heavily on follow-up questions. If they find it interesting, the subject will talk about something ad infinitum. That's my goal in interviewing: to create an environment wherein my subject wants to talk. Don't despair, they'll say something quotable eventually.

What to do if they say something a little *too* quotable? There's no easy rule here. I have yet to write anything truly negative about a subject. Hard-core journalists say the duty of the press is to report the truth, no matter what. There's a conflict of interest that must be settled by each writer in each situation. I've never written for a venue nor heard anything dangerous enough where I felt the "nasty" quote was really necessary. I think it's vital to "pick your wars."

I have one more thing to say. I love writing, and am constantly amazed that someone would actually pay me to have so much fun. The first time I ever saw my byline was thrilling, and the thrill has not lessened one bit.

Chapter Eight

Editors Are Real People, Too

In this chapter, you'll have the opportunity to meet seven adults who work as either editors or contest sponsors, plus Susan Currie, the fourteen-year-old founder and editor of the *Texas Young Writers' Newsletter.*

Susan's *TYWN* is one of the most impressive (yet inexpensively produced) publications for young writers that I've seen. Its professionalism—from a commitment to providing solid writing and publishing information to effective layout and design that enhance the text to the quality of work from young writers published—shines through. Michael Eckert will explain how and why a special section for young writers was developed for the *Times Herald*, the daily newspaper he works for.

Two opportunities from the expanding "cyber" world are represented. Greg Sanders is editor of *Edge*, an e-zine for teens available only by downloading via the Internet. Janet McConnaughey is an assistant SYSOP (systems operator) on CompuServe's Literary Forum and also a reporter for the Associated Press.

Interested in writing for the theater? Then be sure to check out the advice from the coordinator of Baker's Plays High School Playwriting Contest, Raymond Pape. Sandra Haven, editor of *Writers' INTERNATIONAL Forum*, explains the importance of maintaining focus in your manuscripts. Looking for a "by kids, for kids" only market? Then learn what prompted freelance and business writer Gwen McEntire to start *Kids' Byline*. If you're considering "open" contests (those in which everyone competes on an equal basis regardless of age or experience), read the advice from Sandy Whelchel, executive director of the National Writer's

Association. You'll gain perspective into how tough such contests are to win and insight into why you still might want to enter despite the odds.

I hope that putting faces to names, learning a bit about their backgrounds and letting them share what they do behind the scenes will help you to see these professionals as real, everyday people. Use what they've so graciously shared to help you better market your work.

MICHAEL ECKERT

Projects Editor, *Times Herald*
Port Huron, Michigan

Michael Eckert is officially Projects Editor for the Times Herald *newspaper in Port Huron, Michigan, a nice town across the river from Canada and about forty-five miles northeast of Detroit. Practically, a projects editor in this case is responsible for the newspaper's school coverage, outdoors coverage, youth coverage and a couple other specialized and seemingly unrelated areas. Publishing young people's original stories in the newspaper seems like a serendipitous accident, but it's not. A fledgling author brought the* Times Herald *a story and the editors said, "Why not?" A willingness to say yes (that's the part that was no accident) has thus grown into a regular and popular feature in the paper.*

Newspapers nationwide are suffering a pair of potentially lethal problems: General readership has been on a more or less steady decline since the 1960s, and papers' most loyal readers are getting old and dying. People who claim to know how to reverse these trends are called consultants, and they get paid a lot of money. Meanwhile, newspapers have to find practical ways to make their good advice useful.

One oft-repeated bit of advice is that you can increase readership, loyalty and satisfaction—and ultimately circulation and revenue, which are important to editors, too—by getting readers more involved in the newspaper. In other words, give them a sense of ownership in the newspaper. Make it their news in their paper.

That, by the way, differs from the thinking of a couple decades ago, when newspaper executives were also trying to get readers more involved. Then, however, the means was contests, puzzles and prizes. Besides being rather vulgar, "newspaper bingo" tended to have transitory effects on readership. Without that sense of ownership, there is little real loyalty.

One of the hardest nuts to crack for the *Times Herald* and everyone else has been how to get young people involved in the newspaper. We have tried several things, beginning with encouraging high school journalism students to contribute to the coverage on our weekly schools page. We have worked with students to put together some very nice stories, ranging from coverage of a school principal settling a basketball tournament bet by shaving his head to issues-oriented coverage on teen violence, for instance. Our one problem with this is that there are relatively few journalism programs in the *Times Herald* circulation area. We hope to remedy that somewhat by creating a mentoring program this year.

Another tactic we've taken has been the creation and then metamorphosis of the "Eye Page"—which has as its stated goal making sure that young people get their point of view in the paper. Its unstated goal has been to encourage reading and writing, especially by younger, pre-high-school students.

To those ends, we've tried a number of features on the page. We ran a weekly David Letterman-style top-10 list for a while, encouraging young people to call in suggestions for the following week's topic. A memorable one: "The top 10 things that ought to be banned from the beach." The No. 1 suggestion, called in by a young reader, was rocks. The Port Huron area has very rocky beaches.

We ran a weekly trend-spotter feature, again encouraging young readers to call in with their fashion tips (bolstering that encouragement with free movie tickets). For a while, teens kept us abreast of the best TV shows, the hippest haircuts, the coolest clothes.

The problem with these is that they stopped working after a while. You know it's time to stop when the newsroom looks forward to Tuesday afternoon, when everyone gets to think like a thirteen year old for that week's top-10 list.

We also have accepted and encouraged budding young authors to submit their original stories for the page. I think we got four of them the first year. Then, for no reason I can identify, we were deluged with submissions. And it wasn't even from a classroom assignment. We've sponsored essay contests in the past, for instance, that teachers have turned into assignments. The problem with those, beyond being deluged with pencil-written manuscripts, is that it can be really difficult not to grade on a curve. If the second-grade class at Michigamme Elementary School submits essays en masse, you can bet that three of them will be really good and three more will be unintelligible and the rest will fall somewhere in between.

That is what has been surprising about the "Eye Page" submissions. They are nearly all thoughtful, well written and interesting. And we're not even giving out any prizes.

Submitting a story is simple. Get it to me in a form I can read (although, that's not too much of a problem; most nine year olds have word processors, it seems). Please include your picture, and tell me how old you are and where you go to school.

We do edit the stories—a little—and ask that they be kept below about 300 words. We do run longer ones if they merit the extra space, and we even ran one as a serial.

So, has it increased circulation?

Ask us in ten years. Meanwhile, it can't hurt.

SUSAN CURRIE

Editor, *Texas Young Writers' Newsletter*
La Vernia, Texas

Susan Currie, a fourteen-year-old, seventh-grade student at Incarnate Word High School in San Antonio, Texas, hopes to pursue a career as a book or magazine editor but may teach English instead and write on the side. She'd like to develop the Texas Young Writers' Newsletter *to the point where she could turn over many of the business aspects to someone she trusts and have more time to work on her own writing.*

Susan feels that developing the newsletter has taught her a lot about editing and writing. Previously, she'd never written any nonfiction other than for school assignments, and researching articles on writing has given her valuable insight into the publishing world. She says, "I'm probably the only person in my school who can describe all types of publishing rights and procedures." In addition, Susan feels that she learns something from every submission she reads. "If I choose to return it, I study its weaknesses to see what needs development. If I accept it, I look for the elements that were strongest. Then when I write something of my own, I watch for those weaknesses and strengths, and hopefully there are more of the latter!

"Plus, there's always the practical side to this as well. I know a lot more now about the IRS, the post office and running a business than I did when I started."

When I was about three and had first learned to read, I mentally narrated every event in my life. Every step was duly noted, although my story wasn't always very exciting: "She stepped off the curb after looking both ways carefully and walked across the street quickly." If things got too boring, I'd make something up. I learned a lot about words and their relationships from this, however strange it was, and it helped me with my language skills. My mind was a safe place to try out new vocabulary and experiment with sentences.

It wasn't until I was six or so that I walked into my dad's office in our house, pulled off the cover of the electronic typewriter and pounded out my first short story: a four-page tale of love, betrayal and death. It sounded like a soap opera. Although it wasn't much, seeing those words on paper made me think, "Maybe one day *I* could write books like all those on my shelves. Maybe *I* could write stories and have them published in those magazines." And so I wrote.

Later, I started looking for someone to put my name in print for the first time. I read *Writer's Market* thoroughly, typed up perfectly formatted manuscripts and sent off my manuscript and SASE. I quickly found out that many magazines weren't very enthusiastic about publishing a twelve-year-old's work, even if it was pretty good. So, I decided to start my own magazine, to publish only the work of young writers.

After lots of thought and planning, the *Texas Young Writers' Association* was created in the summer of 1994. I was thirteen. We published our first issue that month. I did all of the work on that premiere issue by myself, except for two poems written by my friends online on Prodigy. I laid it all out on my computer, printed it up and sent it off to everyone I knew. The people I met on Prodigy, GEnie, America Online and CompuServe all contributed, sending their work and their much-appreciated advice. Soon, submissions were pouring in from people all over the country. I even had adults sending me their articles to be included in the newsletter, which was tough at first. It was difficult to tell older writers how to change their work so that it could be appropriate for our audience, but eventually I became accustomed to it. I love corresponding with all my contributors, many of whom have gone on to publish in other magazines and who have submitted repeatedly to us.

My favorite part of the newsletter is the work by young writers, usually two poems and a short story every month. But I realized that young writers not only needed a place to publish their work; they also needed a place where they could learn about writing for other markets and about the craft of writing. I really could have used such a source of information when I was first starting out. As a result, we publish an article on the art or business of writing, as well as market information, in every newsletter. All of these elements form a unique resource for young writers.

I have learned so much from running the newsletter. When I evaluate people's work, I am always able to learn something from their writing. I've also learned leadership and communication skills from working with my writers. And even now, at fourteen, I sometimes find myself narrating my life in my head, and I think, "Susan, that's really strange!" And then I continue to do it, remembering how much it helped me in my writing and in my life.

Don't ever let anything stop you from writing, even if you think writing makes you stick out from other people or seem "weird." It does make you different but in a wonderful way; it is your individual talent, and no one can ever take that away from you. It is the power to make others experience a new depth of emotion—bring them to the brink of tears or laugh until their sides hurt. This is the power *you* possess. Develop it, use it, and, most importantly, enjoy it.

GWEN McENTIRE

Editor, *Kids' Byline*
Frederick, Maryland

The path Gwen McEntire traveled from writer to editor of a special magazine not only for kids but written by kids was not a straight one. But, no matter. When the time was right, she reined in any doubts and seized an opportunity. The result has been rewarding.

Here she tells of her own humble (and often bashful) young writer years and how the nub of an idea grew to blossom as a successful magazine for kids and by kids.

First let me say that I feel fortunate that my career has evolved as it has, like steps progressing in a path to an ever more interesting and encompassing vocation. This certainly supports what one of my student writers, Christy Anthony, says: "Take advantage of opportunities. They may never come again, and one opportunity leads to many others."

I always enjoyed writing and would huddle over a notebook when mad at my parents, contemplating and expressing different dark fates. In school, I lacked the confidence to share my thoughts aloud with others. In fact, in freshman college English, I never said one word! Those few times that the professor called on me, I had symptoms of a panic attack; I was intimidated by an environment that spawned what seemed like outrageous creativity . . . the more bazaar, the more he emoted. But the love of writing refused to die; it just went into seclusion.

Sixteen years ago, when my children were young, I was reacquainted with children's stories. I not only read them but began to write them. I fantasized about how *some day* I would see one, with my name affixed, in print. I fantasized about how it would feel. Then the acceptance letter came. My first story, "St. Patrick's Day Blue," was published in 1979 in a national children's magazine. It felt great! For the next few years, I wrote many children's stories.

During that time, I had the opportunity to teach a Saturday

enrichment class for kids in writing and journalism at the University of Toledo. We painstakingly published our own newspaper (without benefit of sophisticated software) and had a lot of fun in the process. I saw the response of young students to seeing their names in print. The idea was born of a publication that featured only students' writing.

Shortly after we moved to Frederick, Maryland, I began working for the local newspaper. For the three years following, and then as director of Community Relations at Frederick Memorial Hospital, I clung to the idea and waited until the timing was right. Luckily, my work experiences proved invaluable toward that goal, for I'd learned something about the production of publications. And since part of my role with *Kids' Byline* involves marketing and promotion, working closely with a Marketing and Development Department was wonderful experience. In fact, I continue to write professionally—newsletters, brochures and newspaper articles—and feel that actively writing is important to my value to the magazine.

I have a problem with magazines that bill themselves as being for children or teens but include mostly material written by adults for these populations. The following excerpt from an essay written by Katie O'Leary, a high school senior, and published in the August/September 1995 issue of *Kids' Byline* sums up why I embrace the philosophy that our publication will consist only of material created by kids:

> It is magic to see words I have written appearing on a computer screen. They are my words, written in my unique way. They form part of a sentence, which is part of an essay, all of which are part of me. Every word I write gives me insight into myself; an opinion I didn't know I had or a word I didn't know I could use effectively . . . the thrill of finding the perfect word may be the most satisfying part of writing. I like to edit my writing to fix awkward sentences . . . the misused words and the unclear thoughts. It is like buffing a rough piece of furniture to a smooth, gleaming finish.
>
> Writing is tangible evidence of accomplishment. If I climb a mountain, I can't hand the mountain to someone as proof

that I've climbed it, but I can hand someone a poem I've written.

Writing is an exploration and a teacher. It is a journey from ideas to complete expression, from vague understanding to precise articulation. The process is often like running in sand—I make progress but with a lot of effort. The result, however, is well worth it: the *A* from my hardest teacher, my writing in print or the appreciation of someone whose opinion matters to me.

In 1994, *Kids' Byline* began involving students in the magazine's production. That, too, was part of my original idea. Realizing the value of practical experience versus reading "about" experiences, I could see only advantages to kids becoming involved. Our first student advisory board consisted of four high school members, along with their journalism teacher. The present board has increased to six high school juniors and seniors. Working with them has been great! Their input and energy are an inspiration.

We focus on content and quality, not submission format, and consider the magazine an adjunct to the classroom, not an extension of basic grammar. We don't like to edit because we believe that the material should represent the work of the writer—not serve as the framework for an "improved" piece. Other than minor mechanical adjustments or slight changes to copy, we will not alter original material. Work is published based on merit, not potential.

As far as advice about what to write or how to get started, we recommend picking a topic you care about. Then spend some time inside your mind. Savor the strength of words. Dare to think a little differently, and consider how to evoke emotion. If you're not caught up in what you write, chances are no one else will be either.

On rare occasions, we assign articles "on spec" and pay for published pieces. These tend to be interviews with interesting individuals or articles about events that would be relevant to a wide readership. If you have an idea you would like to propose, either call us or submit a query letter.

Good generic advice for submitting is to know your publication.

SANDRA HAVEN

Editor, *Writers'* INTERNATIONAL
  Forum
Tracyton, Washington

Sandra Haven is editorial director for Writers' *INTERNATIONAL Forum, a bimonthly magazine that publishes stories from writers around the world. The magazine encourages its readers to send in comments on the stories printed and forwards those comments to the writers.*

She has also worked as a technical writer and editor, has had her articles and essays, as well as her fiction, published in the U.S. and Europe.

In 1994, the Director of the National Pre-Teen Corporation contacted Writers' *INTERNATIONAL* Forum *concerning their interest in young writers and asked their staff to be the final judges in the National Pre-Teen short story competitions. The first place winner from 1994, Kristin Thurston, received a prize from National Pre-Teen Corporation and was also published in* Writers' *INTERNATIONAL* Forum.

Mrs. Haven enjoys receiving manuscripts from young writers and likes to share tips that can help them in their future.

When I started writing this essay, I said to myself, "I wish I could give young writers one special tip to help them all become better writers." I thought of many useful writing techniques. Which should I explain?

Then I realized what I needed was something every writer can use whenever they write. I decided on *focus.*

Focus is the most important tool you can learn to use in writing. When you focus light through a magnifying glass, you concentrate many rays of light and heat into one spot. As you concentrate the rays, that spot becomes brilliant with light and also hot. If you want readers to appreciate your writing, it is important that you focus your ideas. With focus, your writing will be brilliant and hot—as if seen through a magnifying glass.

For instance, when I was young, I enjoyed taking essay tests in school. After I learned all I could about a subject, I could turn those facts into an essay and usually get a good grade for it. However, once I took an essay test and wrote what I *thought* was a fine essay. The teacher liked it too, but I only got a *C* on it. The teacher explained that although it was well written, the essay didn't stick to the subject. The facts she wanted to see in the essay weren't there. I hadn't *focused* on the points asked for on the test.

Later, when I began writing for publication, I remembered the importance of focus. I took classes and attended conferences and joined with other writers who were also learning about creative writing. Then I analyzed each writing project as if it was an essay test. I asked myself, "What is this contest (or magazine or audience) looking for?" Once I knew what I needed to include in my writing for that project, I knew I had found my focus.

Here are some ways to determine your writing focus:

AUDIENCE

First, who is your audience (the person you need to please)? If you are writing for school, then your teacher is your audience. Your writing will need to include the facts and ideas that show him or her that you understand the subject. As a student, you already know how important it is to read or listen to your teacher's directions.

It is just as important to understand what your audience wants when you write for others. Here are some tips:

Contest:

If you want to enter a writing contest, the judges will be your audience. How can you know what they want? The first clue is to carefully read the contest rules and regulations. If it is a contest that has been held before, you may also be able to read the winning entry from previous contests. They will tell you what focus the judges liked last time.

For instance, if you are entering an annual essay contest on the American Dream, your essay may not come to the same conclusions as last year's winning essay, but reading it will help you understand what style or tone the judges chose. Did the last winner use humor to make points? If so, then the judges like that tone. If last year's winner was serious, then the judges will probably still prefer a serious essay.

Publication:

Maybe you want to write something to be published in a magazine. In this case, your audience is the editor. The editor will make the decision about publishing your manuscript.

You can find out what the editor wants by reading the magazine's guidelines. Nearly every magazine will send you free writer's guidelines if you send a self-addressed and stamped envelope and ask for them. *Read and follow these guidelines to the letter!* If you don't follow the guidelines, you will be wasting your time, effort and postage.

You can learn even more by reading that particular magazine. For instance, do the stories have mostly girls as main characters? Do they ever use animals in the stories? Are most of them action stories, or are they stories about relationships? Once you know what type of story they publish most often, you can focus your story in that same way.

SUBJECT

Once you know what your audience will like in general, you will need to decide on your particular subject. It is common for a writer to overdescribe a subject. Narrow your subject down to a single focus.

In Essays:

An essay is defined as "dealing with a subject from a limited or personal point of view." That means focus! For instance, an essay about friendship could include many ideas. If you narrow the essay to the value of making pen pals in other countries, you have made the subject easier for readers to grasp. Then you may want to make it personal by explaining why a pen pal's friendship has become important to you.

In Articles:

An article is an explanation of a subject or idea. When you concentrate on just one focus, your article will have more power.

For instance, if you want to write an article about boats, what size of boat? If you choose small boats, for what purpose? Fishing? Waterskiing? Canoeing? Then narrow your focus even more. Do you want to explain how to safely use that boat, how to enjoy it or how to build one? By choosing a narrow focus, you can create a stronger article.

In Fiction:

Whatever type of story you want to write will dictate the focus. For instance, a mystery will need to be suspenseful, it will need to involve a problem, and your main character should help solve it. These are parts of every mystery. Think through the important parts of the type of story you want to write, and be sure your story includes those parts. Then remove anything that doesn't fit this focus. For instance, if you include a funny scene in a mystery story, it may take away from the suspense.

As Editorial Director of *Writers'* INTERNATIONAL *Forum*, I receive many manuscripts from around the world and from writers of all ages. At least half of them haven't followed our guidelines. Many of the rest are stories with subjects that are too broad. Your writing will stand out from others if you learn this simple lesson about focus:

Focus your writing to an audience and to a subject and you will become a more successful writer!

RAYMOND F. PAPE

Associate Editor, Baker's Plays and
Coordinator for the Annual High School
    Playwriting Contest
Boston, Massachusetts

Raymond Pape knows playwriting. As a literary management intern with the American Repertory Theatre (1986-1987), he read and wrote evaluations for some 150 plays by new American playwrights, and, among other duties, helped choose scripts for readings, workshop and production. While at the University of Massachusetts, he gained experience as a teaching assistant with the theatre department. He's done some performing himself, and he continues to write plays.

In 1995, his play, Out of the Loop, *was produced by Centastage, at the Boston Center for the Arts. Several other plays have also been professionally staged at theaters in Massachusetts and Connecticut. Plus, he's been a finalist and semi-finalist for a number of arts grants, including the Artist's Foundation Grant in 1990 and the 1989 Clauder Competition. He has studied playwriting with Robert Auletta, William Alfred and Virginia Scott.*

He joined the staff of Baker's Plays in January 1988 and is the principal reader for some 600 plays a year. He also works with playwrights in rewriting their plays for production and commissions new work from noted playwrights. Young playwrights have him to thank for creating the Division of Plays from Young Authors.

Here he gives budding playwrights valuable insight into the different requirements of writing plays. Be sure to note the importance that he places on "focus," an important element Sandra Haven wrote about earlier.

The Baker's Plays High School Playwriting Contest has supported young playwrights for six years now. We publish the winning play and offer cash awards to the top three playwrights. Past winners include *Icarus All Over Again,* by Brad Gordon and Gary Rucker, *Throwing Off the Covers,* by Dailyn Rodriguez, *Landslides,* by Jessica Leader and *Removing the Glove,* by Clarence Coo.

In the face of much temptation and adversity, playwriting is becoming a lesser art form. Many talented writers are going to Hollywood or are becoming overwhelmed by the poverty that invariably comes when one is dedicated to one's art.

We thought a contest should give the next generation of talented writers a shot in the arm, so to speak, encouragement to stay in the theater. We're happy to say that, so far, this has been the case. Our "alumni" are at various colleges pursuing playwriting careers. I often get scripts, letters and cards keeping me up to date on their writing. Nothing gives me greater pleasure than seeing these writers continue to develop.

It has also been a great way to acknowledge a voice seldom heard by our national audience. Unlike adults, the high school playwright is in the perfect place to comment on the high school experience, and audiences recognize this and have responded positively. These plays are truly remarkable and worthy of production anywhere.

The scripts that win offer a unique perspective. They go way out of their way to be original. Their scripts do not have a single error, evidence of the fastidious, focused writer. They tend to be from renegades, teens who don't mind spending hours by themselves, writing and reading. These young playwrights also have a great sense of stage and do not fall into the trap of writing a cleverly disguised television script. On the flip side, scripts that do not make the first cut are usually ones written in response to a class assignment or written over a period of a week or so.

Baker's Plays publishes what people want to produce and what we think they would *like* to produce. The decision to publish something always answers to this criteria. What people are producing and what we think they'll produce are variables that change constantly, and we try to respond when a trend takes off in a new direction. Our market is largely high school, but we also publish plays for the university theater, family theater and community theater as well.

I suppose I came to my position here via either an indirect or a direct route, depending on your perspective. I majored in English/writing and minored in theater in a small New England college. I went to graduate school for playwriting, but left the program to intern in the literary management office at American Repertory

Theatre in Cambridge, Massachusetts. It was there that I fell in love with the original script. I read and evaluated a hundred plays from America's brightest and best playwrights and was paid for it, too. It was better than any library card. When my year was up, I wasn't sure where I could expect to work with this experience, but I happened to walk down Chauncy Street in Boston and found Baker's Plays. I have been Associate Editor ever since. So, I suppose, looking back, it was a straight line, but I certainly didn't plan it that way!

WHEN SUBMITTING SOMETHING

Writers should concern themselves less with what kind of font they use, what color font they use, cover designs, fancy paper, express mail postage, etc., and concern themselves more with the *story* they are trying to tell. Scripts that employ the above deception tactics do nothing to improve a playwright's chances of getting published, but instead draw attention *away* from what is essential. The adorned script is the sign of a self-conscious writer and a writer who does not believe his story can stand on its own. When we publish something, it is in a simple, inexpensive, acting edition, without bells and whistles. When a reader/producer purchases the script, she cares about the world of the play, not the packaging.

JUST DO IT

Most people have ideas for things. An idea for a commercial, an invention, a movie or a play. But not everyone will put the time in to bring that idea to the page. Distinguish yourself from the group that forgets their good ideas and put it down on paper!

There will be plenty of obstacles when you decide to write your play: interruptions, distractions, friends thinking that you're weird. But keep on writing! You've got something to say! If you've got something else you need to do, keep a pad and pencil with you and jot down those ideas for the second scene or what-have you so you won't forget.

There are plenty of books on the subject of playwriting, and my advice is to avoid them. At least for now. I know I am generalizing, but they do tend to suck the fun out of it. Like the advertisement says, *Just Do It.* It is much more beneficial (and fun) to learn as you go.

PUT IT ON

The difference between a play and anything else you might write is that it is an active art form. A play is meant to be performed or read aloud. As soon as you feel you've got something worth sharing, let a friend read it. If he or she likes what you've got, get some more friends together and ask them to read it aloud for you. You might be surprised how many masterworks of drama had the humble beginnings of a reading by a group of friends around the kitchen table.

READ AND SEE

"You are what you know." Don't read or see junk! It might take years before a really bad episode of *Who's The Boss?* leaves your brain. Acquaint yourself with the art that appeals to you. Read the arts section of your local paper, raise some funds and go see a play. If you can't stand Top 40 radio, don't listen. Spend an afternoon at the drama section of your library.

Lastly, always do the best job you can before you send a play out to a theater or a publisher. Don't have a single doubt as to whether or not you should have changed something, added something or rewritten something. Do the best job you know how, give it to the mailman and then forget about it. Because when (or if) you get that rejection in the mail six months later, you'll have only one thing to say, "Hey, I did the best I could."

Playwriting, even at its most arduous, should be fun. It will activate your imagination, instill a playful sense of language. You'll also be able to make your friends and family laugh, cry, think. And you will see how vital theater is in our culture and know why so many are supporting it.

JANET McCONNAUGHEY
Assistant SYSOP, Literary Forum
New Orleans, Louisiana

Janet McConnaughey's first publications were sonnets published when she was twelve and thirteen in The Horn Book League, a section for kids' work in The Horn Book, *a magazine for librarians. She is now a reporter for The Associated Press. In her time off, she helps run the Literary Forum and the Writers Forum on CompuServe, writes fantasy and reads just about anything.*

I don't remember not knowing how to read. My mother, who taught me, said that I decided at the age of four that I couldn't let my big brother learn something I didn't know.

When I grew up, I lucked (oh, OK, and worked) my way into a career that lets me talk to people and write stories about them. Working for the AP also means a lot of night work, especially early in one's career. I was working nights when a windfall let me buy my first computer and a friend 1,100 miles away convinced me to join CompuServe so we could correspond by e-mail.

That was in 1983, when CompuServe's forums could be listed on one page. I joined the Literary Forum and the forum for the computer I was then using. I'm not much for hanging around bars, which was about all that was open when I got off work. Litforum and the Model 100 Forum became my after-hours hangouts. Through the seven-line by forty-character screen of my computer, I entered a room where friends were always waiting to talk about books and news and writing.

After five or six years, Alex Krislov, who runs the forum, asked me to become his assistant. When Litforum became The Literary Forum Group with the addition of two more forums in early 1995, I became assistant SYSOP in Writers Forum, too.

It's great fun, and I've met people I'd never have met otherwise, including lots of other writers. With their encouragement, I returned to writing fiction—something I hadn't done for about twenty years. So what does the Literary Forum Group have to offer young writers? To start with, Writers has a Young Writers' Workshop, led by Eldon Garlock 71242,1405. As I write this, it's part of the Students & Teachers section, but there's always a chance that it might get its own section. It's a place to share your work with other young writers and learn what they think works well and what they think could be improved. Eldon, who also runs the Writing Exercises section, leads exercises in the Young Writers Workshop, too.

Litforum has a YouthLit section, where people talk about books written for kids and about writing books for kids. The YouthLit section leader is L.J. Launer (72027,2607).

For that matter, if you're reading books that aren't aimed specifically at kids, you're welcome to join the conversations in any of the other sections or to ask questions about something you don't understand. About the only questions that don't get a quick and sympathetic answer are those that run something like, "Can someone give me a synopsis of ANNE OF GREEN GABLES? I need one by Wednesday."

To find the Literary Forum, GO LITFORUM. To find Writers Forum, GO WRITER.

An important pointer: Most of the conversation is on the message boards rather than in the conference rooms. If you're using CompuServe Information Manager, use the Mark Messages and Retrieve Marked Messages commands to pull discussions—or even entire sections—onto your hard drive so you can read and answer messages off-line.

My ID # is 76704,36. However, I answer messages on the forums faster than by e-mail.

SANDY WHELCHEL

Executive Director, National Writer's
Association
Aurora, Colorado

"Were you a young writer?" I asked Sandy Whelchel when I called to thank her for faxing her essay. I expected an immediate reply, but the line was quiet for a few seconds before she spoke. "Yes, I did write when I was very young, up until age thirteen, then someone squelched my enthusiasm for writing, and I didn't write another thing for a long, long time."

It was Ms. Whelchel's own mother who had discredited her budding interest and talent as a writer and threw all her work out. Ten years later (and with a bit of good luck, she says), she got started working as a branch librarian where writing was a required part of the job. The "squelched" passion for writing started to bloom again. Following four years writing book reviews for the library, she "fell into" two newspaper writing jobs, one of them with the Denver Post. *Today, in addition to her work with NWA and teaching a number of writing courses, she has three published nonfiction books to her credit, five published children's coloring books, hundreds of published newspaper and magazine articles and short stories. Three unpublished novels are still playing the market game.*

Not everyone can count on support from family and friends for his or her writing. But, you needn't suffer in silence. There are others out there ready and willing to lend some practical as well as moral support.

In her essay, I think the most important point that Ms. Whelchel makes is that to have a real chance at winning, your writing has to be good writing, not just good writing for a sixteen year old.

Few writing subjects will receive more comments, both negative and positive, than contests. Some writers love contests and point to certain contests as the embarkation of their careers, while others will complain about contests and feel they are of little value for any writer. Perhaps you, as the writer, need to decide the purpose for entering a contest before deciding to send off an entry.

Most contests I will discuss are open to both beginning and published writers. Unless otherwise stated in the rules, judges only consider the overall merit of the submission and not the age of the writer. Whether the writer is nine or ninety, each category of written material is judged according to predetermined guidelines. Young writers, especially, should take heed ... *winning a contest is tough.* Contest competition is keen, and all entrants should have a firm understanding of this before they enter.

Whether you are a beginning writer or a seasoned veteran, contests can be tough on your self-image and your ego. If you aren't comfortable with having your ego or your work thoroughly dissected, I would recommend not entering a contest.

With those understandings firmly in place, let's take a look at why you might enter a contest and what you can gain by entering—besides the prize money. Since I'm most familiar with the National Writer's Association Contests, I'll use them for illustration.

The NWA Novel Contest is open to any writer—published or unpublished. In 1995, one of our entries came from a published novelist who has two books in print from a major publishing house. Why would an author like this enter our contest? Probably because the entry is in a different genre from this author's previous books. Each NWA contest is read by two published writers, and the top five entries are read by another published novelist. Each of the preliminary judges fills out a judging sheet, which is sent to the entrant, if a self-addressed stamped envelope (SASE) is provided. This means that you can get a better idea of problem areas in your work and perhaps, with revisions, can improve the manuscript so it is marketable.

With this information in mind, a young author must make sure that any contest entry he or she decides to attempt must be as good as any submission from adults. This means the manuscript must be in the very best format possible: typed, double-spaced, free from corrections, containing good sentence structure, grammar and punctuation. The dialogue, narrative, plot and viewpoint of the story must be well written.

NWA currently gives thirteen out of one hundred points for "marketability" of the manuscript. An author must consider whether the story has a place in the market. Is it the type of book that the young author's peers are reading? Will it have a chance of selling to a publisher? These are important questions; ones all authors, young or old, must consider when deciding if they are ready to submit their work.

When submitting to a contest, writers must present the very best possible manuscript. Young authors should not hesitate to talk to teachers, or if possible a published adult author, about their work. Any input from adults will give you a better chance to win the contest and eventually have your work published.

If you don't "win" a contest, what have you gained? Perhaps one of the most important insights you can gain is to learn how strangers view your work. Those who love you and encourage you will always support your endeavors. But what about someone who doesn't know you? Will he or she feel your work is outstanding? A contest is a good way to find out. Contests are difficult to win, but no other "proving ground" for your work is more difficult or similar to the real competition of the publishing world. Remember, there can be only one winner in the contest, but if someone gives you a fair evaluation of your work, and you are able to learn from your mistakes . . . you will be the *ultimate winner*.

GREG SANDERS

Edge Magazine, Managing Editor
Durham, North Carolina

In his youth, Greg Sanders enjoyed writing but never really gave a thought to seriously pursuing it as either a hobby or career. He says, "I saw it as a tool, and being able to do it well meant a lot to me. But I don't have a glorious past as a young writer."

Now, however, in his position as Managing Editor for Edge, *an e-zine available only through the Internet, his own interest in writing has increased, as has his admiration for the talents of young writers. But, he says, while others view him as a writer, he doesn't apply the title to himself yet.*

A graduate of Duke University with a dual major in religion and English, Mr. Sanders's first jobs as an editor were various freelance assignments. Approximately three years ago, he connected with Journalistic, Inc., publisher of Edge's *traditionally published predecessor,* Young Scholar. *In May 1995, the premier issue of* Edge *was published. The basic editorial features remain strikingly similar to the former* Young Scholar, *even down to the amount of editorial content in the electronic equivalent to a forty-eight-page magazine.*

Edge *is part of FishNet, a World Wide Web site (also owned and managed by Journalistic, Inc.) specifically created as a forum for intelligent teens to gather, share and exchange experiences and ideas. "We feel our audience is better served via the electronic medium," says Mr. Sanders. "Kids really like the interactivity available. And we've noticed (and appreciated) that we are receiving much more immediate feedback to what is published in the magazine. It's also more candid."* Edge *anticipates that that interactivity with teens will continue to grow in the coming years.*

If you have access to the Internet, the URL address for Edge *is hhtp://www.jayi.com/jayi*

Whether you are interested in writing, reading Edge *or just communicating with other talented people across the globe, Mr. Sanders hopes you'll visit FishNet.*

Writing for an electronic publication might be a new experience for most writers, but though it's an entirely new medium, I think it doesn't change the writing process so much. You must still be an honest-to-goodness writer.

Edge publishes only nonfiction, and while we have a section devoted to student essays, all our pages are open to young writers. But we certainly won't create different standards for younger writers, and so we expect your work to be of the highest quality.

Unfortunately, a good many would-be *Edge* writers—regardless of age—don't understand that. That's why, in any given two hundred-piece pile of unsolicited submissions, we expect to find five queries that interest us, and, of those, we might actually commission one or two. That's not a particularly astounding success rate, and I think it is attributable to the fact that many people who submit to *Edge* wear the cap of "writer" rather loosely.

I suspect it's the same situation at many other publications, whether print or electronic. Here's a bit of evidence: In browsing through a bookstore one day, I came across a book that suggested something to the effect of "if you can speak, you can write." Well, I suppose speaking is a virtue for a writer, as are a grasp of language, an aversion to typos, a willingness to practice daily and learn from other writers and much more. But if we have to cut it down to a short phrase, I suggest it would be more accurate to say "if you can *think*, you can write."

Writing as a craft is not something to take lightly—that is, one shouldn't consider oneself a writer simply by virtue of being alive. Writing is a way of seeing and interacting with the world, and writing is hard work. Grasp these concepts now and your writing is likely to be miles ahead of that of other writers.

That said, you might just have something valuable to contribute to *Edge*. *Edge* is a magazine about the learning lifestyle, which is a lifestyle in which you constantly learn from all kinds of experiences. It's a lifestyle particularly well-suited to writers. I think some of the best non-fiction happens when a writer puts himself or herself in an interesting situation that results in an interesting experience, finds the best angle in that situation, and tells the story that comes forth.

That's what we ask from any writer. So if you find yourself, as one of our young writers did, on a week-long biological expedition in the Bahamas, we want to hear from you.

As long as you're an honest-to-goodness writer.

PART THREE

Chapter Nine

The Market List

On the following pages, you will find the special market listings for young writers. Yet, as mentioned in chapter three, many of the best and most easily accessible markets are not listed here. They are the pubications you are already familiar with, such as your hometown newspaper or the regional magazine insert that comes with the daily paper, your own school or church publication and the special publications sponsored by clubs and organizations to which you may belong. And for those of you who are members of online information services, don't forget to check what might be available in your special interest areas. They are all potential markets for your work. You may submit material to them using the same formats and advice you have learned here.

Be sure to include a short cover letter when you first submit to local or regional markets, especially ones not listed here. Tell the editor where you are from and include a *brief* bit of personal history in a cover letter, including such things as the name of your school and the grade you're in. You may want to add a line or two about your writing and publishing desires. However, as previously noted, don't waste time telling the editor what a great (or miserable) writer you are, or that you have enclosed (or want to send) a great story, poem or article you wrote. And, under most circumstances, you shouldn't bother mentioning how great (or yucky) your family, friends or teachers find your writing.

Local editors, like editors elsewhere, are usually very opinionated people when it comes to submissions. If you *are* a good writer and *have* submitted a really good manuscript, the editor will know it without your telling her. If the editor doesn't agree with your assessment of your writing ability, no amount of boasting will convince her otherwise. Editors in general are very skeptical about working with people who think too highly of themselves or their work. Let your work speak for itself.

The biggest benefit of submitting work to the types of markets mentioned above is that if a local editor likes your work and finds that you are willing to listen to her comments and ideas, plus can accept editing of your work without much fuss, you may just find yourself being hired to do special writing assignments.

UNDERSTANDING A MARKET LISTING

Markets, which include secular and religious magazines, newspapers, newsletters, theater groups, book publishers and other opportunities, are listed alphabetically, including those accessed through online computer services.

Each listing contains three individual sections of information, which will help you understand (1) the type of publication it is; (2) what material it will consider from young people; and (3) the preferred formats for submitting your work. There are two optional sections: "Editor's Remarks" are quotes directly from editors or their guidelines sheets. They provide additional information to help you understand and evaluate whether the market would be an appropriate place for you to send your work. "Subscription Rates" have been included as an extra service since so many of the publications listed are available by subscription only.

New additions to this edition's market listings are preceded by a check mark (✔). Markets that are of special interest to young people are preceded by an asterisk (*). Markets that require an entry fee are marked with a dollar sign ($). Canadian markets are identified with a maple leaf (✤).

A few listings are also marked with a double cross (‡). This indicates that this market should be considered only by serious teen writers, as competition for acceptance is likely to be tough because you will be competing against adults, the market receives many more submissions than it can use or it has an unusual focus that may not be understood or appreciated by young writers. To help you remember how to interpret the codes and listing information, an "Author's Note" has been placed at the bottom of some listings.

The following chart and sample market listing will help explain the information contained within each section. You may want to review the sections "What's in This Edition" and "More About the Listings" in chapter one, plus the advice in chapter three, "Study and Compare the Opportunities," before reviewing these listings.

MARKET LISTING CHART

SEC.	YOU WILL FIND	PAY SPECIAL ATTENTION TO
1	Name of Publication. Mailing address for manuscripts, guidelines and sample copies. Brief description including how often it is published, the age range, and interests of its readers.	Who reads this publication and the general theme followed in each issue.
2	Types of written material, art and photography, that are considered for publication. Specific material that is not accepted.	Any special columns or departments written exclusively by young writers. Any specific types of material that are never used.
3	More detailed information to help you write and prepare your manuscripts. Payments offered; rights purchased. Word limits; line limits for poetry. Availability of guidelines and samples.	Any special instructions for submitting manuscripts. Whether you need to include a signed statement from your parents, teacher or guardian.
4	Advice and helpful tips especially for young writers, quoted directly from the editor.	What the editors say they do and do not want from young writers.
5	Subscription rates. Subscription mailing address when it differs from the editorial office.	Included as an extra service for young people, parents and teachers.

SAMPLE MARKET LISTING

1 _____ THE ACORN, 1530 7th St., Rock Island, IL 61201. For young people in grades K-12, published six times a year.

2 _____ **Publishes:** Fiction, nonfiction, articles on any subject of interest to young people. Uses 4″ × 5″ black ink drawings on any subject. Uses material from adult authors, as well as young authors, but work must be slanted to students in grades K-12.

3 _____ **Submission Info:** Handwritten material OK if readable. Prefers standard format. Maxiumum length for fiction and nonfiction 500 words; 200-word limit for articles; poetry up to 32 lines. *Always* put author's name, address, age or grade on manuscript. Submissions will *not* be returned without SASE. Reports in one week. Pays in copies. Guidelines available for SASE. Sample copy $2.

4 _____ **Editor's Remarks:** "Just be yourself. Write your feelings; dare to be different. You never know when what you have to say might be of help and encouragement to other young authors."

5 _____ **Subscription Rates:** One year $10 (six issues: February, April, June, August, October, December).

* THE ACORN, 1530 7th St., Rock Island, IL 61201. For young people in grades K-12, published four times a year.

Publishes: Fiction, nonfiction, articles on any subject of interest to young people. Uses $4'' \times 5''$ black ink drawings on any subject. Uses material from adult authors, as well as young authors, but work must be slanted to students in grades K-12.

Submission Info: Handwritten material OK if readable. Prefers standard format. Maximum length for fiction and nonfiction is 500 words; poetry up to 32 lines. *Always* put author's name, address, age or grade on manuscript. Submissions will *not* be returned without SASE. Reports in one week. Guidelines available for SASE. Sample copy $2.

Editor's Remarks: "Just be yourself. Write your feelings; dare to be different. You never know when what you have to say might be of help and encouragement to other young authors. No pay but it isn't necessary to purchase a copy to be published."

Subscription Rates: One year $10 (four issues: March, June, September, December).

AIM—AMERICA'S INTERCULTURAL MAGAZINE, P.O. Box 20554, Chicago, IL 60620-0554. Quarterly publication for high school, college and general public.

Publishes: Some poetry on themes dealing with social issues. However, *no* religious material; do not moralize.

Submission Info: Use standard format; include SASE. Preferred length 2,000 words. Reports in six weeks. Payment $15 to $25. Pays on publication. Sample copy $4.

Editor's Remarks: "The problems in our society are tremendous—drugs, teenage sex, promiscuity, a feeling of being alienated from family, greed, racism, selfishness. We would like to stress that morality does win, that the American Dream can be achieved when members of the group are looking out for others. We are looking for stories that prove all men are brothers. Prove, not by telling but by showing."

Subscription Rates: One year $10.

✔‡* **AMELIA**, 329 "E" St., Bakersfield, CA 93304. (805) 323-4064. Editor: Frederick A. Raborg, Jr. Quarterly publication;

readers predominately college educated, approximate age range of readers 17-90. Attempts to be an effective bridge between small presses, university journals and slick newsstand magazines.

Publishes: All genres of fiction and other creative forms, including poetry and drama. Has no taboo topics, though does not include pornography. Also considers fine pen-and-ink sketches, sophisticated cartoons and photography.

Submission Info: Insists on typed manuscripts from adult writers; will consider handwritten material from students. Fiction and nonfiction should not exceed 4,500 words; poetry 100 lines maximum. Uses many haikus. Send SASE with all submissions and queries. Payment for fiction $35; poetry $2-$25. Pays on acceptance. Reports in two weeks; however, may be up to three months for work under serious consideration. Sample copy $8.95.

Editor's Remarks: "We would like to see evidence in the writing that the student has read both classic and contemporary writers, e.g., Keats, Shelley, Yeats, Whitman, Ginsberg, Dickinson, Steinbeck, Hemingway, Clavell, Vonnegut, Barthelme, etc. If [regarding taboos] for any reason we publish something that might offend, we would contact the parents before sending copies of that issue to anyone underage."

Subscription Rates: Four issues $25. Single issue $8.95.

* AMERICAN GIRL MAGAZINE, 8400 Fairway Place, Middleton, WI 53562. Full-color magazine published bimonthly by Pleasant Company.

Publishes: Children should submit poems, tips, suggestions and responses to polls and questions in *American Girl* magazine.

Submission Info: Guidelines available for adult submissions. See sample issues for more information regarding submissions from young people. Send SASE for guidelines. See guidelines on how to obtain a sample copy or purchase copies at bookstores.

Editor's Remarks: "The mission of Pleasant Company is to educate and entertain children with high quality products and experiences that reinforce positive social and moral values."

Subscription Rates: Single issue retail cost $3.95. One year (six issues) $19.95.

[**Author's Note:** For best chance at having work accepted, read one or more current copies and respond to requests for specific types of material or topics.]

*$ AUTHORSHIP, National Writer's Association, 1450 S. Havana, Suite 424, Aurora, CO 80012. Accepts submissions; students welcomed as members. Published bimonthly.

Publishes: Articles on writing only. No fiction or poetry.

Submission Info: Use standard typed format. Maximum length is 600 words. Payment $10 plus two copies and credit given for professional membership in the National Writer's Association. Submissions will not be returned without SASE. Reporting time one month for unsuitable materials. If it's held longer, we are considering it for publication.

Editor's Remarks: "We would like to see more young people as writers and members."

Subscription Rates: Individual membership includes subscription. For schools or institutions, one year membership costs $18.

[**Author's Note:** NWA has a lot to offer serious young writers; however, membership fee is relatively high.]

* BOODLE: BY KIDS, FOR KIDS, P.O. Box 1049, Portland, IN 47371. (219) 726-8141. Published quarterly. (Formerly called *Caboodle: By Kids, For Kids*.) One hundred percent of magazine is written by children. Audience: children ages 6-12.

Publishes: Student-produced stories, articles, poems, mazes and puzzles. Readers are invited to write and illustrate their own ideas and send them to the editors. Uses about twelve short stories and twenty to thirty poems per issue. Seldom publishes sad or depressing stories about death or serious illness. Especially likes humor and offbeat stories and poems.

Submission Info: Never devotes more than two pages to any one story, so long stories are not acceptable. Handwritten material is OK, if legible. Please include full name, grade when written, current grade, name of school and a statement from parent or teacher that the work is original. Send SASE for reply or if you wish your material returned to you. Guidelines available for SASE. Sample copy $2.50. Student authors receive two free copies of issue in which their work is published. Reports in two months.

Editor's Remarks: "Young writers and artists should read *Boodle* to see what kind of material is published, but do not try to write the same type of material you read. Try to think of something different. What kind of story would you like to read but didn't find in the magazine? The best way to get your story or poem published is to make the editor smile or laugh when she reads it."

Subscription Rates: One year (four quarterly issues) $10.

[**Author's Note:** I have received many notes from young writers who have been happily published in *Boodle*.]

✔ **BREAD FOR GOD'S CHILDREN**, P.O. Box 1017, Arcadia, FL 33821. Monthly magazine for Christian families; designed to be a teaching tool to enhance the knowledge of the Word of God.

Publishes: Two freelance stories and two columns for children and teens. Stories should teach walking in faith and overcoming through Jesus. Articles for "The Teen Page" and "Let's Chat" columns should relate to some aspect of daily living through Biblical principles. Also considers short fillers.

Submission Info: Use standard format; include SASE. Limit articles to 800 words or less. Limit stories for older children and teens to 1,800 words maximum. Limit stories for younger children to 800 words. Pays on publication: $40 for stories for teens; $30 for stories for children; $20 for articles; $7.50 for short fillers. Send SASE for guidelines. If you have not asked for them before, will send two or three sample copies upon request.

Editor's Remarks: "If writers will study several copies of *Bread for God's Children* to get an idea of our thrust, it will be appreciated by us and save you from having a manuscript held up in our office when it really fits another publication."

‡* **CALLIOPE**, 7 School St., Peterborough, NH 03458. World history (East/West) magazine for young people ages 8-14 published five times per year. Each issue focuses on a particular theme.

Publishes: Feature-length material relating to an upcoming theme; authentic historical and biographical fiction, adventure, retold legends, etc., relating to theme. Supplemental nonfiction that includes subjects directly and indirectly related to theme; activities including crafts, recipes, woodworking projects, etc., that can be done either alone or with adult supervision. Poetry, puzzles and games. No wordfinds. Uses crosswords and other word puzzles using the vocabulary of the issue's theme. Also mazes and picture puzzles.

Submission Info: Query first; see current guidelines and theme sheet for details. *All submissions must relate to an upcoming issue's theme.* Theme lists and writer's guidelines available for SASE. Pay varies depending on type of material accepted. Sample copy $4.50 plus 7½″ × 10½″ (or larger) self-addressed envelope with $1.24 postage.

Editor's Remarks: "Unfortunately, we do not have enough space to regularly publish students' work other than the letters, drawings and short poems. We occasionally have contests that involve creative writing. Keep an eye out for these contests. All submissions for feature material, from students and adults alike, are evaluated equally."

Subscription Rates: One year $17.95. Also available on some newsstands.

[**Author's Note:** This is a good market for nonfiction writers who really enjoy researching history; but you *must* query first and follow the editorial procedure exactly. *Calliope* does regularly publish some students' work.]

✔ **CAMPUS LIFE**, 465 Gundersen Dr., Carol Stream, IL 60188. *Campus Life*'s purpose is to help Christian teens navigate adolescence with their faith intact. Target audience: Teens in high school and early college.

Publishes: Personal experience stories from and about teens. Uses very little poetry and fiction. Nonfiction articles need to capture style used in the "Radical View" section.

Submission Info: Query only; no unsolicited manuscripts. Pays $.15-$.20 per word. Reports three to five weeks. Send SASE for guidelines. Sample copy $2. Use standard format; include SASE.

Editor's Remarks: "The first-person or as-told-to first-person story is the best way for new writers to break into *Campus Life.*

❀‡ **CANADIAN AUTHOR**, 275 Slater St., Suite 500, Ottawa, ON K1P 5H9 Canada. Quarterly magazine dedicated to bringing news of Canadian writers, editors and publishers to developing freelance writers.

Publishes: Articles of interest to and about writers and the professional writing business; interested in sharing hints to beginning writers from professionals. See guidelines for specifics regarding submissions, by Canadian authors only, of fiction and poetry.

Submission Info: Query first about article and profile ideas. Use standard format for all submissions. Include SASE or IRCs for foreign submissions. Usually buys first North American serial rights. Payment rates and additional submission information in guidelines, which are available for SASE (in Canada) or self-addressed envelope with IRC.

Editor's Remarks: "Above all, read and study a *recent* issue of *Canadian Author!*"

[**Author's Note:** Notice that writers must query with ideas first.]

*❀ **CHICKADEE MAGAZINE**, 179 John St., Suite 500, Toronto, ON M5T 3G5 Canada. Science and nature magazine for ages 3-8, published ten times per year.

Publishes: Readers' artwork and writing in response to requests in the "Chirp" section of magazine each month. Publishes drawings on a specific topic, a letter with photo from readers and a "chuckle" submitted by a child. *Very* occasionally, publishes short poems by readers in "Chirp."

Submission Info: All materials submitted to "Chirp" become the property of Owl Communications. No payment made for submissions.

Subscription Rates: In U.S., one year (ten issues) $14.95. Mail subscription requests to 255 Great Arrow Ave., Buffalo, NY 14207-3082. (800) 387-4379.

* CHILDREN'S DIGEST, 1100 Waterway Blvd. P.O. Box 567, Indianapolis, IN 46202. Publication for preteens from the Children's Better Health Institute. Stresses health-related themes or ideas, including nutrition, safety, exercise and proper health habits.

Publishes: From readers: original fiction or nonfiction stories, original poetry, readers' favorite jokes and riddles. Material need not be health-related. Stories printed occasionally.

Submission Info: If possible, please type stories. Put your name, age, school and complete address on each page of your work. Fiction and nonfiction stories may be up to 300 words. Material cannot be returned. Jokes and riddles can be sent on postcards. No payment for published reader material. Send SASE for special guidelines for young writers. Sample copy for $1.25.

Editor's Remarks: "We usually select material sent in by children in the 8-13 age group. If you're older than 13, it would be best to find another market for your work. We feel that it is unfair for us to judge the work of young children against the work of teenagers."

Subscription Rates: One year $14.95. Special rate $11.95 is usually offered in every issue.

* CHILDREN'S PLAYMATE, 1100 Waterway Blvd., P.O. Box 567, Indianapolis, IN 46206. Publication for children 6-8 from the Children's Better Health Institute. Stresses health-related themes or ideas, including nutrition, safety, exercise and proper health habits.

Publishes: From readers: original poems, original artwork and favorite jokes and riddles. Does not publish stories written by readers.

Submission Info: Poetry must be original. Artwork must be drawn by the reader. Jokes and riddles can be favorite ones readers have heard. Jokes and riddles can be sent on postcards. (Sorry, no material can be returned.) No payment is made for published reader material. Send SASE for guidelines. Sample copy $1.25. Submissions should be limited to young people ages 6-8.

Subscription Rates: One year $15.95. Special rate of $11.95 is usually offered in every issue.

‡* **COBBLESTONE**, 7 School St., Peterborough, NH 03458. American history magazine for young people published nine times per year. Each issue focuses on a particular theme.

Publishes: Feature-length material if related to an upcoming theme; authentic historical and biographical fiction, adventure, retold legends, etc., relating to theme. Supplemental nonfiction related to theme; activities including crafts, recipes, projects, etc., that can be done either alone or with adult supervision. Poetry, puzzles and games. No wordfinds. Crosswords and other word puzzles using the vocabulary of the issue's theme.

Submission Info: *All submissions must relate to an upcoming issue's theme.* Theme lists and writer's guidelines available for SASE. Pay varies depending on type of material accepted. Sample copy $4.50 plus 7½″ × 10½″ (or larger) self-addressed envelope with $1.24 postage.

Editor's Remarks: "Unfortunately, we do not have enough space to regularly publish students' work other than the letters, drawings and short poems sent to *Cobblestone* for 'Dear Ebenezer.' We occasionally have contests that involve creative writing. Keep an eye out for these contests. All submissions for feature material, from students and adults alike, are evaluated equally."

Subscription Rates: One year $22.95. Also available on some newsstands.

[**Author's Note:** This is a good market for nonfiction writers who really enjoy researching history; but you *must* query first and follow the editorial procedure exactly. *Cobblestone* does regularly publish students' work.]

*$ COMPUSERVE INFORMATION SERVICES,

P.O. Box 20212, 5000 Arlington Centre Blvd., Columbus, OH 43220. The world premier information service featuring a variety of special interest forums open to member subscribers.

Publishes: A variety of publishing opportunities exist on each of the various forums. Some places where young writers are most welcome are: Journalism Forum (GO JFORUM); ShowbizMedia Forum (GO SHOWBIZ); Computer Art & Graphics Forums (GO GRAPHICS); Literary Forum (GO LITFORUM); Motor Sports Forum (GO RACING); Outdoors Forum (GO OUTDOORS);

Pets/Animals Forum (GO PETS); Photography Forum (GO PHOTOFORUM); Students' Forum (GO STUFO); Comic Book Forum (GO COMIC).

Submission Info: Available online. Check the forums' opening bulletins, message boards and library files for guidelines and samples.

Editor's Remarks: "We'd love to have information from young writers in the Motor Sports Forum." (Response by Michael F. Hollander) "Section 15 'Screenwriting' of the ShowbizMedia Forum is where both budding and established screenwriters can find plenty of professional support and respect from their colleagues" (SHOWBIZ Forum).

Subscription Rates: Call (800) 848-8990.

[**Author's Note:** The responses here are typical regarding young writers being welcome.]

* CREATIVE KIDS, Prufrock Press, P.O. Box 8813, Waco, TX 76714-8813. Kids from all over the nation contribute to the largest magazine written by and for kids.

Publishes: Stories, games, puzzles, poetry, artwork, opinion and photography by and for kids ages 8-14. Work must be original and submitted by the author. Work submitted to *Creative Kids* should not be under consideration by any other publisher.

Submission Info: Each submission must be labeled with child's name, birthday, grade, school and home address and must include a cover letter. All submissions must include SASE for reply. Send SASE for detailed guidelines. Sample copy $3.

Editor's Remarks: *"Creative Kids, The National Voice for Kids* bursts with new ideas and activities to entertain, excite and encourage the creativity of kids ages 8-14. The magazine includes exciting examples of the most creative student work to be found in any publication for kids."

Subscription Rates: One year (six issues) $19.95.

* CREATIVE WITH WORDS, P.O. Box 223226, Carmel, CA 93922. Publishes anthologies, many of which are for or by children.

Publishes: *CWW* is devoted to furthering (1) folk/artistic tales and such; (2) creative writing by children (poetry, prose and language arts work); (3) creative writing in special interest groups (senior citizens, handicapped, general family). Particularly interested in prose language arts work, fillers, puzzles and poems from young people. Publishes according to set themes.

Submission Info: Submissions from young writers must be their own work and not edited, corrected or rewritten by an adult. Will work with individual young writers if editing and corrections are necessary. Do not send personal photo unless requested. Use standard format for preparing manuscripts. Poetry must be 20 lines or less. Prose should not exceed 1,000 words. Shorter poems and articles are always welcome. Do not send previously published material. Copyright reverts back to author after publication. No payment is made to contributors, but they do receive a 20 percent cost reduction on publication in which their work appears. No free copies in payment. Send SASE for return of manuscript and/or correspondence. Send SASE for current guidelines and theme list. Address submissions to B. Geltrich.

Editor's Remarks: "*CWW* is an educational publication, which means that it serves both the academic and nonacademic communities of the world. The editors organize one annual poetry contest (only for those nineteen and older), offer feedback on manuscripts submitted, publish a wide range of themes relating to human studies and critically analyze manuscripts for minimal charge."

Subscription Rates: One year (twelve issues, each 50-100 pages) $60.

‡ **CRUSADER MAGAZINE**, P.O. Box 7259, Grand Rapids, MI 49510. Christian magazine for boys aged 9-14; offical publication of the Cadet Corp.

Publishes: Sports articles up to 1,500 words, accompanying black-and-white photos appreciated; crafts and hobby articles, articles about camping and nature (how-to or "God in nature" themes); fast-moving fiction stories of 1,000-1,300 words that appeal to a boy's sense of adventure or sense of humor. Avoid "preachiness" and simplistic answers to complicated problems. Avoid long dialogue and little action. Also boy-oriented cartoons.

All submissions must relate to upcoming theme.

Submission Info: Use standard format, include name and address in upper left corner along with number of words and statement regarding terms of sale (all rights, first rights or second rights). Enclose SASE for return of submission. Payment for manuscripts $.03 per word and up (first rights with no major editing). Cartoons $5 and up for single gags; $15 and up for full-page panels. Puzzle rates vary. Photos $5 for each one used with an article. Send SASE for guidelines and theme sheet.

Editor's Remarks: "A writer desiring to sell fiction to *Crusader* should request a list of themes."

[**Author's Note:** This is the same information supplied to adult writers as found on guidelines.]

✔ **DOGWOOD TALES MAGAZINE**, P.O. Box 172068, Memphis, TN 38187. Published bimonthly for readers of all ages.

Publishes: Only fiction done in good taste. Considers any genre except religious or pornography. Each issue includes special feature story with a southern theme, person or place. Does *not* use poetry or nonfiction.

Submission Info: Use standard format; include SASE. Put name, address and average word count on manuscript. Preferred length 250-3,000 words. Pays in copies. Send SASE for guidelines. Sample copy $3.25.

Editor's Remarks: "Send us your best short story. We select those that are fresh and action moving. We like strong endings. If we reject your manuscript, don't be discouraged. Try us again with another story. Send the one we rejected to another magazine. It might not have been what we're looking for, but it might be perfect for another publisher."

Subscription Rates: One year (six issues) $15.60; U.S. funds only.

✔* **ECLECTIC RAINBOWS**, 1538 Tennessee Walker Dr., Roswell, GA 30075-3152. Editor: Linda T. Dennison. New biannual magazine "committed to making a positive difference," and "dedicated to covering the people, places and things that make a positive difference in our lives and in the universe in which we live."

Publishes: Essays, personal opinion/experience, humor/satire, interviews, short stories (*no* science fiction or horror), reviews, poetry. Particularly interested in environment issues, world affairs, politics, celebrities, humor, astrology and other "New Age" topics. Always express a strong and well-articulated point of view, preferably your own. Also has special "Kid's Korner" column, currently written by an adult. However, editor *very* interested in a young writer aged 13-18 to take over column or receiving suitable articles from young writers. "Kid's Korner" favors environmental pieces or how-to pieces dealing with some strong aspect of growing up. Example: How can we become better parents?

Submission Info: Use standard format. No handwritten or poor-quality dot matrix manuscripts. Send computer or photocopy; do *not* send an original as editor usually makes comments/edits directly on the manuscript. Essays 1,000-3,000 words; short stories 4,000 words maximum; poetry 30 lines maximum; personal experience 1,500 maximum. Send SASE to receive detailed guidelines. Sample $5. Pays up to $25 upon publication. No cash payment for poetry. Purchases one-time rights; will consider reprints.

Editor's Remarks: "I don't expect your writing to have a thirty-year-old's mentality. I *do* expect equivalent writing expertise and a professional attitude. Always remember SASE. Keep in mind our mostly baby-boomer audience: Write with your parents in mind (!) and tell us where you're coming from attitude-wise. Tell us what *you* think we need to know in order to create better communications between the generations. Do it without preaching. Humor is always a good approach. I had wonderful mentors and try to pass it along by helping young writers, so *do* tell me your age and background!"

Subscription Rates: One year (two issues) $10. Single copy $5.

[**Author's Note:** *Eclectic Rainbows* guidelines include this interesting and enlightening tip: "If you can easily think of a half dozen other markets that would be a likely 'fit' for your idea/article—by all means, send it to them instead! They can probably pay you more and faster. What we want is the stuff that is really, really well written—but just doesn't quite 'fit' into any other publication that you know of.''']

✔* EDGE: THE HIGH PERFORMANCE ELECTRONIC MAGAZINE FOR STUDENTS, 4905 Pine Cone Dr., Suite 1, Durham, NC 27707. Prefers electronic communications via World Wide Web: http://www.jayi.com/jayi; e-mail contact: greg@gsanders.pdial.interpath.net. Bimonthly electronic magazine published on the World Wide Web for high school students interested in the learning lifestyle—learning from experiences that take place everywhere.

Publishes: Download sample issue to discover content, style and other details. All sections open to young writers, however the "Full Court Pressure" section is specifically for younger writers; features guest column (balanced, well-thought-out essays) from a different student writer in each issue. Environment, school and politics are good topic choices but also likes topics that are out of the ordinary, as long as topic appeals to other bright teenagers. *No poetry accepted.*

Submission Info: Prefers electronic submissions sent by e-mail. E-submissions should be in text only or ASCII format. Handwritten and typed material sent via regular mail also acceptable; include SASE. No matter the format, include name, mailing address, school name and location and grade. Full Court Pressure submissions 400-800 words. Payment $50. Writer's guidelines available by e-mail or regular mail (send SASE), or download from Web site. Sample copy available only from Web site.

Editor's Remarks: "When you write your essay, write about something that means a lot to you. And make it mean a lot to us and the readers of *Edge*. Our purpose is to give readers the information they need to take advantage of the many learning opportunities—almost always outside of school—available to them."

Subscription Rates: No subscription fee. *Edge* is part of Fish-Net, a Web site for teenagers.

[**Author's Note:** *Edge* is the electronic-only magazine version of what was formerly called *Young Scholar*, listed in previous editions of *Market Guide for Young Writers*.]

‡* **FACES**, 7 School St., Peterborough, NH 03458. Anthropology magazine for young people published nine times per year.

Publishes: Variety of feature articles and in-depth, personal accounts relating to themes. Word length: about 800. Also uses supplemental nonfiction, 300-600 words. Includes subjects directly or indirectly related to themes. Some fiction, activities, photos, poetry, puzzles and games with a connection to an upcoming theme.

Submission Info: Operates on a by-assignment basis but welcomes ideas and suggestions in outline form. Ideas should be submitted at least six months prior to the publication date of related theme's issue. Pays on individual basis. Guidelines with theme list available for SASE. Sample copy $4.50 plus 7½″ × 10½″ (or larger) self-addressed envelope with $1.24 postage.

Editor's Remarks: "Unfortunately, we do not have enough space to regularly publish students' work other than the letters, drawings, and short poems sent to *Faces* for 'Letters Page.' We occasionally have contests that involve creative writing. Keep an eye out for these contests. All submissions for feature material, from students and adults alike, are evaluated equally."

Subscription Rates: One year $21.95.

✔* **FIELD & STREAM JR.**, 2 Park Ave., New York, NY 10016. Published approximately six times per year as a special section in *Field & Stream*. Goal is to pass on the traditions of hunting and fishing to the next generation. Reader age range 8-12.

Publishes: Especially from young writers: short how-to tips. Also straightforward how-to articles, crafts and projects, puzzles and adventure stories. Central topics include hunting, fishing, conservation, nature and sporting ethics. *No poetry accepted.*

Submission Info: Use standard format. Also accepts computer disk submissions, but include a hard [printed] copy. Scrap art appreciated. Articles range from 50-500 words. Short fillers should be 50-100 words. Address all submissions to THE EDITOR at above address. Detailed guidelines available for SASE. Sample copy $4. Reports within thirty days. Pays on acceptance.

Editor's Remarks: "Study past *Field & Stream Jr.* sections to determine the types of articles we are looking for. Write about something you know well."

Subscription Rates: For information, write *Field & Stream*, P.O. Box 55652, Boulder, CO 80322-5652.

* THE FUDGE CAKE, P.O. Box 197, Citrus Heights, CA 95611-0197. Bimonthly newsletter designed to showcase the works of young writers ages 6-17.

Publishes: Short stories and poetry from writers ages 6-17. No artwork accepted.

Submission Info: Type or neatly print submissions on 8″ × 11″ white paper. Send SASE for information flyer and detailed guidelines. Sample copy $2.50.

Subscription Rates: Six issues $10 in U.S.; $12 Canada.

‡ FUTURIFIC MAGAZINE, Futurific, Inc. Foundation for Optimism, 305 Madison Ave., Concourse 10B, New York, NY 10165. Published twelve times a year by Futurific, Inc., a nonprofit educational organization dedicated to finding a better understanding of the future.

Publishes: Material analyzing any issue in current events. All material must show what *improvements* are coming in the near future. No gloom and doom stories, and do not try to tell readers how they should live their lives. Wants material that tells what *will* happen.

Submission Info: Buys one-time rights. Payment negotiated. Material will only be returned with SASE. Presently only black-and-white photos and artwork are used. Sample copy available for $5.

Editor's Remarks: "We've had nineteen years of accurate forecasting, reporting solutions not problems."

Subscription Rates: One year for individuals $70; institutions $140.

[**Author's Note:** Be sure you understand the special focus of this magazine before submitting material.]

* THE GOLDFINCH: IOWA HISTORY FOR YOUNG PEOPLE, State Historical Society of Iowa, 402 Iowa

Ave., Iowa City, IA 52240. Award-winning quarterly history magazine for 4th-7th graders, focused on Iowa, Midwestern and U.S. history. Each issue devoted to one theme in Iowa history.

Publishes: Special section called "History Makers" that publishes activities, photographs, artwork, class projects, essays created by young people that relate to the issue's theme.

Submission Info: Submissions should include age, grade, school. Feel free to include photos. Include SASE with submission. Pays in copies. Send for free writer's guidelines and list of upcoming themes. Sample copy $4.

Editor's Remarks: "*The Goldfinch* encourages submissions from young people, but *all* submissions must correspond to an upcoming theme to be considered for publication. Writers should write for a copy of our Young Writers' Guidelines before submitting work. An SASE should accompany all correspondence."

Subscription Rates: One year (four issues) $10.

[**Author's Note:** The special focus here is history related to Iowa.]

❧ **GREEN'S MAGAZINE**, P.O. Box 3236, Regina, SK, S4P 3H1 Canada. Quarterly literary magazine for general audience, including libraries and many writers.

Publishes: See writer's guidelines for specifics. Material targeted to a general audience. Study sample copy.

Submission Info: Send complete manuscripts with SASE or self-addressed envelope (SAE) with adequate IRCs. Send cover letter and biographical information with manuscripts. Buys first rights but can be reassigned to authors on written request with SASE or SAE plus IRC. Do not send multiple submissions. Generally reports in eight weeks. Payment in two copies. Send SASE or SAE with IRC to receive writer's guidelines. Sample copy $4.

Editor's Remarks: "We do not go out of our way to publish young writers but report happily that we have published many, including preteens."

Subscription Rates: One year (four issues) $12. Single issues $4 each.

‡ **GUIDE MAGAZINE**, 55 W. Oak Ridge Dr., Hagerstown, MD 21740. Weekly Christian publication for young people ages 10-14; aim is to foster a greater sense of self-worth, assurance and a concern for others in its readers.

Publishes: Devotional, adventure, personal growth and Christian humor stories. Present stories from a young person's viewpoint, written in the active voice, concisely and with clarity. Avoid stories with violence, hunting, etc. Prefer true or based on true stories. Uses very little poetry.

Submission Info: Use standard format; be sure to include name, address, phone and Social Security number in upper left-hand corner of first page. Include SASE with submissions and requests for guidelines and sample copy. Pays on acceptance; complimentary copies sent when published. Reports in two weeks. Considers first rights, reprints and simultaneous submissions.

Editor's Remarks: "When writing for *Guide*, please strive to set forth a clearly evident Christian principle, without being preachy. (This doesn't mean kids don't have important issues to address. It just means there are effective and ineffective ways to deal with their problems.) In general, *Guide* is interested in creative approaches to topics that will provide young people with ideas and tools to help enrich their lives in Christ."

Subscription Rates: One year (fifty-two issues) $35.97. Higher outside U.S. Send check or money order to above address or call (800) 765-6955.

[**Author's Note:** These are the same guidelines given to adult writers.]

* **HIGHLIGHTS FOR CHILDREN**, 803 Church St., Honesdale, PA 18431. Published monthly for youngsters ages 2-12.

Publishes: Poems, drawings and stories from readers. Also runs many reader-response features a year, to which readers submit their creative responses. For writers 16 or older, also reviews submissions of short stories, factual features, puzzles, party plans, crafts, finger plays and action plays. Seldom buys verse.

Submission Info: For writers up to age 15, drawings may

be in color or black and white. Prose may be no more than two double-spaced typed pages or three double-spaced handwritten pages. Acknowledges all material submitted. However, material is not returned; *do not enclose SASE*. No payment made for contributions from writers 15 or under. For writers 16 or older, consult regular freelance guidelines available free. Fiction should not be more than 800 words; pays $.08 and up per word. Science and factual articles within 800 words bring $75 and up. Other material brings $25 and up. Those 16 and older should send complete manuscript with SASE. All submissions need to include name, age and complete home address. Personal photo is unnecessary.

Subscription Rates: One year $26.00. Three years $70.00. Write *Highlights for Children*, 2300 W. Fifth Ave., P.O. Box 269, Columbus, OH 43216.

[**Author's Note:** Be sure to read the foreword to this book, written by Kent Brown, editor of *Highlights*.]

‡ **HOME EDUCATION MAGAZINE**, P.O. Box 1083, Tonasket, WA 98855. Bimonthly (68 pages) magazine for homeschooling families.

Publishes: Nonfiction articles, interviews and essays about home-based education. Regular staff-written column, called "Higher Education," features articles about how homeschooled youngsters have furthered their education through going on to college, locating apprenticeships or finding jobs. Also uses black-and-white and color photos of children and families in all kinds of situations, not necessarily those traditionally thought of as "educational." Artwork and cartoons will be considered, but we do not publish poetry or fiction.

Submission Info: Accepts submissions in any format. Prefers articles between 1,000 and 2,500 words. If handwritten, take care to write as neatly as possible. Include name and address on each page of all articles and on photos, artwork and other submissions. Guidelines available for SASE. Sample copy $3.50. Purchases first North American serial rights. Pays $.45 per column inch for articles, $5 each for inside black-and-white photos (send normal size prints, not enlargements), and $50 for color cover photos (send transparencies/slides). Rates vary for other material; write for specific information. Include SASE for reply or return of submissions. Cannot acknowledge submissions not accompanied by SASE.

Editor's Remarks: "We are particularly interested in articles describing young writers' homeschooling experiences."

Subscription Rates: One year (six issues) $24. Foreign countries write for rates. Available in most public libraries. Free 24-page catalog available.

[**Author's Note:** Not a suitable market for young writers who attend public or private schools.]

* HOW ON EARTH! *Youth supporting compassionate, ecologically sound living*, P.O. Box 339, Oxford, PA 19363-0339. *HOW ON EARTH! (HOE!)* is a nonprofit, all volunteer quarterly vegetarian magazine for and by youth concerned about environmental, animal, global and social justice issues. Geared toward youth ages 13-24. Youth are also involved in all aspects of planning, development and production.

Publishes: Research articles, poetry, creative writing and essays concerning ecology, ethics, animals, global issues, social justice, health, vegetarianism, vegetarian lifestyle and activism. Original artwork and photographs accepted. Food articles and vegetarian recipes suitable for young people are encouraged, as are articles containing practical information for compassionate, ecologically sound living. Authors must be age 24 or younger.

Submission Info: Accepts typed or handwritten material, if legible. Send SASE for writer's guidelines. Sample copy $6. Payment for submitted material not offered at this time.

Editor's Remarks: "We encourage young writers, artists and activists interested in environmental, animal, global and social justice issues to get involved with *HOW ON EARTH!* We also welcome young people with other skills who want to volunteer. All material must be original, factual and preferably presented in a positive, educational manner. *HOW ON EARTH!* welcomes ideas, input and participation from its readers in every way possible."

Subscription Rates: One year (four issues) $18.

* HUMPTY DUMPTY'S MAGAZINE, P.O. Box 567, Indianapolis, IN 46206. Published by the Children's Better Health Institute for preschool level children ages 4-6.

Publishes: Black-and-white or color drawings by readers ages 4-6. Submission Info: no payment for published reader materials. Editors advise readers to keep copies of their contributions because unused material cannot be returned. Publisher owns all rights to material printed.

Editor's Remarks: "We cannot promise to publish what you send because we receive many, many letters from children all over the world. We do promise to read and consider all the material sent to us, though! We are sorry, but because of the large amount of mail, we cannot write to each of you personally."

Subscription Rates: One year (eight issues) $15.95 in U.S. currency. Subscription office: P.O. Box 7133, Red Oak, IA 51591-0133.

* INK BLOT, 901 Day Rd., Saginaw, MI 48609. Monthly newsletter designed to provide a new outlet for young writers and artists; distributed to local schools, libraries and hospital waiting rooms.

Publishes: Nonfiction essays, short stories, poetry, acrostics. Will consider other types of short manuscripts and black-and-white artwork. Especially in need of short fillers. No photos.

Submission Info: Handwritten is accepted; typed material preferred. Students should include age, grade and school name. Short fillers should be 25-75 words long. Poetry limited to 30 lines. Maximum length for essays and stories 500 words. No submissions returned, however, contributors retain copyright to their materials. If SASE is sent with submission, you will receive free copy of newsletter containing your published work. Guidelines available for SASE. Sample copy $1 plus SASE. (Make check or money order payable to Margaret Larkin.)

Editor's Remarks: "We like to receive material written from your heart. Write your feelings into words. Remember to send your best work. Double-check for grammar, spelling and writing errors before mailing. We want to promote a positive outlook to our readers. We do not want negative or derogatory material."

Subscription Rates: No subscriptions available. Monthly copies may be obtained for $1 each plus SASE.

✓* **IT'S YOUR CHOICE MAGAZINE**, P.O. Box 7135, Richmond, VA 23221-0135. Informal newsletter format; published monthly. Readership: ages 11 and up. Mission: to arouse interest in ethics.

Publishes: Fiction and nonfiction with ethical implications (such as the choices or acts of high-ranking political figures). *No poetry or photos.* Accepts submissions from anywhere; articles in foreign languages are published in the original language with an accompanying English sidebar. Special "TEEN PAGE: Young Voices Speak Out on the Issues" offers the opportunity to research social issues of current issues. Resource leaders are individuals 11 and up (sometimes younger) who distribute questionnaires and return them in SASEs.

Submission Info: Use standard format; 1,000 words maximum. Guidelines for #10 SASE. Sample copy $2. Pays up to $1 per word. Reports approximately four weeks, longer if held for consideration.

Editor's Remarks: "Examples of current topics of interest: crime, captial punishment, abortion, euthanasia, learning behavior, religious belief, sexual behavior, failure of school systems, failure of criminal justice system, personal responsibility (concept of duty, etc.), environment, behavior/decision making by government officials, dishonesty/cheating, self-destructiveness."

Subscription Rates: One year $9.84; foreign $20.80.

[**Author's Note:** See profile of Michael LaFontaine in chapter seven.]

* **JACK AND JILL**, 1100 Waterway Blvd., P.O. Box 567, Indianapolis, IN 46202. Publication for children 7-10 from the Children's Better Health Institute. Stresses health-related themes or ideas, including nutrition, safety, exercise or proper health habits.

Publishes: From readers, original poetry and favorite jokes and riddles. Occasionally, publishes original stories (500 words or less) and original drawings.

Submission Info: Submissions do not have to be health related. Please write your name, age, school and complete address on each submission. Jokes and riddles can be sent on postcards. Material cannot be returned. No payment is made for published reader material. Send SASE for guidelines for young writers. Sample copy $1.25.

Editor's Remarks: "We usually select material sent in by children in the 7-10 age group."

Subscription Rates: One year $14.95. Special rate $11.95 is usually offered in every issue.

✔* **KIDS' BYLINE**, P.O. Box 1838, Frederick, MD 21702. Bimonthly magazine that provides a forum for students to publish their creative work. Targeted to grades 4-12. Readership: Grade 1-grandparents. Except for "Letter from the Editor," written entirely by young people. Student advisory board helps review material.

Publishes: Focuses mostly on writing but encourages art and photos to enhance magazine. No graphic violence. Also encourages "Letters to the Editor."

Submission Info: Stories should be short. Type or carefully handwrite submissions. Submit seasonal material four months in advance. Include author's name, address, telephone and age on submissions; school name optional. Include SASE with *all* submissions. Authors and artists receive three copies of issues containing their work. Send SASE for guidelines. Sample copy $3.

Editor's Remarks: "We don't like to edit. We want the material published to be the work of the writer—not the framework for an 'improved' piece. Work is published based on merit, not potential. Write about what you care about. Think of creative ways of expression. We shy away from factual accounts of historic events, geographic areas, etc. Savor the strength of words. Play with them. If you're having fun or *feeling* what you write, our readers will too."

Subscription Rates: One year (six issues) $15. Single issue $3.

[**Author's Note:** See the profiles of editor Gwen McEntire in chapter eight and student advisory member Christy Anthony in chapter seven.]

* KIDS N' SIBS, 191 Whittier Rd., Rochester, NY 14624. May also write to editor Elizabeth Fogg via Internet e-mail: dhcy@uhura.cc.rochester.edu. Free newsletter focusing on sharing views and experiences of disabled children and siblings.

Publishes: Anything that people want to write is acceptable, as long as it's in good taste and relates to newsletter's theme. Prefers submissions made by those 18 and under but will publish stories by older writers if they are personal accounts of their childhood and what it was like for them then as a disabled child or sibling of one. Also interested in information on different disabilities and diseases.

Submission Info: Submissions longer than one column or page will be used, with author's permission, as a series. No guidelines available. May contact Elizabeth Fogg by regular mail or e-mail. Send SASE for free sample. No payment. However, contributor's will receive free copy with published piece.

Editor's Remarks: "This newsletter is for anyone that has an interest in disabilities and handicaps. Feel free to write for us or just subscribe! Currently there aren't any 'rewards' for submitting an article because there isn't any charge for subscription."

Subscription Rates: Free; may charge for subscriptions in future.

✔* KIDS' WORLD, 1300 Kicker Rd., Tuscaloosa, AL 35404. E-mail address on GEnie: D.KOPASKS-ME. Editor: Morgan Kopaska-Merkel. Biannual (January and July) magazine featuring writing and art from young people up to age 17.

Publishes: Prefers poems, short stories and art. Also considers jokes, puzzles, games and other material. *No submissions from those over age 17. No horror accepted.*

Submission Info: Type or neatly handwrite submissions; include SASE. Also accepts electronic submissions. Send SASE for guidelines. Sample copy $1. Payment one copy.

Editor's Remarks: "For all kids: Have your parent or teacher check your work for grammar, spelling and punctuation. Un-rhymed poetry is OK. If you do *not* send SASE, you will not receive a reply. *Kids' World*'s foremost purpose is to provide a good place for aspiring writers to get started. Don't be afraid to submit! Pictures are especially needed. I only reject about one in twenty submissions, and feel free to submit more than one thing at a time."

Subscription Rates: Four issues (over two years) $3.75. Spec-ify which issue to start subscription or "next issue." Make check payable to David Kopaska-Merkel.

[**Author's Note:** The editor is a young writer herself. *Kids' World* is in its third year.]

* KOPPER BEAR PRESS, P.O. Box 19454, Boulder, CO 80303. May also reach via CompuServe: Howard S. Bashinski 70732,2505. Book publisher dedicated to helping exceptional authors ages 13-21 get published in high-quality format.

Publishes: Fiction, nonfiction, short stories, novels, novellas, essays, etc., from young people ages 13-21. Is very interested in receiving book-length manuscripts. No longer accepting poetry.

Submission Info: Will accept typed or handwritten work, but be sure you keep a copy as submissions are not returned. For additional information, e-mail to the above CompuServe number.

Editor's Remarks: "We want to read *everything*, except poetry. We promise a thorough reading of everything we receive and usually provide feedback, if requested. We are especially looking for well-written longer short stories and novels."

[**Author's Note:** This exciting new market opportunity for young writers began in April 1993. *It is not a vanity or subsidy press.*]

* LIFEPRINTS, P.O. Box 5181, Salem, OR 97304. (503) 581-4224. Published four times annually by Blindskills, Inc., a nonprofit organization for visually impaired adults and youth. Available in large print, cassette and braille. International reader-ship.

Publishes: Career, sports and leisure articles, topics of interest to students, fashion, study skills, social skills, book reviews, notices about technology and other aids available to visually impaired persons, and personal experience pieces by visually impaired adults and youth.

Submission Info: *Must* be written by visually impaired individuals. Send SASE for guidelines, and study a sample copy in either large print or braille. Visually impaired adults write on a volunteer basis. Visually impaired students who submit articles that are published receive a small honorarium from monies donated for that purpose. Sample copy available $6; specify format desired. Brochure available for SASE to all persons interested in learning more about *Lifeprints*.

Editor's Remarks: "Our emphasis is on experimental articles and methods used by successful visually impaired students and adults. We welcome submissions from middle and high school, as well as college youth. *Lifeprints* is a role model publication that, by example, inspires its readers to realize their vocational and selected lifestyle potential. We now have printed guidelines. However, it is best to study a sample issue."

Subscription Rates: Subscription/donation of $20 is suggested annually.

[**Author's Note:** This a good example of a magazine with a narrow focus. Note that submissions are restricted to those who are visually impaired.]

✔* **THE LOUISVILLE REVIEW**, Children's Corner, Dept. of English, 315 Bingham Humanities, University of Louisville, Louisville, KY 40292. "The Children's Corner" is a special section of *The Louisville Review* featuring the writings by students K-12. Readership: Mostly adults.

Publishes: Poems and short fiction from students K-12.

Submission Info: Use standard format; *must* include SASE and written permission to publish, if accepted, from a parent or guardian. Submit between September and December; reports by May. Payment one copy. Sample copy $4.

Editor's Remarks: "We are looking for vivid imagery, fresh language and originality. Our magazine comes out once or twice a year."

Subscription Rates: (Not indicated.) Single issue $4.

* LOW COUNTRY PARENT, 22 W. Bryan St., #202, Savannah, GA 31401. (912) 238-5982. (Formerly *Savannah Parent*.) Family, newspaper-style magazine with special section featuring submissions by writers ages 4-12 from Savannah and South Carolina's Low Country.

Publishes: Short poems and illustrations preferred. Other short creative writings are used as space permits. Seasonal submissions encouraged.

Submission Info: Submissions may be handwritten or typed. Maximum length approximately four paragraphs. Note: No rejection slips sent. Submissions are held and used as space permits. Each contributor receives an attractive parchment certificate suitable for framing. SASE needed if work is to be returned. However, it is usually returned along with the certificate and a copy of the paper in which the work appears. Guidelines and a sample copy are available for $1 to cover postage and handling.

Editor's Remarks: "The children's 'Creative Expressions' page appears in the centerfold of each issue of *Low Country Parent*, and it is highlighted with spot color. The choice spot selected for the 'Creative Expressions' page reflects the integral part the editor considers this page to be. It is intended to provide a forum for local children to share their creative endeavors, while experiencing the excitement of seeing their work and name in print."

Subscription Rates: One year (five issues) $10.

[**Author's Note:** Don't live in this area? Look for similar opportunities in your own area!]

✔* MAJESTIC BOOKS, P.O. Box 19097M, Johnston, RI 02919. Publishes anthologies of stories by writers under age 18.

Publishes: Stories and essays suitable for children of all ages. Occasionally accepts stories.

Submission Info: Use standard format; include SASE with all submissions and requests; indicate age of author. No guidelines. Payment one copy; occasionally pays small flat fee. Sample copy for $3.50 or $2 plus a 6"×9" SASE with $1.24 postage.

Editor's Remarks: "Use *your* imagination and be original. We prefer stories that leave a reader thinking long after the last word is read. Manuscripts are judged against others of the same age group, and we use anything that is considered good for that age group. Make sure to include your age. We comment on manuscript if requested."

[**Author's Note:** See profile of Greg Miller in chapter seven.]

* MERLYN'S PEN: THE NATIONAL MAGAZINES OF STUDENT WRITING, "MIDDLE SCHOOL EDITION," GRADES 6-9, P.O. Box 1058, East Greenwich, RI 02818. (401) 885-5175. Magazine written by students in grades 6-9. Four issues a year.

Publishes: Stories, plays, poems, essays on important issues, review letters, word games, opinions, critiques of writing in magazine and art by students in grades 6-9. Also considers puzzles. Letters to the editor are welcome.

Submission Info: *Merlyn's Pen* no longer considers unsolicited submissions. All submissions (art and literature) *must* now include *Merlyn's Pen* Official Cover Sheet. Authors and artists may call or write to receive a copy of the required cover sheet. Manuscripts without the cover sheet will be returned unread. Submissions with the cover sheet will receive a response within ten weeks. Upon acceptance, a statement of originality must be signed. For each published piece, authors and artists receive payment and three copies of the issues in which their work appears.

Editor's Remarks: "We find that young fiction writers who are successful in *Merlyn's Pen* choose subjects, characters and plots that come from personal experience. For example, they set stories in places they know (school, home, vacation spots, etc.), write about characters their own age and choose conflicts that they've handled themselves (peer pressure, parents, growing up, sports, etc.). Writing about anything else is bound to be nonspecific, unclear and, therefore, unconvincing and unpublishable. More advanced writers can disregard this advice!"

Subscription Rates: For one year (four issues during school year) $21.00 each for one to nine subscriptions; $7.95 each for ten or more subscriptions. Two-year individual subscriptions $33.95. Special student-at-home prepaid discount: One year $17.50; two years $33.50.

* MERLYN'S PEN: THE NATIONAL MAGAZINES OF STUDENT WRITING, "SENIOR EDITION," GRADES 9-12, P.O. Box 1058, East Greenwich, RI 02818. (401) 885-5175. Magazine written by students in grades 9-12. Four issues a year.

Publishes: Stories, plays, poems, essays on important issues, review letters, word games, opinions, critiques of writing in magazine and art by students in grades 9-12. Also considers puzzles. Letters to the editor are welcome.

Submission Info: *Merlyn's Pen* no longer considers unsolicited submissions. All submissions (art and literature) *must* now include *Merlyn's Pen* Official Cover Sheet. Authors and artists may call or write to receive a copy of the required cover sheet. Manuscripts without the cover sheet will be returned unread. Submissions with the cover sheet will receive a response within ten weeks. Upon acceptance, a statement of originality must be signed. For each published piece, authors and artists receive payment and three copies of the issues in which their work appears.

Editor's Remarks: "We find that young fiction writers who are successful in *Merlyn's Pen* choose subjects, characters and plots that come from personal experience. For example, they set stories in places they know (school, home, vacation spots, etc.), write about characters their own age and choose conflicts that they've handled themselves (peer pressure, parents, growing up, sports, etc.). Writing about anything else is bound to be nonspecific, unclear and, therefore, unconvincing and unpublishable. More advanced writers can disregard this advice!"

Subscription Rates: For one year (four issues during school year) $21.00 each for one to nine subscriptions; $7.95 each for ten or more subscriptions. Two-year individual subscriptions $33.95. Special student-at-home prepaid discount: One year $17.50; two years $33.50.

✔$‡ THE MISSOURI REVIEW, 1507 Hillcrest Hall, University of Missouri, Columbia, MO 65211. This literary magazine, published three times a year, appeals to a broad age range.

Publishes: The editors invite submissions of poetry, fiction and essays of a general literary interest with a distinctly contemporary orientation. Stories should be between 10-30 pages in length. The magazine publishes 3-5 poets per issue and features 6-12 pages of poetry per poet. Please keep in mind the length of features when submitting poems. Also, please clearly mark the outer envelope as fiction, poetry or essay. Also accepts cartoons, but no art or photography.

Submission Info: Submissions should be typewritten and double spaced, and must include SASE. Pays on publication.

Subscription Rates: Subscriptions are $19 for one year, $35 for two years and $45 for three years. Sample copy is $7.00.

✔* **NATION MAGAZINE**, Twisted Teen Publishing Co., 5998 Taylor Rd., Painesville, OH 44077. May also contact via Internet: Repsi SK@AOL.com. Published monthly except July and December. Readership: Teens and young adults to age 25. Unique magazine that focuses on friendship and is intended as an economical substitute for maintaining out-of-state and long-distance relationships.

Publishes: Letters and essays detailing the experiences, observations and social dialogue pertaining to life and living in general of its subscribers and contributors. Individuals up to age 25 may contribute. Additional participation is encouraged by way of personalized messages (sentences or short paragraph notes) in the "Parenthesis!" section or by communicating directly with the author.

Submission Info: Use standard format; ASCII format for electronic submissions. See sample issue for additional details and issue deadlines. Prefers letters or essays be *no less* than 250 words. Sample copy $1.50.

Editor's Remarks: "The best topics to write about are those that most enthuse the individual. More of a community than a magazine, *Nation* acts as a place to build friendships and maintain old acquaintances in a sincere and altruistic environment of loving and dynamic individuals. All submissions are edited for grammatical errors. Personal writing styles are left intact, although occasional sentence structure and particular wordings may be altered for clarity. *Nation* also reserves the right to edit any undue profanity and/or obscene or sexual content. The expression of radical concepts and freedom are supported to the farthest degree possible in maintaining a general readership without censorship."

Subscription Rates: Available for $1.50 per issue and can be purchased in either single issue, quarter-, half- or full-year subscriptions. Make checks payable to Peter Kowalke.

[**Author's Note:** I'm especially impressed with the quality and interesting focus of this magazine. It's a magazine equivalent to "round-robin" letter correspondence. While you don't have to have a subscription to contribute, its focus is basically defeated without one. I had the pleasure of meeting *Nation*'s teen editor and publisher, Peter Kowalke, at the 1995 Clonlara School Home Based Education Program National Conference in Toledo.]

* NEW ERA MAGAZINE, 50 E. North Temple Street, Salt Lake City, UT 84109. Official monthly publication for youth (ages 12-18) of the Church of Jesus Christ of Latter-day Saints.

Publishes: All types of writing—fiction, articles, poetry. Also seeks color or black-and-white slides or prints. Also uses short, humorous anecdotes about Mormon life, ideas for Mormons (refer to magazine for format) and material for FYI ("For Your Information") section, which features news of young Latter-day Saints from around the world. Considers submissions of artwork only for annual contest, unless portfolio has been shown to art director. All material must uphold Church standards (example: modesty in dress). Written material must have an LDS (Mormon) point of view.

Submission Info: Use standard format. Include SASE. Except for short pieces, best to query by letter, showing an example of your proposed writing style. Preferred length is 150-2,000 words. Reports in six to eight weeks. Seasonal material should be submitted six months to one year in advance. Payment on acceptance. Send SASE for detailed guidelines and story ideas sheets. Sample copy $1.

Editor's Remarks: "We're after material that shows how the Church of Jesus Christ of Latter-day Saints is relevant in the lives of young people today. It should capture the excitement of being a young Latter-day Saint. We have a special interest in personal experience; personality profiles; activities involving

LDS youth; and the experiences of young Latter-day Saints in other countries. Please don't send general library research or formula pieces without the *New Era* slant."

Subscription Rates: One year $8.

✔* NEW MOON: THE MAGAZINE FOR GIRLS AND THEIR DREAMS, P.O. Box 3620, Duluth, MN 55803-3620.

Bimonthly international magazine for every girl who wants her voice and her dreams taken seriously. Edited entirely by girls ages 8-14.

Publishes: Nonfiction profile articles of girls and women from the present and past; narratives of personal experience (difficult and pleasant); opinion pieces, poetry and some short fiction; cartoons, puzzles, artwork and photography by and about girls. Especially seeks submissions from girls ages 8-14.

Submission Info: Include name, age, address and phone number. Articles run 300-600 words; poetry 25 lines or less. Black-and-white photos preferred, but crisp color acceptable. Artwork in black ink/pencil on plain white paper preferred. Don't fold artwork; send flat or in mailing tube. Send SASE for cover art or writer's guidelines. Pays with copies and percentage of reprint revenue. Sample issue $6.50.

Editor's Remarks: "*New Moon*'s girl editors seek well-written, original work that covers the depth, range and variety of girls' experiences, feelings, opinions, concerns and dreams. Let the girl's voice and soul come through. Make it real. *New Moon* celebrates girls, explores the passage from girl to woman and builds healthy resistance to gender inequities."

Subscription Rates: One year (six issues) $25. Add $10 for postage to Canada; $12 to all other countries. U.S. funds only. Send check or money order to *New Moon*, P.O. Box 3587, Duluth, MN 55803-3587. Classroom discounts and free library sample available.

‡* ODYSSEY, 7 School St., Peterborough, NH 03458.

Magazine published nine times a year focusing on science for young people.

Publishes: Feature-length articles and question and answer interviews with scientists (750-900 words) related to theme. (Primary research is essential.) Supplemental nonfiction (people, places and classroom activities to discover) related to theme. Hands-on activities (models, experiments, etc.) that can be done alone or in a classroom setting. Science fiction or science-related stories, myths and legends (750-900 words) and poems related to theme.

Submission Info: Query first; see current guidelines and theme sheet for details. *All submissions must relate to an upcoming issue's theme.* Theme lists and writer's guidelines available for SASE. Pay varies depending on type of material accepted. Sample copy $4.50 plus 7½" × 10½" (or larger) self-addressed envelope with $1.24 postage.

Editor's Remarks: "We occasionally publish theme-related articles, poems and stories written by students, but they must be of professional quality. 'Future Forum' includes student opinions on science-related topics, and 'Ask Uly' answers students' science-related questions. We regularly publish 'envelope art.' We have an annual art contest and several writing contests throughout the year."

Subscription Rates: One year (nine issues) $22.95. Also available on some newsstands.

[**Author's Note:** This is a good market for nonfiction writers who really enjoy researching science, but you *must* query first and follow the editorial procedure exactly. Notice that *Odyssey* does regularly publish students' work.]

‡❋* **OUR FAMILY**, P.O. Box 249, Battleford, SK, S0M 0E0 Canada. Monthly magazine published for Catholic families, most of whom have children in grade school, high school or college.

Publishes: Nonfiction related to the following areas: people at home, people in relation to God, people at recreation, people at work, people in the world, biography (profiles about Christians whose living of Christian values has had a positive effect on their contemporaries) and inspirational articles. Also spiritual reflection, humorous anecdotes, poetry on human/spiritual themes, cartoons (family type), photos. *No fiction.*

Submission Info: Send for theme list and detailed guidelines for nonfiction and photos by enclosing SAE and $.50 (Canadian currency) or IRC. (Average cost to return manuscript is $1.10 in Canadian currency.) Sample copy $2.50.

Editor's Remarks: "The majority of our readers are adults. If young people write for us, they must understand that they are writing and competing in an adult market. Because our publication stresses the personal experience approach, young people could find a slot in our publication by writing as teenagers focusing on teenage concerns. We make no age distinctions. If a particular article/poem/filler effectively reaches a certain segment of the family, we are pleased to purchase it for publication in our magazine."

✔$* **POETS AT WORK,** Jessee Poet, VAMC 325 New Castle Rd., P.O. Box 113, Butler, PA 16001. Bimonthly magazine for poets of all ages.

Publishes: Poems by subscribers. In each issue an editor-designated "Distinguished Poet" gets a page all alone featuring his or her poetry. Also a postcard is inserted so subscribers can mail a note of congratulations to the distinguished poet.

Submission Info: Poems must be in good taste; no more than 20 lines long. Five or more poems may be submitted at one time. Include SASE. Sample copy $3.

Editor's Remarks: "No poet is too young or too old or too inexperienced. *Poets at Work* is a place to be encouraged, to learn and to enjoy fellowship with others who share a love of this field of expression. I have no special columns for young writers or any writers. I believe that my youngest poet is 12 and the oldest 93. *Poets at Work* is clean, thoughtful and fun. One thing that I *always* write in my publication is that I enjoy mail and like to hear from my poets; however, one subject is not open for discussion. *You may not criticize any of my poets.* We are all writing poetry because we have something to share—our dreams, hopes, plans, nightmares, etc. If one can write freely (in good taste) and be assured that no criticism will be forthcoming, one can stretch and grow."

Subscription Rates: One year (six issues) $18.

SHOFAR, 43 Northcote Dr., Melville, NY 11747. Published October through May for Jewish children ages 8-13. Managing Editor: Gerald H. Grayson.

Publishes: Nonfiction, fiction (500-700 words), poetry, photos, puzzles, games, cartoons. (Artwork on assignment only.) *All material must be on a Jewish theme.* Special holiday issues. Black-and-white, color prints purchased with manuscripts at additional fee.

Submission Info: Complete manuscripts preferred. Queries welcome. Submit holiday theme pieces at least four months in advance. Will consider photocopied and simultaneous submissions. Buys first North American serial rights or first serial rights. Pays on publication: $.10 per word plus five copies. Send 9" × 12" SASE with $.98 postage for free sample copy.

Editor's Remarks: "All material must be on a Jewish theme."

✔* SHOW AND TELL, 93 Medford St., Malden, MA 02148. Editor/Publisher: Donna Clark. Monthly publication that seeks to publish fiction that illustrates a good balance of fiction elements, not necessarily with an emphasis on award-winning stories. Age range: high school to senior citizens.

Publishes: Prefers high-quality, intelligent, light, humorous fiction for adults and juveniles. Accepts most genres *except* horror, the occult (including psychics, witches, spirits, devils, etc.), sexual and fiction about political, social and religious issues.

Submission Info: Prefers standard format. Neatly handwritten manuscripts of 300 words or less acceptable. Length 200-5,000 words. *Exceptional* novellas of 5,000-15,000 words considered. Not every issue contains a juvenile story. To subscribers pays $7 plus copy; $5 to nonsubscribers. Reports in one month. Send SASE for guidelines. For sample copy send $2 plus 9" × 12" envelope with two first-class stamps.

Editor's Remarks: "I am, above all, seeking classic fiction that stands on its own. I want a story that sticks with me long after I've finished reading it. I'm looking for characterization that rings true, as well as plots that remind me of something I know as a human being. Above all, endings must be spectacular—satisfying, consistent with characters and plot. Not necessarily happy but not depressing (e.g., the main character commits suicide anyway)."

Subscription Rates: One year $20.

[**Author's Note:** Be sure to send for guidelines to fully understand the types of stories *Show and Tell* does and does not want to see.]

* SKIPPING STONES: A MULTICULTURAL CHILDREN'S MAGAZINE, P.O. Box 3939, Eugene, OR

97403. International nonprofit quarterly children's magazine featuring writing and art by children 7-18. Writing may be submitted in any language and from any country. Awarded 1995 Golden Shoestring Award by Educational Press Association of America.

Publishes: Original artwork, photos, poems, stories, pen pal letters, recipes, cultural celebrations, songs, games, book reivews; writings about your background, culture, religion, interests and experiences, etc. May send questions for other readers to answer or ask your pen pal to send a letter. Submissions welcome in all languages. (Work published in the language submitted, with English translation.)

Submission Info: Prefers original work (keep your own copy). Short pieces preferred. Include your age and a description of your background. Can be typed, handwritten or handprinted. Free copy of the issue in which your work appears. Material not copyrighted for exclusive use. Reproduction for educational use encouraged. Guidelines available; please enclose SASE or SAE with IRC if possible. Sample copy $5. (Enclose SASE with submissions if possible.) Address submissions to Arun Toké, editor.

Editor's Remarks: "*Skipping Stones* is a place for young people of diverse backgrounds to share their experiences and expressions. Our goal is to reach children around the world, in economically disadvantaged as well as privileged families, including underrepresented and special populations within North America. Please tell us about yourself in a cover letter. For instance: What is your cultural background? What languages do you speak or write? What is important to you? What are your dreams for the future? What inspired you to write or create your submission?"

Subscription Rates: In the U.S.: one year $20; institutions

$30. Foreign: $30 in U.S. funds. Third World libraries and schools or low-income U.S. families may purchase one-year subscriptions for $15. Free subscriptions available when situation warrants. Contact editorial office for information.

* SKYLARK, Purdue University Calumet, 2200 169th St., Hammond, IN 46323. (219) 989-2262. *Skylark* magazine annually reserves fifteen to twenty pages out of one hundred for the work of young writers usually 8-18 years old.

Publishes: Prose, poetry and graphics from young writers that show an original bent and have a positive impact. Materials illustrated by author are welcome.

Submission Info: Manuscripts must be typed, double-spaced and mailed with SASE. Poetry 18 lines or less. Prose 800 words or less. Graphics should be suitable for 8½″ × 11″ page, may include black-and-white photos or ink sketches on white paper. No color or light pencil or lined paper. No simultaneous submissions. Payment is one free copy of publication. Entries from schools earn the teacher one free copy, too. Schools are credited in issue where student's work is published. Teachers encouraged to submit portfolios of their students. Reporting time four months. Guidelines available for SASE. Sample copy $7 postpaid.

Editor's Remarks: "Our best advice to a young writer: Go with your own feelings and state them as clearly as you can. We look for the spontaneous and creative. Manuscripts should be edited and grammar should be correct."

Additional Editor's Remarks to Parents/Teachers: "In the Young Writer Section, we publish work by young writers only. If their work is applicable in other sections (e.g., special theme), it will be placed there. However, *Skylark* is a magazine for adults, so much of its contents will include adult themes and perhaps some adult language. Parents and teachers who may not like controversial or mature material in the same book with work by young writers should keep this in mind."

✔* THE SOW'S EAR POETRY REVIEW, 19535 Pleasant View Dr., Abingdon, VA 24211-6827. Quarterly poetry magazine.

Publishes: Poetry only. *No fiction or essays.* Includes a few poems by school-age poets in some issues.

Submission Info: Use standard format. No length limit, but shorter poems have better chance of acceptance. *Always* send SASE with submissions. Payment one copy. Reporting time unpredictable. Sample copy $3.50.

Editor's Remarks: "We are very selective and reject far more poems than we can publish, both by adult and young poets. We look for the same qualities in poems by young poets as those we hope to find in all poems—real poems make the strange familiar or the familiar strange or both. We look for honesty, courage, risk taking, deeply felt emotions and an awareness that a poem is not just an expression of those emotions but a reworking of them through language."

Subscription Rates: One year (four issues) $10.

✔* **SPIRAL CHAMBERS**, % Twisted Teen Publishing Co., 5998 Taylor Rd., Painesville, OH 44077. May also contact via Internet: Repsi SK@AOL.com. Internationally syndicated poetry column distributed to over forty different small-press magazines of diverse origin and content.

Publishes: Poetry, especially from new and upcoming poets.

Submission Info: Use standard format or ASCII text for electronic submissions. *Must* include note to Twisted Teen granting permission to reprint work in *Spiral Chambers*. Send SASE for further information and sample.

Editor's Remarks: "With a total readership every month in the thousands, *Spiral Chambers* is ceaselessly questing for new and upcoming poets. Editors of magazines are also encouraged to contact Twisted Teen for free distribution and further information."

* **SPRING TIDES**, Savannah Country Day Lower School, 824 Stillwood Dr., Savannah, GA 31419. Literary magazine written and illustrated by children ages 5 to 12.

Publishes: Stories and poems with or without illustrations. Illustrations may be black and white or in color.

Submission Info: Any child, ages 5 to 12, may submit material.

Limit stories to 1,200 words and poems to 20 lines. Material submitted should not be under consideration by any other publisher. All work must be accompanied by SASE. Label each work with child's name, birth date, grade, school, home and school address. Also include a statement signed by the child's parent or teacher attesting to the originality of the work submitted. All material should be carefully proofread and typed. All material must be original and created by the person submitting it. Students who have material accepted will receive a copy of the issue in which the work appears. Send SASE for guidelines. Sample copy $5.

Subscription Rates: Per copy price $5, plus $1.25 postage/handling. Georgia residents add 6 percent sales tax. Order from above address.

✔* **STONEFLOWER**, 326 Lands End, Rockport, TX 78382-9770. Editor/Publisher: Brenda Davidson-Shaddox. Literary journal that devotes a portion of spring edition to poems and drawings by youth up to age 16.

Publishes: Prefers poems and drawings from young writers up to age 16 for inclusion in spring edition, but will consider short fiction. Especially interested in new ideas, fresh approaches and contemporary issues important to young people.

Submission Info: Use standard format. *No response* without SASE. Limit poems to 30 lines; short fiction to 1,000 words. Drawings should be done in pen and ink or dark pencil. Good quality photocopy of artwork acceptable. Submissions should include short bio with name, age, address, school, any past publishing or exhibition credits (including awards, shows or other creative recognition), hobbies and other interests and hopes for the future. Pays $5 for published story; $2 for poems; $5 for drawings. Send SASE for detailed guidelines for teachers and young writers.

Editor's Remarks: "*Stoneflower* is not directed at young readers specifically. It is a 'standard' (if there is such a thing) literary journal. I include a section for young writers and artists because of my interest in supporting them. Even if you are fortunate enough to have a teacher who encourages and supports your efforts, there is often little outlet for what you accomplish. I especially think that it is important that you have exposure to readers other than just other young readers, and my hope is that *Stoneflower* will help provide that. Please choose only your best work for submission, and pay attention to the guidelines. We will assess work according to age (e.g., a ten-year-old's work will not be compared with that of a sixteen-year-old's)."

Subscription Rates: Request information.

* STONE SOUP, THE MAGAZINE BY YOUNG WRITERS AND ARTISTS, Children's Art Foundation, P.O. Box 83, Santa Cruz, CA 95063. (800) 447-4569. Founded in 1973. Each issue includes an activity guide with projects designed to sharpen reading and writing skills. Five issues published yearly.

Publishes: Stories, poems, personal experience, book reviews and art by children through age 13.

Submission Info: *New policy: All submissions must be accompanied by SASE and include contributor's home address and phone number.* (Foreign contributors need not include return postage.) Writing need not be typed or copied over. Stories may be any length. Writing in languages other than English considered; include translation if possible. No simultaneous submissions. Children interested in reviewing books should write the editor, Ms. Gerry Mandel, stating name, age, address, interests and the kinds of books they like to read. Children interested in illustrating stories should send two samples of the artwork, name, age, address and a description of the kinds of stories they want to illustrate. Reporting time four weeks *if* SASE was enclosed. CAF reserves all rights. Authors of stories and poems whose work is published receive $10, book reviewers receive $15 and illustrators receive $8 per illustration. All published contributors receive a certificate, two copies and discounts on other purchases. Guidelines are available at no charge. Sample copy $3.

Editor's Remarks: "We can't emphasize enough our interest in your experiences. If something that happened to you or something you observed made a strong impression on you, try to turn that experience or observation into a good story or poem. Whether your work is about imaginary situations or real ones, use your own experiences and observations to give your work depth and a sense of reality."

Subscription Rates: *Stone Soup* is mailed to members of the Children's Art Foundation. Rates: One year (five issues) $24; two years $42; three years $58. Canada and Mexico add $5 per year. Other countries add $15 per year. All checks must be in U.S. funds or equivalent amount in foreign currency.

[**Author's Note:** It's believed that *Stone Soup* has been published longer than any other literary magazine by and for creative young writers and artists.]

* STRAIGHT, 8121 Hamilton Ave., Cincinnati, OH 45231. Published quarterly for Christian teens, ages 13-19. Distributed through churches, youth organizations and private subscriptions.

Publishes: Poetry, stories, and articles from teens. Material must be religious/inspirational in nature and appeal to other teens.

Submission Info: Submit manuscript on speculation. Enclose SASE, birthday (day and year) and Social Security number. Reports in four to six weeks. Buys first and one-time rights; pays $.03-$.05 per word. Samples automatically sent to contributors. Guidelines and sample issues available for SASE. Pays a flat fee for poetry.

Editor's Remarks: "Most teen work that I reject does not fit our editorial slant (religious/inspirational). A look at our guidelines or a sample copy will help teen writers in deciding what to submit. Also, I'd like to encourage teens to write about things they know but not necessarily 'common' or general topics. We see scores of poems about rainbows and loneliness and friends but hardly any about 'How I feel about working at McDonalds,' 'What happened when I tried something new . . .' or 'Why I believe in. . . .' Also, a tacked-on moral does not make a religious story. Make your *characters* Christian, and the religious slant will take care of itself."

✔* SURPRISE ME, P.O. Box 1762, Claremore, OK 74018. Editor: Lynda Nicolls. New biannual publication founded on the hope of providing a home for those souls who believe life's purpose is to serve truth and beauty.

Publishes: Poetry, essays, short stories and black-and-white artwork. Interests lean toward mysticism, religion, nature, art, literature, music, dance, relationships, love and peace. *Not interested in profanity or intolerance.*

Submission Info: Use standard format; submit six pages or fewer, include name, address and page number on every page. Send with #10 SASE and a cover letter with short bio. Clear photocopies of artwork acceptable. Pays with two copies. Send SASE for guidelines. Sample copy $4.

Editor's Remarks: "The age range of my magazine's readers and contributors is from teens to the elderly. I'm open to submissions from all ages. I receive about 1,000 poems and 500 stories annually, using 10 percent of these. I am currently [as of May 1995] overstocked on manuscripts but still open to submissions of artwork."

Subscription Rates: One year, U.S. individual (four issues) $16; institutions $20. Canada and Mexico $20. Overseas $24.

* TEEN POWER, P.O. Box 632, Glen Ellyn, IL 60138. Sunday School take-home paper for young teens ages 11-15; published quarterly in weekly parts.

Publishes: True, personal experience stories of how God has worked in the life of a teen. Also poetry from teens, nonfiction articles and puzzles.

Submission Info: Double-spaced typewritten manuscripts only, 500-1,000 words. Always include SASE for return of manuscript or reply. Pays $.06-$.10 per word on acceptance. Reports in eight weeks. Send business-size (#10) SASE to receive a sample copy and writer's guidelines.

Editor's Remarks: "Our goal is to help teens apply biblical principles for Christian living to their everyday lives. Everything we publish must have a strong, evangelical Christian basis."

Subscription Rates: One year $9.95. Slightly higher in Canada.

✔* TEXAS YOUNG WRITERS' NEWSLETTER, P.O. Box 942, Adkins, TX 78101-0942. Editor: Susan Currie. May be contacted electronically via America Online: TYWN@aol.com. Published nine times a year, *TYWN* is primarily a market for manuscripts by young writers ages 12-19. Reaches wide audience: homeschool families, public and school libraries, teachers and adult writers. *TYWN*'s first source of submissions was the electronic community of young writers on Prodigy.

Publishes: Poetry, short stories, essays, humor and personal experience pieces only from young writers ages 12-19. Open to short nonfiction articles (600-800 words) related to writing and publishing from experienced writers; include cover letter describing your publishing experience and qualifications.

Submission Info: Use standard typed format, or disk files in Windows Write or Word for DOS format or submit via e-mail. Maximum length for poems 55 lines; other material should be no longer than three or four typed, double-spaced pages. Include SASE with submissions. Responds in four weeks. Pays with two copies for poetry and five copies for short stories. Send SASE for separate guidelines for young writers and adults.

Editor's Remarks: "If your work is not published the first time you submit, don't be discouraged. There are many reasons why your work might not have been chosen; we may have too many submissions right now, or your work might be too long, or we might just like you to develop the work a little further. Mail your work now! We wish you the best of luck."

Subscription Rates: One year (nine issues) $10.

* THUMBPRINTS, 928 Gibbs, Caro, MI 48723. Monthly newsletter published by the Thumb Area Writer's Club.

Publishes: Poetry, short fiction, articles, essays, information, how-to, opinions, etc. Accepts general information but prefers manuscripts that relate to writing, publishing or the writer's way of life. Also interested in short profiles of writers.

Submission Info: Material must be typed following standard formats. Will consider handwritten material only from writers 12 and under. Send SASE with submissions. Limit stories and articles to 1,000 words. Prefers items 500 words or less. Poems should not be longer than 64 lines. Pays in copies. Sample issue $.75. You do not need to live in Michigan to submit material; however, the work of club members and subscribers will be given first consideration. Send SASE for yearly theme list for ideas.

Editor's Remarks: "We've published many young writers in the past."

Subscription Rates: One year for nonmembers $9.

[**Author's Note:** Unlike the annual contest sponsored by TAWC, *Thumbprints* is *not* restricted to Michigan residents. Anyone may submit material.]

✔$* THE TRADING NEWS, P.O. Box 5504, Coralville, IA 52241. May be contacted electronically via America Online: kidsclub@aol.com. Newsletter published six times per year by Clubs for Kids™, an organization of national correspondence clubs for young people ages 7-13.

Publishes: Creative work of Young Collectors Club members.

Submission Info: Send SASE for details. Membership (open to 7-13 year olds) includes club I.D. card and decoder, club pencil, gold seal membership certificate and a subscription to club newsletter.

Editor's Remarks: "Founded by children's writer and editor Amy Ruth, Clubs for Kids™ offers fun, educational and affordable alternatives to today's entertainment options. Club members belong to an organization that takes them seriously and encourages them to create, explore and nurture their interests in collecting and writing."

Subscription Rates: Send SASE for details.

* TURTLE MAGAZINE, P.O. Box 567, Indianapolis, IN 46206. Published by the Children's Better Health Institute for preschool level children ages 2-5.

Publishes: Black-and-white or color drawings by readers ages 2-5.

Submission Info: No payment for published reader materials. Editors advise readers to keep copies of their contributions because unused material cannot be returned. Publisher owns all rights to material printed.

Editor's Remarks: "We cannot promise to publish what you send because we receive many, many letters from children all over the world. We do promise to read and consider all the material sent to us, though! We are sorry, but because of the large amount of mail, we cannot write to each of you personally."

Subscription Rates: One year (eight issues) $15.95 in U.S. currency. Subscription office: P.O. Box 7133, Red Oak, IA 51591-0133.

---

* **U*S*KIDS**, 1100 Waterway Blvd., P.O. Box 567, Indianapolis, IN 46202. Publication for children 5-10 from the Children's Better Health Institute. Stresses health-related themes or ideas, including nutrition, safety, exercise and proper health habits.

Publishes: From readers, original drawings and poetry for the "Best for the End" column.

Submission Info: Submissions do not have to be health related. Please write your name, age, school and complete address on each submission. Material cannot be returned. No payment for published reader material. Send SASE for guidelines for young writers. Sample copy $1.25.

Editor's Remarks: "We usually select material sent in by children in the 5-10 age group."

Subscription Rates: One year $20.95. Special rate $14.95 is usually offered in every issue.

---

‡♣ **WEST COAST LINE**, 2027 E. Academic Annex, Simon Fraser University, Burnaby, BC V5A 1S6 Canada. Focuses on contemporary writers who are experimenting with or expanding the boundaries of conventional forms of poetry, fiction and criticism.

Publishes: Poetry: poems in extended forms; excerpts from works in progress; experimental and innovative poems. Fiction: short stories; excerpts from novels in progress; experimental and innovative writing. Nonfiction: critical and theoretical essays on contemporary and modernist writing; interviews; statements of poetics; reviews. Other work: bibliographies; edited letters and manuscripts; translations into English of innovative contemporary writing.

Submission Info: Must be typed; use standard format; MLA format. Prefers printed manuscript and computer disk copy. Maximum lengths: poetry to 400 lines; fiction to 7,000 words; nonfiction and "other" not indicated. Recommends that potential contributors send a query letter before submitting a manuscript. SASE or IRC required for return of manuscript. Pays $3-$4 per page after publication; copyright reverts to writer after publication of issue. Takes up to four months to evaluate a submission. Guidelines available on request. Send SASE. Sample copy $10.

Editor's Remarks: "Our editorial slant shows a special concern for contemporary writers who are experimenting with or expanding the boundaries of conventional forms of poetry, fiction and criticism; also interested in criticism and scholarship on Canadian and American modernist writers who are important sources for current writing. Please note: American postage is *not* legal tender in Canada. If you use U.S. postage on SASE, you will *not* hear back from us."

Subscription Rates: One year (three issues) $20. One year for institutions $30. U.S. subscribers pay in U.S. funds. Single copy $10.

[**Author's Note:** Only mature young writers (high school or college age) should consider this market.]

$✦ WHITE WALL REVIEW, 63 Gould St., Toronto, ON M5B 1E9 Canada. (416) 977-1045. Founded in 1976. Published annually, *WWR* is 144-160 pages, digest-sized, professionally printed, perfect bound with glossy card cover, using black-and-white photos and illustrations. Editors change every year.

Publishes: Poetry, short stories and photography. Work should be "interesting, preferably spare art. No style is unacceptable. Nothing boring, self-satisfied, gratuitously sexual, violent or indulgent."

Submissions: Manuscripts must be typed. Short stories should not be more than 3,000 words in length. No poem should be longer than five pages. A maximum of five poems may be submitted at one time. Accepts black-and-white unmounted photography. No slides. Accepts manuscripts from September to first week in December. Send manuscripts to "The Editors." Cover letter, SASE and $5 per envelope reading fee required; include short bio. Reports "as soon as we can (usually in April or May)." Comments on all submissions, accepted or not. No simultaneous submissions. Pays one contributor's copy. Sample copy $8.

Editor's Remarks: "We are known for publishing first-time or little-known writers. We look for creativity but not to the point of obscurity."

Subscription Rates: One year (one issue): $9 in Canada; $9.50 in U.S. and elsewhere.

* WHOLE NOTES, P.O. Box 1374, Las Cruces, NM 88004. Special issue of writing by young people published in even-numbered years. Seeks to recognize outstanding work from across the country.

Publishes: Poems, especially free verse, by young people up to and including age 21. All poetic forms considered, including haiku, riddles, sonnets, long poems, prose poems and free verse. Some black-and-white drawings are used. Special young writers' issue published in December of even-numbered years.

Submission Info: Typed poems preferred. We will read neat handwriting, if necessary. Drawings must be in black ink, ready to print. Do not send original drawing; a clean photocopy is best. Be sure to include SASE so you receive a prompt reply. Prefers not to receive multiple or simultaneous submissions. Reporting time is as quickly as possible, usually two to three weeks. Pays with one free copy of issue containing published work. Send SASE for copy of writer's guidelines. Sample copy $3.

Editor's Remarks: "We look for poems that are clearly written, with fresh images. Poems about the natural world as well as the human one are welcomed. A surprise at the end is a delight, if it's not forced. We want the poem to come from your imagination."

Subscription Rates: One year (two issues) $6; two years $10.

*$ WORLD PEN PALS, 1694 Como Ave., St. Paul, MN 55108. Sponsored by International Institute of Minnesota (a United Way affiliated agency). Promotes friendship through understanding, providing service for all nationalities.

Publishes: A letter-writing program that links more than 20,000 students ages 12-20 from 175 countries and territories around the world with students in the U.S. Does not link students within the U.S. Small service fee applies. Short letters telling about pen pal experiences appear in newsletter.

Submission Info: Send SASE for complete details. Offers "Suggestions," a guideline sheet for letter writing, and a newsletter called *Pen Pal Post*, along with the name and address of your new pen pal.

Editor's Remarks: "It is fun for students to receive letters from another country. As pen pals correspond, they become good friends even though separated geographically and culturally. Their interest grows in other languages and customs. Some pen pals even visit one another after corresponding."

Subscription Rates: Fee is $4.50 for each pen pal requested. Groups of six or more may apply for a fee of $3.00 per person; names and addresses of pen pals will be sent to the group's leader.

[**Author's Note:** Writing to a pen pal, especially one from another country, is an excellent way for young writers to hone their writing skills as they write about their personal experiences.]

✔ **WRETCHED TRUTH**, Julie Luce, Editor, 514 W. Avenue J-5, Lancaster, CA 93534. Bimonthly publication for people of all ages, discussing the environment, animal welfare and vegetarianism.

Publishes: Humorous and serious stories, essays, opinions and poetry; artwork and cartoons.

Submission Info: Use standard format; include full name, address, daytime phone number and SASE. Limit stories and essays to 700 words. Pays with one copy. Sample copy $2.50.

Editor's Remarks: "This is a publication for and about everyday people who want to make a difference in this world. *Wretched Truth*'s readers would like to read how you would make this world a better place."

Subscription Rates: One year (six issues) $15. Make payment payable to Julie Luce.

✔* **WRITE ME A STORY**, c/o Michael Eckert, *Times Herald*, P.O. Box 5009, Port Huron, MI 48061-5009. Feature of special "Eye Page" ("a closer look at what's happening from a younger point of view") published in Wednesday issues of newspaper.

Publishes: Short stories by students. Will consider personal experience and opinion pieces.

Submission Info: Prefers standard format or neatly handwritten. Include your name and age, address, phone, school and a photo. Preferred length 300 words; *occasionally* runs longer ones.

Editor's Remarks: "Submitting a story is simple. Get it to me in a form I can read (although that's not too much of a problem; most 9 year olds have word processors, it seems). Please include your picture, and tell me how old you are and where you go to school. We do edit the stories—a little—and ask that they be kept below 300 words. We do run longer ones if they merit the extra space, and we even ran one as a serial.

Subscription Rates: Write or call for details. *Times Herald*, 911 Military, Port Huron, MI 48060. (810) 985-7171.

[**Author's Note:** See profiles of Michael Eckert in chapter eight and Alicia Gauthier in chapter seven.]

✔$* **THE WRITE NEWS,** P.O. Box 5504, Coralville, IA 52241. May be contacted electronically via America Online: kidsclub@aol.com. Newsletter published six times per year by Clubs for Kids™, an organization of national correspondence clubs for young people ages 7-13.

Publishes: Creative work of Young Writers Club members.

Submission Info: Send SASE for details. Membership (open to 7-13 year olds) includes club I.D. card and decoder, club pencil, gold seal membership certificate and a subscription to club newsletter.

Editor's Remarks: "Founded by children's writer and editor Amy Ruth, Clubs for Kids™ offers fun, educational and affordable alternatives to today's entertainment options. Club members belong to an organization that takes them seriously and encourages them to create, explore and nurture their interests in collecting and writing."

Subscription Rates: Send SASE for details.

* **WRITERS' INTERNATIONAL FORUM, JUN-IOR EDITION,** P.O. Box 516, Tracyton, WA 98393-0516. Publication that brings writers together to exchange ideas and im-

prove their skills and marketability. (Formerly *Writers' Open Forum*.)

Publishes: Junior Editions feature short stories (2,000 words maximum, 500-1,500 preferred) exclusively on subjects of interest to youth or that include young people as major characters. Also prints essays (up to 1,200 words) on subjects that concern the lives of young people; must make a point or offer some insight and should be encouraging in nature. Readers are encouraged to write in comments on manuscripts published. Some comments are printed in future issues; all comments are sent on to authors. "Writer to Writer" column features tips, ideas, questions and answers (up to 300 words) regarding writing.

Submission Info: Use standard format. Be sure to number pages, include accurate word count and write *End* at bottom of last page. Include SASE for return of material. Cover letter required; include a brief note about yourself. Young writers should note age, grade and school. Payment $5 upon publication and two copies of publication. Submission guidelines available for SASE. Sample copy $5.

Editor's Remarks: "We encourage material that is written for, about and/or by those from 8 to 16 years of age. In all stories, we look for both a theme (an idea behind the story) and plot (actions or decisions that the main character must make in order to solve a problem). All submissions that follow our guidelines receive a personal reply; subscribers additionally receive a brief critique."

Subscription Rates: One year (six issues) $14; $24 in U.S. funds for foreign destinations.

✔* **THE WRITERS' SLATE**, F. Todd Goodson, Coeditor, English Dept., East Carolina University, Greenville, NC 27858-4353. Published three times a year; features student writing K-12.

Publishes: Student writing in a variety of forms, including poems, narratives and expositions. Also student reviews of children's and young adult literature. Accompanying artwork also accepted.

Submission Info: Use standard format; include SASE. Clearly mark writer's name, address, school, grade, teacher's name and school address. Deadlines: November 15 for winter issue; May 15 for fall issue. Spring Issue for Writing Contest winners only.

Editor's Remarks: "Each issue highlights student writing in a variety of forms."

Subscription Rates: One year (three issues) $12.95; two years $22. Student rate one year $10; two years $17. Mail to *The Writers' Slate*, P.O. Box 664, Ottawa, KS 66067.

✔* **YOUNG EQUESTRIAN**, Submissions Editor, Tamara Duncan, 22 Spencer Trail, St. Peters, MO 63376. Magazine published bimonthly by Horse Cents for children ages 9-16 about horses, horse care, riding and other horse-related subjects.

Publishes: Nonfiction articles about riding, horse health and care, breed profiles, showing, horse-related activities (such as model horses), careers, young rider profiles (written in lively, anecdotal style). Factually accurate fiction; no anthropomorphic horses or ponies. Also art, photographs, cartoons, fillers, puzzles, word games, quizzes and "Parent's Page." Especially from young writers: true experience and personal opinion essays.

Submission Info: Use standard format, include SASE. Length for articles and "Parent's Page" 200-1,200 words; fillers 20-200 words; true experience and essays from young writers up to 800 words. Fiction up to 1,200 words; up to 5,000 words if suitable for serialization. Artwork and photographs in black and white or color, prints or slides. Recognizable persons not in a public setting (such as a show) *must* sign a model release. Buys one-time rights. Will consider reprints. Pays in copies and subscriptions. Send SASE for guidelines. Send submissions directly to Submissions Editor at above address. Sample copy $2.75; request from address below.

Editor's Remarks: "The publisher currently mixes articles and stories from adult writers and articles sent in by kids, but I'd like to limit these to first-person, true experience or opinion pieces and place them in a special section (e.g., 'Young Writers and Riders')."

Subscription Rates: Send general correspondence and subscription orders to *Young Equestrian*, P.O. Box 626, Minden, NV

89423. One year (six issues) $12; in Canada $16 and foreign $21 (in U.S. funds). Nevada residents add 6.5 percent sales tax.

* **YOUNG PLAYWRIGHTS ROUNDTABLE**, c/o The Coterie, 2450 Grand Ave., Suite 144, Kansas City, MO 64108-2520. Theatre staff members help young writers plan and write plays. Membership limited to Kansas City Youth.

* **YOUNG SALVATIONIST MAGAZINE**, c/o Lesa Davis, P.O. Box 269, Alexandria, VA 22313. Published monthly except summer for high school/early college aged youth by The Salvation Army.

Publishes: Nonfiction articles that deal with real life issues teenagers face and that present a Christian perspective on those issues. Fiction along same lines as nonfiction. Rarely uses fillers or poetry.

Submission Info: Use standard format. SASE required for return of material. Pays $.10 a word on acceptance. Reports in one month on unsolicited manuscripts. Sample issue, guidelines and theme list available for 8½" × 11" SASE with three first-class stamps.

Editor's Remarks: "Before sending your manuscript, please take time to request sample copy and theme lists. We like to work with new writers, but all material must fit our guidelines."

Subscription Rates: One year $4 (U.S. funds).

‡* **YOUTH UPDATE**, 1615 Republic St., Cincinnati, OH 45210-1298. Monthly publication from St. Anthony Messenger Press to support the growth of teenagers (ages 14-18) in a life of faith through the application of Catholic principles to topics of timely interest.

Publishes: One 2,300 word article per issue. No poetry, fiction or sermons accepted.

Submission Info: *Query first*, include SASE. Send SASE for writer's guidelines and sample. Pays $.14 per word.

Editor's Remarks: "*Youth Update* has published adult-teen collaborations before with great success."

Subscription Rates: One year $12.

[**Author's Note:** Note that this market uses only one article per issue and you *must* query first.]

Chapter Ten

The Contest List

There are many different types of contests listed in this guide. Some are sponsored through various publishers, some by individual writing groups and others by for-profit companies and not-for-profit associations. Contests are listed alphabetically, including those accessed through online computer services.

Each listing contains three individual sections of information, which will help you understand (1) general information about the contest and its sponsor; (2) how entering the contest might benefit you; and (3) prizes awarded. There are also two optional sections: "Sponsor's Remarks" provide extra insight into the history or goals of the contest and/or advice for producing a winning entry. "Subscription Rates" have been included as an extra service for those interested in receiving a sponsor's publication on a regular basis.

New additions to this edition's contest listings are preceded by a check mark (✔). Contests that are of special interest to young people are preceded by an asterisk (*). Contests that require an entry fee are marked with a dollar sign ($). Canadian markets are identified with a maple leaf (✤).

A few listings are also marked with a double cross (‡). This indicates that this contest should be considered only by serious teen writers, as competition is likely to be against adults and/or very difficult. To help you remember how to interpret the codes and listing information, an "Author's Note:" has been placed at the bottom of some listings.

Contest listings were researched and chosen using the same criteria as that used for market listings. See details on page 33.

The following chart and sample contest listing will help explain the information contained within each section. You may want to review the sections "What's in This Edition" and "More About the Listings" in chapter one, plus the advice in chapter three, "Study and Compare the Opportunities," before reviewing these listings.

CONTEST LISTING CHART

SEC.	YOU WILL FIND	PAY SPECIAL ATTENTION TO
1	Name of Contest. Mailing address for entries, forms, and complete list of rules. Brief description including who is eligible, frequency of contest. Name of sponsor.	Who sponsors this contest and the general theme of each contest. The goal of the contest.
2	General information about the contest. Deadlines for entries. Eligibility requirements. Entry fees, if any. How the contest is judged. Availability of rules and samples.	Any contest designed specifically for young people. Note any age limits. How to enter. Any restrictions.
3	Prizes awarded including cash, certificates, merchandise, and publication and display of winning entries.	The number of prizes awarded. How entries may be published or displayed. How often and how many times you may enter.
4	History of the contest, plus advice and tips for entering and winning, quoted directly from the sponsor or entry form.	Advice to help you submit a winning entry.
5	Subscription rates if sponsored by a publication. Subscription mailing address when it differs from contest entry address.	Included as an extra service for young people, parents and teachers.

SAMPLE CONTEST LISTING

1 _____ GUIDEPOSTS YOUTH WRITERS CON-
TEST, 16 E. 34th St., New York, NY 10016. Sponsored
annually by *Guideposts* magazine for high school juniors
and seniors.

2_____ **General Info:** Open to any high school junior or senior,
or students in equivalent grades in other countries.
Entrants must write a true first-person story about a
personal experience. All manuscripts must be the student's original work and must be written in English.
Use standard format. Maximum 1,200 words. Entries
must include: home address, phone number, and name
and address of entrant's school. Write for rules and
current deadlines. Winners will be notified by mail
prior to announcement in *Guideposts*. Prize-winning
manuscripts become the property of *Guideposts*.

3_____ **Prizes:** Eight cash awards totalling $20,000 in scholar-
ships, plus seventeen honorable mentions. All winners
and honorable mentions receive a portable electronic
typewriter. Scholarships to the accredited colleges or
schools of winners' choice will be: First prize $6,000;
second $5,000; third $4,000; fourth through eighth
$1,000. Prizes are not redeemable in cash, are non
transferable, and must be used within five years after
high school graduation.

4_____ **Sponsor's Remarks:** "A winning story doesn't have
to be complicated or filled with drama. It only has to
come from the heart, and be an honest and straightforward account of an experience that touched you deeply
or changed your ideas or outlook. Think of something
that happened to you at home, at school or at a job:
an exciting close call, or a tough personal decision that
took moral courage. Then write about it as if you were
telling a story to a friend. Don't be shy about revealing
your innermost feelings."

5_____ **Subscription Rates:** In the United States one year
$9.95. In Canada one year $10.95. Sample copy for $.52
stamp.

* ACHIEVEMENT AWARDS IN WRITING, NCTE, 1111 W. Kenyon Rd., Urbana, IL 61801. The National Council of Teachers of English has sponsored this awards program for thirty-six years. Only writers who are nominated may enter.

General Info: To encourage high school students and to recognize publicly some of the best student writers in the nation, the NCTE gives achievement awards in writing to more than eight hundred graduating students each year. Only students who are juniors in the contest's academic year may be nominated. High school juniors from public, private and parochial schools in the U.S. and Canada and from American schools abroad are eligible. Each high school selects its own nominee or nominees: one or more juniors agreed upon by the English department, not chosen by an individual teacher. A current official nomination blank for each nominee must be submitted to NCTE. Write for details.

Prizes: In 1993, 876 awards possible.

Sponsor's Remarks: "Because NCTE is a nonprofit educational association, it has no funds to award scholarships to winners. Their names and addresses, however, are printed in a booklet that is mailed in October to directors of admissions and freshman studies in 3,000 colleges, universities and junior colleges in the U.S. Accompanying each booklet is a letter in which NCTE recommends the winners for college admission and for financial assistance, if needed. Booklets are also sent to state supervisors of English, to NCTE affiliate organizations and to the winners and their high school principals."

AIM MAGAZINE'S SHORT STORY CONTEST, P.O. Box 20554, Chicago, IL 60620. Annual contest sponsored by quarterly publication for high school, college and general public.

General Info: No fee to enter. Stories judged by *AIM*'s editorial staff. Deadline is August 15.

Prizes: First prize $100; second prize $50. Winner is published in autumn issue.

Sponsor's Remarks: "To purge racism from the human bloodstream—that is our objective. To do it through the written word. We want to show that people from different ethnic and racial backgrounds are more alike than they are different. They all strive for the same things—education, jobs, good health, etc."

Subscription Rates: One year $10. Single copies $4.

*❀ AIR CANADA AWARD, CAA, 275 Slater St., Suite 500, Ottawa, ON K1P 5H9 Canada. Annual competition sponsored by Air Canada, administered by the Canadian Authors Association. Open to Canadian writers under 30; writers must be nominated to enter.

General Info: Award goes to the Canadian writer under age 30 (at April 30 in the year of the competition) deemed most promising. There are no restrictions as to the field of writing and a winner may be chosen for work in several fields. Writers may be renominated until they reach the age limit. Nominations are made through CAA branches or other writing organizations to the Canadian Authors Association. Nominee does not need to be a CAA member. Nominations must be postmarked no later than April 30. A trustee appointed by the awards chairperson reviews the entries and recommends a winner. The recommended approach to nominating a writer is to submit a one-page outline of why the writer shows promise along with samples of the writer's work or reviews of that work. Full-length works need not be sent; copies of a few pages are sufficient.

Prizes: The airline offers winner a trip for two to any destination on Air Canada's routes. Awards are presented each June at the Annual Awards Dinner.

Sponsor's Remarks: "It takes many years for a Canadian writer to achieve national (and, increasingly, international) recognition. But Air Canada believes the signs of greatness can usually be detected before the writer reaches 30. Past winners include Gordon Korman, Larry Krotz, Mary deMichele, Wayne Johnston, Evelyn Lau and Leslie Smith Dow. Give a promising writer in your community this opportunity."

✔* AMELIA, 329 "E" St., Bakersfield, CA 93304. (805) 323-4064. Editor: Frederick A. Raborg, Jr. Quarterly publication; readers predominately college educated, age range of readers 17-

90. Attempts to be an effective bridge between small presses, university journals and slick newsstand magazines.

General Info: Open to all high school students. Student may make one entry only from the three genres: short story (1,500 words maximum), essay (1,500 words maximum) or poem (up to 100 lines). Entries should be signed by parent, teacher or guardian to verify originality. Use standard typed format. Annual deadline: May 15 (postmark). Send SASE for detailed guidelines.

Prizes: Publication in *Amelia* plus $200.

Sponsor's Remarks: "There is no entry fee for this contest. We offer it in the hope that young writers still are striving to equal the talent of generations past, but, perhaps more important to the age group, we hope to generate keen interests in reading and the return of excellent fiction and poetry to mainstream periodical publications."

Subscription Rates: One year (four issues) $25. Sample $8.95.

* AMERICA & ME ESSAY CONTEST, Farm Bureau Insurance, Lisa Fedewa, Contest Coordinator, P.O. Box 30400, Lansing, MI 48909. Yearly contest that encourages Michigan young people to explore their roles in America's future.

General Info: Open to any eighth-grade student in any Michigan school. Students must participate through their school systems. Interested students and schools should contact the main office or a Farm Bureau insurance agent in their area for complete information and requirements. Each school may submit up to ten essays for judging. A first-, second- and third-place winner will be selected from each school. Each first-place essay is automatically entered into the statewide competition, from which the top essays are selected. Essays must relate to yearly theme and may be up to 500 words long. (Topic examples from recent years: "America & Me—How We Will Work Together," "Why My Education is Important to the Future of America.") Schools must preregister.

Prizes: First- through third-place winners in each school receive certificates. First-place winner's name also appears on plaque that hangs permanently in his or her school. The top ten statewide winners each receive a plaque, plus they share $5,500 in savings bonds. Individual prizes range from $1,000 to $500 in savings bonds. In addition, the top ten essays plus selected excerpts from other essays are compiled into a booklet and distributed to schools, government leaders and the general public.

Sponsor's Remarks: "This (1994-95) is the contest's 26th year. Since it was started in 1968, more than 140,000 students have participated. Average participation each year is now more than 10,000 students. The final ranking of the top ten winners is made by a panel of VIP judges that in the past has included Governors Engler, Blanchard and Milliken and former President Gerald Ford."

Subscription Rates: Samples of the compiled essays are available through Farm Bureau at the above address.

[**Author's Note:** This contest is restricted to Michigan youth.]

* THE AMERICAN BEEKEEPING FEDERATION ESSAY CONTEST

ESSAY CONTEST, P.O. Box 1038, Jesup, GA 31545. Annual contest coordinated between the American Beekeeping Federation and state 4-H offices.

General Info: Contest is open to *active* 4-H club members only. Essays must be 750-1,000 words long, written on the designated subject only. All factual statements must be referenced; failure to do so will result in disqualification. Essays should be submitted to the state 4-H office. *Do not submit essays directly to the American Beekeeping Federation office.* Each state 4-H office is responsible for selecting the state's winner. State winners will be forwarded to the national level. Essays will be judged on accuracy, creativity, conciseness, logical development of the year's topic argument and scope of research. Contact your local or state 4-H office for details, topic for current contest and state deadlines. Contest information is also available from the ABF at the above address.

Prizes: Cash awards to top national winners: first place $250; second place $100; third place $50. Each state winner receives an appropriate book about honey bees, beekeeping or honey. All national entries become the property of the ABF and may be published. No essays will be returned.

Sponsor's Remarks: "This national essay contest has been established to stimulate interest among our nation's youth in honey bees and the vital contributions they make to mankind's well-being."

* AMHAY MORGAN HORSE LITERARY CONTEST, P.O. Box 960, Shelburne, VT 05482-0960. Sponsored by the American Morgan Horse Association. Open to all young people under the age of 22.

General Info: In either essay or poetry form (1,000 words or less), tell *in your own words* what the contest theme statement means to you. Essays and poetry will be judged on general style, originality, grammar, spelling and punctuation. No entry fee required, but you must attach an official entry form to your poem or essay. Work submitted may be used for promotional purposes by AMHA. Participants must be under 22 as of December 1, the contest deadline. Write the AMHA for current theme and entry form.

Prizes: Cash awards of $25 will be presented to the winner in both the essay and poetry categories. Ribbons will be awarded to the second- through fifth-place winners. Winning entries are published in "The AMHA News & Morgan Sales Network."

Sponsor's Remarks: "Winning entries are often published in *The Morgan Horse*, a glossy magazine with an international circulation of 10,000."

*$ ARTS RECOGNITION AND TALENT SEARCH, National Foundation for Advancement of the Arts, 800 Brickell Ave., #500, Miami, FL 33131. Scholarship opportunities for high school students interested in dance, music, theater, visual arts and writing, including jazz, voice and photography.

General Info: Contact your teacher, guidance counselor or principal for complete registration packet. The ARTS program is designed for high school seniors and other 17 to 18 year olds with demonstrable artistic achievements in dance, music, theater, visual arts (including film and video) and writing. Application materials sent to individuals upon request. Fee of $25 for each discipline or discipline category entered; more for late entry.

Prizes: Winners receive between $100 and $3,000 in cash.

NFAA earmarks up to $300,000 in cash awards for ARTS applicants whose work has been judged as outstanding by a national panel of experts. Selected candidates are also invited to Miami, Florida, for a week of live adjudications [judging], consisting of auditions, master and technique classes, workshops, studio exercises and interviews. NFAA pays travel, lodging and meal expenses for the cash award candidates. Additional college scholarships and internships worth over $3 million have also been made available to all ARTS participants, whether or not they were award winners.

Sponsor's Remarks: "ARTS is a unique program in that applicants are judged against a standard of excellence within each art discipline, *not* against each other. ARTS does not predetermine the number of awards to be made on any level or in any discipline."

* BAKER'S PLAYS HIGH SCHOOL PLAYWRITING CONTEST, Baker's Plays, 100 Chauncy St., Boston, MA 02111. Annual contest open to any high school student.

General Info: Plays should be about "the high school experience" but can also be about any subject so long as the play can be reasonably produced on the high school stage. Plays may also be of any length. Multiple submissions or collaborative efforts accepted. *Teachers may not submit student's work.* Scripts must be accompanied by the signature of a sponsoring high school drama or English teacher, and *it is recommended that the script be given a public stage reading or production prior to the submission.* The manuscript *must* be typed and *firmly bound*, and come with SASE. Please include enough postage for the return of the manuscript. All plays must be postmarked by January 31. Playwrights will be notified in May. Send SASE for contest information.

Prizes: First place receives $500, and the play will be published under the *Best Plays From the High School* series by Baker's Plays the September of the contest year. Second place receives $250 and Honorable Mention; third place receives $100 and Honorable Mention.

Sponsor's Remarks: "The purpose of the contest is to promote play writing at the high school level, to promote the production of that work and to encourage the next generation of playwrights."

*$ BYLINE STUDENT CONTESTS, P.O. Box 130596, Edmond, OK 73013. Special contests for students during school year sponsored by *Byline* magazine, which is aimed at writers of all ages.

General Info: Variety of monthly writing contests for students 18 years and younger beginning with September issue and continuing through May each year. Prefers typewritten entries on white bond paper 8½″ × 11″. Most contests have a small entry fee, which provides cash awards to winners. Others have no entry fee and are often used as class assignments by writing and English teachers. Send SASE for details of upcoming contests. Sample copy $4.

Prizes: Cash prizes and possible publication.

Sponsor's Remarks: "We do not print student work except as winners of our monthly student writing contests."

Subscription Rates: One year (eleven issues) $20.

[**Author's Note:** Good contest for eager young writers.]

*$✦ CANADIAN AUTHOR ANNUAL STUDENT CREATIVE WRITING CONTEST, CAA Student Writing Contest, Box 32219, 250 Harding Blvd. W., Richmond Hill, ON L4C 9R0 Canada. Sponsored by *Canadian Author*, a quarterly magazine dedicated to bringing news of Canadian writers, editors and publishers to developing freelance writers. Open to Canadian high school, college and university students only.

General Info: Only manuscripts not published previously, except in a student class anthology, are eligible. Genres and fees are $5 per short story of 2,000 words or less; $5 per article of 2,000 words or less; $5 for two to three poems of not more than 30 lines. Entrants must be enrolled in secondary schools, colleges or univerities and must be Canadian residents or Canadian citizens living abroad. Students may enter each category as many times as they wish, but each entry costs $5. Entries must be typed and double-spaced on one side of letter-sized white paper. Make sure title, but not entrant's name, is on each page. On official entry form or a separate sheet of paper, type or print following information: title(s) of entries, category entered, student's full name, address, phone or fax number, school attended, student number. Include check or money order for full amount payable to CAA with entry. *No entries will be returned.* Copyright ownership remains with entrant. Write for details, yearly deadlines and official form.

Prizes: First-place prize of $500, plus four Honorable Mentions, awarded in each genre and category. First-place winners published in *Canadian Author.* All winners receive one year subscription to magazine.

Sponsor's Remarks: "*Canadian Author* sponsored its 12th annual creative writing contest for high school, college and university students in 1995."

*✦ CHICKADEE COVER CONTEST, 179 John St., Suite 500, Toronto, ON M5T 3G5 Canada. Annual contest sponsored by *Chickadee*, a science and nature magazine for children 3-8, published ten times per year.

General Info: Create a cover for *Chickadee* magazine based on a new topic announced each year. Use markers, crayons, paints or make a collage (if you don't use tape) to make your cover. Your cover must be exactly the same size as a real *Chickadee* cover. Leave room at the top for the word *Chickadee. Don't* print the word yourself. Include another piece of paper with your name, age, address and postal code. Don't write on your picture. Mail your entry flat with a piece of cardboard. Look for the contest announcement and deadline for submissions in the October issue.

Prizes: Winner and runners-up are published in the February issue.

Subscription Rates: In the U.S., one year (ten issues) $14.95. Mail subscription requests to 255 Great Arrow Ave., Buffalo, NY 14207-3082. In U.S. and Canada: (800) 387-4379.

‡$ CHRISTOPHER COLUMBUS SCREENPLAY DISCOVER AWARDS, 433 N. Camden Dr., Suite 600, Beverly Hills, CA 90210. Sponsored by the Christopher Columbus Society for the Creative Arts, a division of the C.C.S. Entertainment Group. The Group was created in 1990 to discover new screenplays and to develop them.

General Info: Open to all writers. *Only* nonproduced, nonoptioned feature screenplays may be submitted. Entrant is allowed to submit more than one screenplay. Application/release form and nonrefundable $45 registration fee *must* be sent with each entry. See detailed guidelines for deadlines in two categories: Discovery of the Month, Discovery of the Year. Judging criteria based on execution, originality and salability.

Prizes: See guidelines for specific details. However, awards include feedback by phone, a personal meeting with professionals in the field and help with further development of your screenplay. Selected "Discovery of the Month" screenplays automatically qualify as finalists for "Discovery of the Year," and the writer can submit a second screenplay at no cost. Screenplays are introduced to top agents, producers and studios. Award certificates are issued.

Sponsor's Remarks: "Through our monthly and yearly contests, our unique development process and our access to major agents, producers and studios, we are able to bridge the gap between writers and the established entertainment industry."

[**Author's Note:** Consider your options carefully before submitting to this competition due to the high registration fee and the tough competition.]

✔$* CLUBS FOR KIDS™, P.O. Box 5504, Coralville, IA 52241. Offers fun, educational and affordable alternatives to today's entertainment options.

General Info: The "Young Writers Club" and the "Young Collectors Clubs" sponsor a variety of contests throughout the year exclusively for club members. Send SASE for membership form.

Prizes: Include children's books and honorable mention certificates.

Sponsor's Remarks: "Club members belong to an organization that takes them seriously and encourages them to create, explore and nurture their interests in collecting and writing."

$ COMPUSERVE MEMBER ESSAYS, CompuServe Magazine, User ID 76004,3302. Monthly winners. No charge to submit essay.

General Info: Compete for $50 worth of connect time. Write a 200-word essay describing an original way you've used the Information Service and send it to User ID number 76004,3302. Include your full name, address and User ID number. There is no charge to submit essay, but you must be a CompuServe member (or family member).

Prizes: Fifty dollars and software. Winning essays published in "Monitor" section of *Print* magazine.

‡✔$ CONTEMPORARY POETRY SERIES, University of Georgia Press, 330 Research Dr., Athens, GA 30602-4901. Annual poetry collection competition; two divisions.

General Info: Poets who have never had a full-length book of poems published may submit manuscripts during the month of September each year. Chapbook publication does not disqualify a writer from this round, nor does publication of a book in some other genre. Poets with at least one full-length (poetry) book publication with any press including University of Georgia Press should submit entry during January each year. Competition is open to writers of English, whether or not they are citizens of U.S. Poems included in manuscripts may have been published in journals or anthologies. Collected or selected poems will also be considered in the January selection period. Single-spaced manuscripts are $10. Nonwinning manuscripts are discarded after competition. Authors may submit manuscripts to other publishers during judging; however, you must notify University of Georgia Press immediately if a collection submitted elsewhere is accepted for publication. Send SASE for complete details.

Prizes: Four entries selected for publication in the University of Georgia Press's "Contemporary Poetry Series." Two winners selected from "emerging talent" and two from poets in "mid-career."

Sponsor's Remarks: "Because the press is interested in both encouraging emerging talent and in helping to maintain poets in midcareer, two separate rounds of manuscript selection are held each year."

[**Author's Note:** Beware. Even though this contest judges work by "emerging talent" separately, it is still a very tough competition. It would be wise to read past winning collections before deciding to enter.]

* CREATIVE KIDS, Prufrock Press, P.O. Box 8813, Waco, TX 76714-8813. Kids from all over the nation contribute to the largest magazine written by and for kids.

General Info: Various ongoing and new contests. Examples: T-shirt, illustration, recipe, photo, postcard, bookmark.

Prizes: Vary. Prizes have included $50 savings bond, artist's sets, baking sets, 35mm camera. All winners receive recognition in the magazine.

Subscription Rates: One year (six issues) $19.95.

** CRICKET LEAGUE CONTESTS, P.O. Box 300, Peru, IL 61354. Monthly contests for young people sponsored by *Cricket* magazine.

General Info: Contest themes vary from month to month. Refer to a current issue of the magazine. Throughout the year, contests are sponsored in four categories: art, poetry, short story and photography. There are two age groups for each contest: 10 and under and 11 and up. All contest rules must be followed. Rules are listed in each issue. If you are 14 years old or younger, you must have your parent's or guardian's permission to send your entry. Each entry must be signed by your parent, guardian or teacher saying it is your own original work and that no help was given. If you're older than 14, you must sign your own work verifying that it is original. Deadlines are the 25th of each month.

Prizes: Winners receive prizes and certificates and most place-winners' entries are published in the magazine.

Sponsor's Remarks: "The *Cricket* League has sponsored contests since the magazine's inception in September of 1973. Through these contests, children have an opportunity to express their creativity in writing and the visual arts."

Subscription Rates: Single copy $3.95. One year $29.97. Two years $49.97. Three years $69.97.

‡ DELACORTE PRESS CONTEST FOR FIRST YOUNG ADULT NOVEL, Bantam Doubleday Dell BFYR, 1540 Broadway, New York, NY 10036. Annual book contest to encourage the writing of contemporary young adult fiction.

General Info: Annual contest for American and Canadian writers who have not previously published a young adult novel. Submissions should consist of a book-length manuscript with a *contemporary* setting that will be suitable for readers ages 12 to 18. Manuscripts should be no shorter than 100 typed pages and no longer than 250 typed pages. Include a brief plot summary with your cover letter. See additional format requirements and deadlines on guidelines sheet. Each manuscript must be accompanied by SASE large enough to accommodate manuscript; otherwise, the manuscript cannot be returned. Manuscript entries may not be submitted to other publishers while under consideration for the prize. Authors may not submit more than two manuscripts to the competition; each must meet all eligibility requirements. Foreign language manuscripts and translations are not eligible. Judges are the editors of Delacorte Press Books for Young Readers. Judges reserve the right not to award a prize. Send SASE anytime to receive complete guidelines.

Prizes: Winner receives book contract (publisher's standard form) for a hardcover and a paperback edition, including a $1,500 cash prize and $6,000 advance against royalties.

Sponsor's Remarks: "Our YA novel contest is not primarily for *young* writers. It is for anyone who has never published a YA novel."

[Author's Note: Suitable but tough contest for teens with novel-length manuscripts.]

✓$ DOGWOOD TALES MAGAZINE JUNE '96 WRITER'S COMPETITION, P.O. Box 172068, Memphis, TN 38187. Short story competition open to all ages.

General Info: Short story must be previously unpublished. Any genre or style accepted. Maximum length 3,500 words. Use standard format. Send copy of your original story, fee of $10 and cover letter with name, address and request to be included in competition. Deadline for submissions June 30, 1996. All entrants receive free copy of magazine. Include SASE only if you would like list of winners. Manuscripts will not be returned; no acknowledgement of receipt made. All winners notified by August 31, 1996. Send SASE for guidelines.

Prizes: Winning entries published. First prize $75; second prize $25. Winners also receive two copies and a one-year subscription. All entries considered for future publication. If you have not received notice of winning or future publication by August 31, 1996, you may submit your entry elsewhere—but not before August 31.

Sponsor's Remarks: "Send us your best short story. We select those that are fresh and action moving. We like strong endings."

Subscription Rates: One year (six issues) $15.60; U.S. funds only.

[**Author's Note:** Be sure to read market listing for *Dogwood Tales* and a sample copy to see what type of short stories are generally favored. Also send for *current* competition guidelines.]

✔$ ECLECTIC RAINBOWS CREATIVE NONFICTION CONTEST, Linda T. Dennison, Editor, 1538 Tennessee Walker Dr., Roswell, GA 30075-3152. Sponsoring magazine, published biannually, is "committed to making a positive difference."

General Info: Any essay approach is acceptable. Examples: factual, personal opinion or experience, humor. Length: 2,000 words maximum. Entries must be unpublished, and not accepted for publication at time of entry. You may submit your entry to other contests and publications pending notification of winning entries. Limit entries to three or less. Fee is $10 for first entry; $8 per additional entry. Include SASE. Deadline July 1. Submissions should relate in some way to the sponsor's ideal. *Do not put your name on the work itself.* See detailed rules sheet for special format requirements. Send SASE for rules.

Prizes: Cash awards plus publication in summer issue. First place $100; second place $75; third place $50. Nonwinning essays considered for publication; pays $25 plus copies.

Sponsor's Remarks: "All entries are coded by the editor to ensure the fair play of anonymity. Judging is conducted by an independent panel of three professional writers not on the *Eclectic Rainbows* staff."

Subscription Rates: One year (two issues) $10. Single copy $5.

✓$ ECLECTIC RAINBOWS POETRY CONTEST,

Linda T. Dennison, Editor, 1538 Tennessee Walker Dr., Roswell, GA 30075-3152. Sponsoring magazine, published biannually, is "committed to making a positive difference."

General Info: Length: 36 lines maximum. Entries must be unpublished and not accepted for publication at time of entry. You may submit your entry to other contests and publications pending notification of winning entries. Up to ten poems may be entered. Fee is $5 for one to three entries; $1 per additional entry. Include SASE. Deadline July 1. Submissions should relate in some way to the sponsor's ideal. *Do not put your name on the poem itself.* See detailed rules sheet for special format requirements. Send SASE for rules.

Prizes: Cash awards plus publication in summer issue. First place $100; second place $75; third place $50. Nonwinning essays considered for publication; pays $25 plus copies.

Sponsor's Remarks: "All entries are coded by the editor to ensure the fair play of anonymity. Judging is conducted by an independent panel of three professional writers not on the *Eclectic Rainbows* staff."

Subscription Rates: One year (two issues) $10. Single copy $5.

✓$ ECLECTIC RAINBOWS SHORT STORY CONTEST,

Linda T. Dennison, Editor, 1538 Tennessee Walker Dr., Roswell, GA 30075-3152. Sponsoring magazine, published biannually, is "committed to making a positive difference."

General Info: Length: 2,000 words maximum. Entries must be unpublished and not accepted for publication at time of entry. You may submit your entry to other contests and publications pending notification of winning entries. Limit entries to three or less. Fee is $10 for first entry; $8 per additional entry. Include

SASE. Deadline July 1. Submissions should relate in some way to the sponsor's ideal. *Do not put your name on the story itself.* See detailed rules sheet for special format requirements. Send SASE for rules.

Prizes: Cash awards plus publication in summer issue. First place $100; second place $75; third place $50. Nonwinning essays considered for publication; pays $25 plus copies.

Sponsor's Remarks: "All entries are coded by the editor to ensure the fair play of anonymity. Judging is conducted by an independent panel of three professional writers not on the *Eclectic Rainbows* staff."

Subscription Rates: One year (two issues) $10. Single copy $5.

*$ EXCELLENCE IN STUDENT LITERARY MAGAZINE PROGRAM, NCTE, 1111 W. Kenyon Rd., Urbana, IL 61801. Program to recognize excellence in student literary magazines sponsored by the National Council of Teachers of English.

General Info: Open to all senior high, junior high and middle schools throughout the U.S. and Canada and American schools abroad. Only one entry may be submitted per school. In cases where a school publishes more than one magazine or more than one issue per year, a selection committee should be formed at the school to select the best entry. Two or more schools *may not* join to submit one entry. Districtwide magazines produced by student staff are eligible if such magazines are developed in a district that *does not* have individual school literary magazines. Note: The following types of magazines are *not* eligible: K-elementary magazines and other kinds of pubications, e.g., newspapers, yearbooks. Evidence of plagiarism will disqualify a magazine. Magazines submitted must have been published between September of the previous year and July of the entry year. Three copies of the entry form and three copies of the literary magazine should be received by the State Leader no later than July 1. Write to above address for more information, official entry form and list of State Leader addresses. Entry fee $25.

Prizes: Initial judging will determine the entry's placement in one of five categories, the three most prominent being Excellent, Superior and the Highest Award.

Sponsor's Remarks: "Do not send entries to NCTE. Identify your State Leader from the list. This program is intended as a means of recognition for students, teachers and schools producing excellent literary magazines; as an inducement for improving the quality of such magazines; and as encouragement for all schools to develop literary magazines, seeking excellence in writing and schoolwide participation in production."

‡✔$ **FLANNERY O'CONNOR AWARD FOR SHORT FICTION**, University of Georgia Press, 330 Research Dr., Athens, GA 30602-4901. Annual short story competition.

General Info: Competition is open to writers in English, whether published or unpublished. Stories that have previously appeared in magazines or anthologies may be included. Stories previously published in book-length collection of author's own work may not be included. Collections that include long stories or novellas are acceptable; estimated length of novella 50-150 pages. Novels or single novellas will not be considered. Use standard format; author's name should appear only on the cover sheet. Fee $10. Authors may submit more than one manuscript as long as each is accompanied by a $10 check, meets all eligibility requirements and does not duplicate material submitted to us in another manuscript. Manuscripts must be submitted between June 1 and July 31. Those postmarked after July 31 are returned unopened. Authors may submit manuscripts to other publishers during judging; however, you must notify University of Georgia Press immediately if a collection submitted elsewhere has been accepted for publication. Send SASE for complete details.

Prizes: Two winners each receive cash awards of $1,000, and their collections are subsequently published by The University of Georgia Press under a standard book contract. The Press may occasionally select more than two winners.

Sponsor's Remarks: "Young writers need to be aware that this contest attracts entries from both new talent as well as seasoned, published professionals."

[**Author's Note:** Beware. This is a very tough competition that attracts a large number of entries each year.]

↙* GANNON UNIVERSITY'S TRI-STATE HIGH SCHOOL CONTEST, % Berwyn Moore, Assoc. Prof. of English, Gannon University, University Square, Erie, PA 16541. Poetry competition.

General Info: Open to high school students in Pennsylvania, New York and Ohio. Each student may submit two poems. No restrictions of form or content. Entries must be typed. In upper left corner, put name, address, home phone and grade. In upper right corner, put teacher's name, school name, address and phone number. Deadline February 1. No fee to enter. Poems judged by Gannon's English Department faculty. Each poem is read by three judges to determine finalists. Judges look for originality of subject, free verse or traditional forms that *complement* subject and precision of language and imagery.

Prizes: First place $50; second place $35; third place $20. Top three winners also receive signed book by famous poet plus publication in program book. Up to as many honorable mention awards given as poems warrant; recipient receives certificate and has name listed in program book. All winners receive complimentary copies of program books and posters.

Sponsor's Remarks: "Contest is part of Gannon's Annual Awards Night held in April. Judges' goal is to reward quality. Students receive recognition for their poetry, journalism and research writing. The Awards Night features a famous poet to present a reading. Past poets have included Gwendolyn Brooks, Donald Hall, Galway Kinnell, Lucille Clifton, W.D. Snodgrass and William Matthews."

↙‡$ GLIMMER TRAIN'S SHORT-STORY AWARD FOR NEW WRITERS, 812 S.W. Washington St., Suite. 1205, Portland, OR 97205. Sponsored by Glimmer Train Press, Inc.

General Info: Held twice yearly. Open to any writer whose fiction hasn't appeared in a nationally distributed publication with a circulation over 5,000. No theme. Length: 1,200-7,500 words. Up to two story entries may be sent together in the same envelope for single entry fee of $11. Include name, address and phone number on first page of story. *Staple* (rather than paper clip) manuscript pages together. Write "Short-Story Award for New Writers" on outside of envelope. No SASE needed; materials will not be returned. Entries must be postmarked during the months of February/March or August/September. Send SASE for detailed guidelines.

Prizes: Winner receives $1,200 and publication in *Glimmer Train Stories*. First and second runners-up receive $500 and $300, respectively, and honorable mention. Winners telephoned by July 1 for February/March entries and January 1 for August/September entries.

Sponsor's Remarks: "Please, no heavy dialect, story fragments, poetry, children's stories or nonfiction. We tend to choose stories for their ability to move us emotionally and for their absolute clarity in storytelling."

Subscription Rates: Single issues available for $9 in most bookshops or directly from address above.

‡$ GROLIER POETRY PRIZE, 6 Plympton St., Cambridge, MA 02138. Annual competition cosponsored by the Grolier Poetry Book Shop, Inc. and the Ellen La Forge Memorial Poetry Foundation, Inc.

General Info: Open to all poets who have not published either a vanity, small press, trade or chapbook of poetry. Entry fee is $6. Each poet should submit in duplicate only one manuscript of up to five poems that have never been published. Poems submitted elsewhere for publication are not eligible. Manuscript should not exceed 10 double-spaced pages. Each manuscript should be accompanied by a separate page that lists the author's name, address, phone number and titles of submitted poems. Author's name should not be included in the body of the manuscript. Guidelines sheet available for SASE. Copyright allows the Foundation to publish them in any of its subsequent anthologies. Deadline is May 1. Winners selected and informed in June. Judges remain anonymous.

Prizes: Two poets will receive an honorarium of $150. Up to four poems by each winner and two by each of the four runners-up will be chosen for publication in the *Grolier Poetry Prize Annual.*

Sponsor's Remarks: "The primary purpose of the Award is to encourage and recognize developing writers."

Subscription Rates: Copies from 1995 for $7. Place orders with Grolier Poetry Book Shop, Inc. Make checks payable to the Foundation.

✔$* IT'S YOUR CHOICE MAGAZINE WRITING CONTESTS, P.O. Box 7135, Richmond, VA 23221-0135. *It's Your Choice Magazine* is a journal of ethics and morality with an international circulation. Special contest open to grade school students.

General Info: Topic subject: ethics/morality. Entries may be either fiction or nonfiction. Monthly deadlines and awards. School district levels may send manuscripts in "batches" at any time but must be received by March 31. Entry fee is $1 for each manuscript submitted (check or money order). Only one entry per student allowed. First page of manuscript must bear author's name, home address, word count and the words "1996 It's Your Choice Student Writing Contest Entry." Length limits: for elementary students 50 words; middle school students 200 words; high school students 500 words. School district levels may send in one batch only for each year's contest. Manuscripts will be returned if SASE accompanies entry. Winning entries become the property of *It's Your Choice*, Future Wend Publications. Also sponsors second contest division open to general public; see guidelines and required registration form for details. Send SASE for complete details.

Prizes: Cash prizes and certificates, along with brief presentation ceremony sent directly to school officials. Cash awards for *each* participating school district: elementary $25; middle school $50; high school $100. Winners notified by mail sent to their home addresses. Awards made as soon as a winner has been selected in each "batch." Awards announced in June issue.

Sponsor's Remarks: "All articles and stories must be related to ethics/morality issues in an essential way. 'Tacking on' a couple of statements about ethics/morality to a story you have already written will not do. We regard ethics as the scientific study of the rightness or wrongness of human behavior in any context, which opens the field to a wide variety of articles. Do not overwrite; manuscripts 10 percent under or over word limits acceptable."

Subscription Rates: One year (twelve issues) $9.84. Sample copy $2 (except June, Contest Winners, $5).

* KENTUCKY STATE POETRY CONTESTS, % Jo Emary, 1134 Delmar Dr., Radcliff, KY 40160. Note some contest categories have modest entry fees, others have no fees. Sponsors a variety of annual poetry contests.

General Info: One category for elementary school students grades 1-3; one category for grades 4-6; and one category for high school students grades 7-12. Other categories open to all writers. No entry fee for student categories. Fees for other categories vary according to number of manuscripts entered. Poems must be the original work of the poet. Teacher or parent may *suggest* subject matter or offer advice on poetry techniques and may stress adherence to rules, importance of correct spelling, grammar and punctuation, neatness and legibility. Student entries may be untyped but copy must be neat and legible. *Must* include SASE. No poems returned; keep your own copy. Do not submit poems currently submitted in another contest or for publication. Send SASE for details and list of current categories.

Prizes: Only first-place winners will be published. Varying cash awards and certificates awarded.

Sponsor's Remarks: "This contest cannot be successfully entered without a new contest sheet each year, as the contest may not always be the same! Contest chairman may change without notice, and we cannot handle entries without SASE."

[**Author's Note:** These contests are not restricted to residents of Kentucky. Anyone may enter.]

✔* THE LOUISVILLE REVIEW CHILDREN'S CORNER CONTEST, Attn: Children's Corner, *TLR*, Dept. of English, 315 Humanities, University of Louisville, Louisville, KY 40292. *TLR* has been a national literary magazine since 1976. Contest open to students K-12.

General Info: Original, previously unpublished, poetry and fiction manuscripts by students in grades K-12. *No entry fee*, but submissions *must* be accompanied by SASE *and* a statement from a parent or guardian giving *TLR* permission to publish the work if accepted. Deadline for entries December 31. Also sponsors open contests in poetry and fiction with cash award; entry fee $10. Send SASE for contest rules.

Prizes: Selected entries published in *The Louisville Review*'s "Children's Corner" section.

Sponsor's remarks: "We are looking for vivid imagery, fresh language and originality. Our magazine comes out once or twice a year."

Subscription Rates: One year $8. Sample copy $4.

✔* MAJESTIC BOOKS WRITING CONTEST, P.O. Box 19097M, Dept. C, Johnston, RI 02919. Annual contest begun in 1992. Open only to Rhode Island students ages 6-17.

General Info: Contest is for original, unpublished work by Rhode Island students ages 6-17. Entries are judged against others received from same age group. Entries must be postmarked between September 1 and the second Friday in October each year. Each entry must include name, age, grade, school and a statement of authenticity signed by the author and a parent, guardian or teacher. Entries must be neatly prepared. Manuscripts are not returned. Send SASE after August 1 for complete contest rules and submissions guidelines.

Prizes: Forty stories chosen each year and published in a quality-bound softcover book. Winners receive one free copy. Every student who enters receives a personalized certificate.

Sponsor's Remarks: "Our goal is to encourage students to not only write to the best of their ability but to take pride in their success. Winners are invited to a special presentation ceremony. Write the best story you can, polish it and send it in. Originality is our biggest requirement. We also choose one piece of artwork for our cover, so if you are multitalented or know a good artist, write for those guidelines also."

‡ MARGUERITE DE ANGELI PRIZE CONTEST,

Bantam Doubleday Dell BFYR, 1540 Broadway, New York, NY 10036. Annual first book for middle grade readers competition to encourage the writing of fiction that examines the diversity of the American experience in the same spirit as the works of Marguerite de Angeli.

General Info: Open to U.S. and Canadian writers who have not previously published a novel for middle grade readers. Submissions should consist of a fiction manuscript suitable for readers 7-10 years of age that concerns the diversity of the American experience, either contemporary or historical. Do *not* submit art with your manuscript unless you have illustrated the work yourself. If you do submit artwork, do not send the originals. If you submit a dummy, also submit the text separately using standard format. Manuscripts should be no shorter than 40 typed pages and no more than 96 typed pages. Include a brief plot summary with your cover letter. Authors may not submit more than two manuscripts; each must meet all eligibility requirements. Title should also appear on each manuscript page. Entries must be postmarked no earlier than March 31 and no later than June 30. Send SASE for complete rules sheet. Contest results announced in October. Manuscripts sent to Doubleday may not be submitted to other publishers while under consideration for the prize.

Prizes: One hardcover and paperback book contract, in addition to a cash award advance of $1,500 and a $3,500 advance against royalties.

Sponsor's Remarks: "Marguerite de Angeli told simple stories about the lives and dreams of active, impulsive and inquisitive children, whose adventures often brought them into contact with persons of other races and cultures. With books such as *The Hannah!, Elin's Amerika, Bright April, Up the Hill, Henner's Lydia, Petite Suzanne, Jared's Island* and *Yonie Wondernose*, de Angeli helped children of many cultures to understand and appreciate each other and showed all children that they were important parts of a diverse, larger society."

[**Author's Note:** Suitable but tough contest for teens with novel-length manuscripts.]

*$ MERLYN'S PEN LITERARY MAGAZINE CONTEST AND CRITIQUE, P.O. Box 910, East Greenwich, RI 02818.

Sponsored by *Merlyn's Pen: The National Magazines of Student Writing* for intermediate and high school literary magazines.

General Info: Separate divisions for high schools and middle schools compete for the Golden Pen Award, honoring the best overall entry. Three optional categories—Best Design, Best Writing, Best Art and Photography—to recognize specific outstanding aspects may also be entered. Judges use a comprehensive checklist and a 500-point rating scale to evaluate the magazines submitted. Each entry receives a personalized critique in which an experienced reviewer evaluates its strengths and weaknesses. Entry forms are included in the last two issues of *Merlyn's Pen* each school year. Note: Schools do *not* need to subscribe to enter. Entries need to be postmarked no later than June 30. Winners of awards are notified in mid-September and featured in *Merlyn's Pen*'s third issue of the school year. To receive an entry form and more information, send SASE or call (800) 247-2027. Minimum fee to enter school literary magazine is $60.

Prizes: Two recipients of the Golden Pen Award receive recognition in *Merlyn's Pen*—with pictures of each magazine's staff advisor. Each of the recipients' schools also earns a Golden Pen trophy. Merlyn's Silver Award (450-500 points) and Merlyn's Bronze Award (400-449 points) also awarded. Winners of the special categories receive a plaque.

Sponsor's Remarks: *"Merlyn's Pen: The National Magazines of Student Writing* is dedicated to recognizing and publishing the best in student writing and artwork. This contest is designed for school magazines that emphasize creative writing. Our judging includes a detailed critique of art and photography because they so often are a part of literary magazines. But this contest and critique is not appropriate for 'arts' magazines whose main focus is the visual arts."

Subscription Rates: For one year (four issues during school year) $21 each for one to nine subscriptions; $7.25 each for ten or more subscriptions. Special student-at-home discount for prepaid orders: one year $7.50, $33.50 two years. Two-year individual subscriptions $33.95.

* MICHIGAN STUDENT FILM & VIDEO FESTI-VAL, % Margaret Culver, Harrison High School, 29995 W. 12 Mile Rd., Farmington Hills, MI 48334.

Only event of its kind in the U.S. that showcases productions from children in grades K-12. Sponsored annually by Detroit Area Film & Television (DAFT) and funded by a number of individuals and organizations.

General Info: Festival is open to film and video work done by students who live in Michigan. Students compete in either the elementary, junior or senior levels, depending on their age. There is a special category for students with disabilities, although they may choose to compete in their age brackets instead. Professional artists, educators, media professionals and interested community members serve as judges. Additional information available. Schools and other interested community organizations may borrow, free of charge, a copy of a past Festival videotape. Write to above address. Entries for Festival are due in March.

Prizes: First Division medals and Special Certificates are given to the best entries. In addition to "Best of Show" awards, a number of special awards and scholarships are sponsored. "Best of Show" winners are shown at the Festival, usually held in May. Selected winners appear on WTVS *Visions of a New Age: Today's Young Media Makers*. All entries receive some kind of reward. Event is juried, and students receive the judges' comments on evaluation forms that are returned with their entries.

Sponsor's Remarks: "Last year (1995), approximately three hundred entries from over 80 sites in Michigan competed for awards, making it one of the biggest Festivals of its 26 year history. However, the Festival does not put a great emphasis on competition. The major focus of the Festival is to positively reinforce student participation in film and video. Many Festival winners have gone on to receive great success in the film and video industry. The 1994 'Best Film' winner, senior Dan Scanlon, has been featured in *National Geographic World* and has earned an Emmy nomination for his award-winning entry. Doug Chiang, a past Festival winner, is an outstanding special effects master, whose feature film credits include *Switch, Ghost, Back to the Future 2* (and *3*), *Terminator 2* and *The Doors*. Doug has earned two Academy Awards for special effects in *Death Becomes Her* and

Forrest Gump. Chen Rohwer was the youngest person to qualify as one of the ten finalists for the Mark Silverman/Robert Redford Sundance Institute Fellowship and is being considered as the director for a Madonna music video."

✔$* MISSISSIPPI VALLEY POETRY CONTEST,

P.O. Box 3188, Rock Island, IL 61204. Nonprofit contest for all ages. Students encouraged to enter.

General Info: Any young person of school age is eligible. Entry fee $3 for up to five poems. Send SASE for complete rules and guidelines. Judging by a panel of experienced published poets and writers.

Prizes: First-place high school level $75; junior high $50; elementary $50. No publication of winners at this time.

Sponsor's Remarks: "Subject matter at writer's discretion. Young writers are encouraged to read works of various poets before entering. Now in our 24th year, we especially aim at developing a love for poetry and writing skills among elementary, junior high and high school students."

✔$‡ THE MISSOURI REVIEW EDITOR'S PRIZE,

1507 Hillcrest Hall, University of Missouri, Columbia, MO 65211. Open to writers of any age.

General Info: The contest includes prizes for short fiction, essays and poetry. Page restrictions are 25 or fewer typed, double-spaced pages for fiction, 10 for poetry. Entries must be previously unpublished and will not be returned. Entry fee is $15 per entry. Each fee entitles the entrant to a one-year subscription to *MR*, an extension of a current subscription or a gift subscription. Please clearly mark the outside of the envelope as fiction, essay or poetry. Include an index card with the author's name, address and telephone number in the left corner and, for fiction and essay entries only, the work's title in the center. Enclose SASE for notification of winners. The deadline is October 15.

Prizes: One winner and three finalists will be chosen in each category. The prizes are $1,000 for short fiction, $1,000 for essay and $500 for poetry. Winners will be published and the finalists announced in the following spring's issue of *The Missouri Review*.

‡ NATION/I.F. STONE AWARD FOR STUDENT JOURNALISM, % The Nation Institute, 72 Fifth Ave., New York, NY 10011. Annual award recognizes excellence in undergraduate college journalism.

General Info: Contest is open to all undergraduates enrolled in a U.S. college. Articles may be submitted by the writers themselves or nominated by editors of student publications or faculty members. While entries originally published in student publications are preferred, all articles will be considered provided they were not written as part of a student's regular course work. This year, for example, all entries must have been written or published between June 30, 1994 and June 29, 1995. Each writer, editor or faculty member may submit up to three separate entries. A series of related articles is considered a single entry. Investigative articles are particularly encouraged. No restrictions as to scope, content or length. Call (212) 463-9270 for further information.

Prizes: The article that, in the opinion of the judges, represents the most outstanding example of student journalism in the tradition of I.F. Stone will be published in a fall issue of *The Nation*. Winner also receives cash award of $1,000.

Sponsor's Remarks: "Entries should exhibit the uniquely independent journalistic tradition of I.F. Stone. A self-described 'Jeffersonian Marxist,' Stone combined progressive politics, investigative zeal and a compulsion to tell the truth with a commitment to human rights and the exposure of injustice. As Washington editor of *The Nation* magazine and founder of the legendary *I.F. Stone's Weekly*, he specialized in publishing information ignored by the mainstream media (which he often found in *The Congressional Record* and other public documents overlooked by the big-circulation dailies)."

✓$* NATIONAL POETRY COMPETITION, Chester H. Jones Foundation, P.O. Box 498, Chardon, OH 44024. Annual competition open to all.

General Info: Entrants must live, work or study in the U.S. or be an American or Canadian citizen. No competitor may receive more than one prize. Each competitor may submit up to ten poems; each poem submitted is judged separately. All entries must be in English and must be the unaided work of the competitor and must not have been previously published or broadcast. Author's name (or pseudonym) must not appear on the manuscript and must be given on the entry form only. Use standard format. Maximum length 32 lines. Receipt of entries will be given if SASE enclosed. Fee (in U.S. funds) for first poem submitted $2. Fee for each additional poem $1. Send SASE for entry form and current information.

Prizes: Entries from prize winners and runners-up are published in a chapbook-style anthology. Authors of any poem selected for the anthology receive one free copy. The Foundation reserves first right to publish winners' poems; thereafter, copyrights revert to the authors.

Sponsor's Remarks: "Chester H. Jones was a resident of Cleveland. He was a printer with a lifelong interest in writing. The Foundation that bears his name is a nonprofit organization set up to further his wish of discovering new talent in poetry."

Subscription Rates: Anthology collections available for purchase for $3.50; information included on contest brochure.

* NATIONAL WRITTEN & ILLUSTRATED BY ... AWARDS CONTEST FOR STUDENTS, Landmark Editions, Inc., 1402 Kansas Ave., Kansas City, MO 64127. Annual book contest for students.

General Info: Original books may be entered in one of three age categories: 6-9, 10-13 and 14-19. Each book must be written and illustrated by the same student. Entry must be signed by parent/guardian and teacher. Homeschooled students may enter, but entry must be signed by a librarian or teacher other than a parent/guardian. Send a self-addressed business-size (#10) envelope with $.64 postage for complete rules and guidelines.

Prizes: Winners receive all-expense-paid trips to Landmark's offices in Kansas City, where editors and art directors assist them in the final preparation of text and illustrations for the publication of their books. Winners also receive publishing contracts and are paid royalties.

Sponsor's Remarks: "Contest is sponsored to encourage and celebrate the creative efforts of students. Every year students nationwide submit more than seven thousand original book entries. Winning books are selected by a national panel of distinguished educators, editors, art directors and noted authors and illustrators of juvenile books."

* NEW ERA WRITING, ART, PHOTOGRAPHY AND MUSIC CONTEST, 50 E. North Temple St., Salt Lake City, UT 84150. Sponsored annually by *New Era Magazine.* Open to all English-speaking Latter-day Saints [Mormon youth] in good standing, ages 12-23.

General Info: Separate categories for various types of writing (feature articles, poetry and short story), art (original designs, illustrations, paintings, drawings, prints, sculpture or crafts), photography, hymn writing, songwriting and a special category for arts entries that don't fit within another category (examples: plays, computer games and programs, videos, instrumental music, etc.). Entrants desiring a scholarship (rather than cash award) must be in a position to accept scholarship in fall of contest year. All work must be original and not previously published. Details and entry form appear in *New Era* (see September issue). Form must be completed and signed by local church leader.

Prizes: Cash award or scholarship to Brigham Young University, BYU-Hawaii Campus or Ricks College. Note: Nonwinning entries suitable for publication will be paid for at usual rates.

Sponsor's Remarks: "The editors of *New Era* will be the judges of the contest. Entries will be judged on originality, perceptivity, overall excellence and appropriateness for publication in the *New Era.* All entries should reflect LDS values."

Subscription Rates: One year $8.

‡$ NICHOLL FELLOWSHIPS IN SCREENWRITING, Academy of Motion Picture Arts & Sciences, 8949 Wilshire Blvd., Beverly Hills, CA 90211. Annual international screenwriting competition, open to new writers.

General Info: Writers who have not sold or optioned a story or screenplay for film or television are eligible. Writers must submit a completed application form, an original (noncollaborative) feature-length screenplay and a $30 entry fee. Entries must be in standard screenplay format; 100-130 pages. Deadline May 1. Send SASE to receive contest rules and application form available after January 1. Judges are looking for an intriguing, original story and exceptional craft.

Prizes: Up to five fellowships of $25,000 are awarded each year. The Academy acquires no rights to the work and does not participate in the marketing nor in any other aspect of the script's commercial future.

Sponsor's Remarks: "The purpose of the program is to foster the development of the art of screenwriting by providing financial support for up to five writers for one year. This award cannot be used to begin, continue or complete a formal education program. (In other words, this is not a scholarship program.) Since the program's inception in 1986, there have been thirty fellowship recipients, ranging in age from 22 to 61. Entrants' ages have ranged from 14 to 85. In 1992, there were 3,514 entrants."

[**Author's Note:** Suitable only for older teen writers who have studied screenwriting. Be sure to *professionally* format your entry.]

* NORTH AMERICAN INTERNATIONAL AUTO SHOW SHORT STORY CONTEST, Detroit Auto Dealers Association, 1800 W. Big Beaver Rd., Troy, MI 48084. Contest open to all Michigan residents. Two judging divisions: high school and "open."

General Info: All stories must be fictional and original and may not have appeared in any publication prior to the annual NAIAS held in January. There is no theme requirement. However, stories must be in good taste. Stories with a pornographic theme or obscene language will be immediately disqualified. Entries must be typed double-spaced on 8½″×11″ paper. Length must not exceed 2,500 words. All stories must be in English. Each entry must be attached to a cover sheet containing the author's name, address and phone number. Author's name must appear on each page of the entry. Entry limit: two per person. There are two judging divisions, one for high school students (grades 9-12) and one "open" division, which usually attracts entries from college students or graduates. Send SASE to above address to receive current competition rules and deadline (usually in November).

Prizes: Winners are announced during NAIAS in January. Awards are first place $1,000; second $500; third $250. Winning stories may be published in the Auto Show Program at the sole discretion of the Detroit Auto Dealers Association (DADA). All authors retain all rights to their work.

Sponsor's Remarks: "The contest is not open to Detroit Auto Dealers Association members, their families or family members of the judges. Entries will be judged by an independent panel comprised of knowledgeable persons engaged in the literary field in some capacity."

✔$* NPT YOUNG WRITER'S COMPETITION, National Pre-Teen Corporation, 214 Fifth Ave., Lehigh Acres, FL 33936. Annual contest sponsored by National Pre-Teen Achievement Program. Open competition; entrants do *not* need to participate in NPT Program.

General Info: Entrants may enter up to two short stories and two poems. Junior division ages 8-10; Senior division ages 11-13. Short stories require $25 fee per submission. Story must have a young person as major character, a plot in which problem or situation must be resolved and resolution resulting from main character's action or decision. *Writers' INTERNATIONAL Forum* manuscript guidelines must be followed. (See market listing page 244.) Story length should be between 500 and 2,000 words. Fee for poem is $10 per submission. Maximum length 20 lines. Submit two copies of each entry; include SASE for return of manuscript. Deadline is October 15; late entries automatically placed in next year's contest. Send SASE for complete details.

Prizes: Ten U.S. Savings Bonds (worth from $50 to $300) awarded in short story contest. Five prizes in each division. Certificates to top ten in each division. Winning entries may be published in *Writers' INTERNATIONAL Forum*. Poetry winners in each division receive $50 Savings Bond; certificates awarded to top five in each poetry division.

Sponsor's Remarks: "We encourage young people to begin and/or continue to express themselves with thoughts and words. To give them the opportunity to achieve their dreams of using the written word to expand their own creativity. As always, write what you know . . . what you feel and tell it well. Preliminary judging coordinated by Lee County Council of the Arts, Ft. Myers, Florida. Final judging by *Writers'* INTERNATIONAL *Forum.*

[**Author's Note:** For more information, see the profiles of Sandra Haven (chapter eight) and Kristin Thurston (chapter seven).]

$ NWA ARTICLES & ESSAYS CONTEST, National Writer's Association (formerly NWC), 1450 S. Havana, Suite 424, Aurora, CO 80012. Annual contest open to all writers.

General Info: Any nonfiction article or essay is eligible provided it does not exceed 5,000 words. Submissions must be in standard typed format. You may enter as many manuscripts as you wish, but each must be accompanied by an entry form, $12 entry fee and SASE with sufficient return postage. Judging will be based on originality, freshness of style, significance and marketability. Send SASE for details and entry form. Critique available for additional fee. Deadline is December 31. Judging sheets are included if SASE accompanies entry.

Prizes: First place $200; second $100, third $50; fourth through tenth—choice of books; eleventh through twentieth—honorable mention certificate.

Sponsor's Remarks: "The purpose of this contest is to encourage writers in this creative form and to recognize those who excel in nonfiction writing."

[**Author's Note:** Notice that NWA contests *allow* writers to submit their manuscript entries to a publisher. If you do, you should tell the publisher so in a cover letter.]

$ NWA NOVEL CONTEST, National Writer's Association, 1450 S. Havana, Suite 424, Aurora, CO 80012. Annual contest open to all writers.

General Info: Any genre or category of novel manuscript may be entered. Only *unpublished, unbound* manuscripts eligible. Use standard typed format. English only. Maximum length is 90,000 words; longer manuscripts may be submitted upon payment of an additional entry fee. Send appropriate SASE if you wish your manuscript returned. Entry fee for each novel is $25. Contest opens December 1. All materials, complete with entry form and fees, must be postmarked no later than April 30. Entries may be submitted to publishers while contest is in progress. Top three entries offered to NWA's literary agents for consideration. Send SASE for complete details and entry form. Critiques available for additional fee.

Prizes: First place $500; second $250; third $150; plus other awards for fourth through twentieth places.

Sponsor's Remarks: "Our purpose is to help develop creative skills, to recognize and reward outstanding ability and to increase the opportunity for the marketing and subsequent publication of novel manuscripts."

[**Author's Note:** See profile of NWA Executive Director Sandy Whelchel in chapter eight.]

$ NWA POETRY CONTEST, National Writer's Association, 1450 S. Havana, Suite 424, Aurora, CO 80012. Annual contest open to all writers.

General Info: All poems are eligible: lyric, ballad, free verse, experimental and traditional. Entry must be accompanied by entry fee, entry form and SASE. Your name and address must appear on the first page of your poems. Only unpublished poems are eligible. Authors retain all rights and may submit their entries to publishers while contest is in progress. Judging based on originality, technique, significance and emotional values. Entry fee for poems 40 lines or shorter is $8; see details regarding longer poems. Awards given at annual conference. Send SASE for complete details and entry form. Critiques available for additional fee. Opens July 1; closes September 30.

Prizes: First place $100; second $50; third $25; fourth $15; other prizes awarded through twentieth place.

Sponsor's Remarks: "Our purpose is to encourage the writing of poetry, an important form of individual expression but with a limited commercial market."

$ NWA SHORT STORY CONTEST, National Writer's Association, 1450 S. Havana, Suite 424, Aurora, CO 80012. Annual contest open to all writers.

General Info: Any type of fiction is eligible provided it does not exceed 5,000 words. You may enter as many manuscripts as you wish, but each must be accompanied by an entry form, $12 entry fee and SASE. Although only unpublished short stories are eligible, authors retain all rights and may submit their entries to publishers while contest is in progress. Short stories between 5,000 words and 10,000 words may be entered for a $24 fee. Judging based on originality, imagination, freshness of style, significance, emotional value and marketability. Send SASE for complete details and entry form. Critiques available for additional fee. Opens April 1; closes July 1.

Prizes: First place $200; second $100; third $50; plus other awards through twentieth place.

Sponsor's Remarks: "Our purpose is to encourage writers in this creative form and to recognize those who excel in short story writing."

* PAUL A. WITTY OUTSTANDING LITERA-TURE AWARD, % Cathy Collins Block, Ph.D., Professor of Education, Texas Christian University, P.O. Box 32925, Fort Worth, TX 76129. Sponsored by Special Interest Group, Reading for Gifted and Creative Students, International Reading Association.

General Info: Entries from elementary, junior high and high school judged separately. Two categories: prose and poetry. Elementary prose limited to 1,000 words. Entries from secondary students must be typed and may exceed 1,000 words, if necessary. Set of five poems required. Entries judged on creativity, originality and beauty of expression. Entry blanks and more information sent to teachers for SASE.

Prizes: National awards, $25 and plaques; also certificates of merit.

Sponsor's Remarks: "Begun in 1979 to honor Dr. Paul Witty, between 500 and 1,000 entries are received yearly. Our goal is to encourage gifted writers and their teachers by recognizing and rewarding their achievements. We grant awards as deserved, from one to six in past years, although two different years, no entry was deemed award quality. From contact with winners, I learn that most of them write continuously and go to their folios to select entries."

✔$* **POETS AT WORK CONTESTS**, Jessee Poet, VAMC 325 New Castle Rd., P.O. Box 113, Butler, PA 16001. Sponored by bimonthly magazine for poets of all ages. Some contests require entry fee; some do not.

General Info: Approximately twenty-two poetry contests sponsored each year. Some have end-of-the-month deadlines; some quarterly deadlines. Requirements, such as for themes and line limits, vary. Average entry fee $1 per poem. Send SASE for current contest flyer. New contest flyers published three times a year. Entries accompanied by SASE automatically receive winners' list and next contest flyer.

Prizes: Various cash awards, some based on number of entries received, others have set amount. Publication of winning entries depends on which contest(s) entered.

Sponsor's Remarks: "I encourage young writers to subscribe to *Poets at Work*. One of the things that you need most is to have your poetry published and enjoyed by others, and you will learn by reading the poetry of others. You will also have the opportunity to practice different forms of poetry if you study the rules and examples of the various contests that I provide. I always have one *free* contest, which allows up to five entries."

Subscription Rates: One year (six issues) $18.

*✤$ **THE PRISM AWARDS**, 90 Venice Crescent, Thornhill, ON L4J 7T1 Canada. Contest sponsored by The Kids Network, Scotiabank and Air Canada. The Kids Network works directly with winners to produce professionally written and published books. Open to Canadian children only.

General Info: Restricted to Canadian children ages 7-14. Entry fee of $2 required. Each story must be between 4 pages and 18 pages and in one of the story categories listed on the official entry form. Entry form must be signed by the child writer and parent attesting that the story is the original work of the child. The same story may not be submitted to The Prism Awards more than once. Children may submit one manuscript each year. Manuscripts cannot be coauthored but must be the original work of one child and not edited or changed by an adult. Over forty judges review manuscripts according to preset criteria that emphasize conceptual thinking. Judges appreciate manuscripts that are double-spaced. Official entry form is required, available in October of every year. Strict January deadline is on form. No late entries accepted.

Prizes: There is one winner in 7-10 age group, one in the 11-14 age group for *each* story category listed on entry form. Winners receive a $500 cash award and a crystal prism trophy. They also join The Kids Netword Training program and work with a team of professional editors and have the possibility of being published as part of The Kids Netword series of books. Child authors whose books are published receive royalties.

Sponsor's Remarks: "The best way to look at The Prism Awards program is to say it opens the door for 'original thoughts from enterprising young Canadian minds.' If you think you have something you'd like to write about and you love to write, we encourage you to enter the program. Very few of The Prism Award winners ever thought they would win! We see it as a way for kids to share with other kids their talents, interests, wildest imaginings and innermost feelings."

Subscription Rates: Write to above address to be placed on mailing list to receive official entry form, or fax your request to (905) 451-2035. Be sure to include your complete address.

* PUBLISH-A-BOOK CONTEST, Raintree/Steck-Vaughn, P.O. Box 27010, Austin, TX 78755. Yearly contest for children in grades 4-6 in U.S. and Canada.

General Info: New contest theme announced each fall. Stories, 700-800 words in length, must relate to year's theme and be written by children in grades 4, 5 or 6. *Entrants must be enrolled full time in an accredited public or private school.* Each student must be sponsored by a teacher or school or public librarian. All entries become the property of the publisher and will not be returned. Sponsors should submit children's stories in typed, double-spaced format. Illustrations are not accepted. Cover sheet should include all information (name, address, grade level, school and telephone number) for both young author and sponsor. Judging criteria includes adherence to theme, potential for illustration, use of language. Rules (poster format) available free by calling (800) 531-5015. Submission deadline is January 31 of each year.

Prizes: Four grand-prize-winning entries will be published in professionally illustrated, hardcover book form and become part of the current series bearing the contest name. Winners also receive a $500 advance against royalties as well as ten copies of their published books. The sponsor named on each of the winning entries receives twenty free books from the Raintree/Steck-Vaughn Library catalog. Twenty honorable mention young authors each receive $25; their sponsors receive ten free books.

Sponsor's Remarks: "Teachers and librarians may sponsor as many children as they wish in the PAB contest. We encourage teachers and librarians to use the contest as a classroom activity or to encourage a young writer. A photo and biography of the author is given in the back of each of the winning entries. Authors are invited to dedicate their books to special people in their lives."

*$ QUILL AND SCROLL INTERNATIONAL WRITING/PHOTOGRAPHY CONTEST, Quill and Scroll, School of Journalism, University of Iowa, Iowa City, IA 52242-1528. Contest open to grades 7-12.

General Info: Competition open to all high school and junior high students. Each school may submit two entries in ten categories: editorial, editorial cartoon, investigative reporting (individual and team), news story, feature story, sports story, advertisement and photography (news feature and sports). Entries must have been published in school paper or professional paper. Entries must be tearsheet form. Two-dollar entry fee must accompany each entry. Contest rules are sent, in late December, to all schools on mailing list. Guidelines and entry form also appear in the December/January issue of *Quill and Scroll* magazine. If your school does not receive information about this contest, request information from the above address. Materials will be sent to the journalism advisor, principal or counselors at your school. See contest guidelines sheet for format and information for each category. Deadline is February 5. Note: Senior national winners are automatically eligible for the Edward J. Nell Memorial Scholarship in Journalism.

Prizes: National winners will be notified by mail through their advisors and receive the Gold Key Award and will be listed in April/May issue of *Quill and Scroll*. Senior winners intending to major in journalism at a college or university that offers a major in journalism are eligible for $500 scholarships. All winners are published in *Quill and Scroll*.

Sponsor's Remarks: "Currently enrolled high school and junior high students are invited to enter the National Writing/ Photo Contest. Awards are made in each of the ten divisions."

Subscription Rates: One year $12.

*$ QUILL AND SCROLL YEARBOOK EXCEL-LENCE CONTEST, Quill and Scroll Society, School of Journalism, University of Iowa, Iowa City, IA 52242-1528.

General Info: Contest evaluates yearbook spreads in ten different categories and overall theme development. Photo categories must include original photo as well as yearbook spread. Contest is open to students in grades 9-12. Students must attend a high school that is chartered by *Quill and Scroll* (more than 13,000 schools are chartered). Each school may submit two spread sheet entries in each of the categories. These are student life, academics, sports action photo, academic photo, feature photo, graphic and index. Only one entry may be submitted for the theme development division (twelve themes). Submit $2 entry fee for each division. Entry applications will be sent to each member school in late August. Request applications or membership information from the above address. Deadline November 1.

Prizes: Winners receive a Gold Key Award and are eligible to apply for the Edward J. Nell scholarship during their senior year. Winners are published in *Quill and Scroll* magazine.

Subscription Rates: One year $12.

* READ, 245 Long Hill Rd., Middletown, CT 06457. Educational magazine that cosponsors a variety of reading, writing and video-making contests throughout the year.

General Info: These contests upcoming for 1995-1996. Similar contest every year. See magazine issue indicated for details. Announced in issue #2, LetterWriters Ink pen pal exchange program; deadline October 20, 1995. Students write letters, submit them to editorial office and, within two months, receive responses from students in a class somewhere in the U.S. Issue #3, Writing and Art Awards; writing categories include short fiction or plays, first-person essays and two-dimensional artwork; deadline December 15, 1995. Issue #4, Ann Arlys Bowler Poetry Prize; deadline December 22, 1995. Issue #5, Letters About Literature; students write letters to the authors of a book that changed their way of thinking about some issue; cosponsored by the Center for the Book at the Library of Congress; deadline December 8, 1995. Issue #9, Video Voyages; students get their chance to write, direct and produce their own class videos; cosponsored by The Panasonic Company; deadline March 17, 1996.

Prizes: For Bowler and WAA: First place $100. For Letters: trip to Washington, D.C. For Video: video equipment.

[**Author's Note:** Entry in these contests is not limited to *Read* readers.]

✔ RICHARD J. MARGOLIS AWARD OF BLUE MOUNTAIN CENTER, 101 Arch St., Ninth Floor, Boston, MA 02110. Annual award.

General Info: Open to journalists, poets or essayists whose work combines warmth, humor, wisdom and a concern with social issues. Applications should include at least two examples of the writer's work (published or unpublished, 30 pages maximum) and a short biographical note including a description of his/her current and anticipated work. Send three copies of each writing sample. Deadline July 1. Award announced in October.

Prizes: Cash award $1,000.

Sponsor's Remarks: "The award is given each year to a promising new writer. Previous winners include Richard Manning (1992) and Judith Levine (1993)."

✔$* SCHOLASTIC ART & WRITING AWARDS,
The New York Foundation for the Arts, The Scholastic Writing Awards, P.O. Box 517, New York, NY 10013. Open to students in grades 7-12; numerous writing categories. Sponsors separate Art Awards competition.

General Info: All students in grades 7-12 who are currently enrolled in public or nonpublic schools in the U.S., U.S. territories, U.S.-sponsored schools abroad and Canada are eligible. Two award groups: Group I—grades 7, 8 and 9; Group II—grades 10, 11 and 12. Categories include short story, short short story, essay/nonfiction/opinion writing, dramatic script, poetry, humor, science fiction/fantasy. Writing portfolio category open only to students in Group II. Works may be submitted into only one category (with the exception of portfolios). Example: A science fiction short story may be entered in either the science fiction category *or* the short story category but not both. Send SASE for complete rules (including word lengths and entry fee payment options) and official entry form. Entry fee is $3 per manuscript.

Prizes: Cash awards include maximum of ten Gold Awards for each group—$100; maximum of fifteen Silver Awards—certificate. Four scholarships of $5,000 each awarded for best portfolios submitted by graduating students. Selected winning entries appear in some issues of Scholastic magazines. Each entry form for additional cash and certificate awards offered.

Sponsor's Remarks: "The Scholastic Writing Awards were founded in 1923 to honor young people who have dedicated themselves to the craft of writing. Our objective is to foster the confidence of young writers and to invite students to broaden their horizons while winning national recognition. The Scholastic Art & Writing Awards are the largest and longest running programs of their kind in the country."

✔$* SHOW AND TELL'S WRITE ON JUVENILE
RESPONSIBLE WRITING CONTEST, Donna Clark, Editor, 93 Medford St., Malden, MA 02148. Those from East Coast and South submit to above address. Those from Midwest and West Coast submit to Tom Conger, 2830 S. 2750 E., Salt Lake City, UT 84109. Sponsored by monthly publication that seeks

to publish fiction that illustrates a good balance of fiction elements, not necessarily with an emphasis on award-winning stories. Age range: High school to senior citizens. Special contests for youths ages 7-18.

General Info: Contest seeks to find and showcase literary abilities of youths ages 7-18. No adult may help entrant except in typing. Three age categories, entry fees and requirements: (1) Small Fry—ages 7-10, $1 per story up to 600 words long; (2) Medium Rare—ages 11-14, $3 per story up to 1,000 words; (3) Well Done—ages 15-18, $5 per story up to 1,200 words. Prefers standard format; neatly written stories from ages 7-10 acceptable. Provide name and address of local library and newspaper with entry. Submit entries between September 1 and November 30. Stories judged on character and plot creativity. Send SASE for complete rules and official entry form.

Prizes: Cash awards for first and second place range from $5 to $25 depending on age category. All entrants receive certificate of participation. Winners published in special January short story issue of *Show and Tell*. Winners also announced in their local newspapers, and free copies of winning collection sent to their local libraries.

Sponsor's Remarks: "We believe writing should make sense but should not be so sophisticated that it can't be understood. We're looking for young authors who can write a great story that captures the wonder of simplicity. We'll know if an adult 'helps.' The East Coast judge edits a national fiction publication. The West Coast judge also edits and writes adult fiction. We both have a big heart for children and between us have six kids who write fiction. We believe writing is one of the highest forms of creativity and is best found in a kid!"

Subscription Rates: Short story collection issue $3, available beginning January 1. Request from East Coast address.

✔$* SKIPPING STONES YOUTH HONOR AWARDS,

P.O. Box 3939, Eugene, OR 97403. New annual awards program sponsored by *Skipping Stones*, an international nonprofit quarterly children's magazine featuring writing and art by children ages 7-18. Annual theme. Contest open to youth age 16 and under.

General Info: Entries accepted written in English and other languages. Open to writings and artwork that promote multicultural awareness, nature and ecology, social issues, peace and nonviolence. Theme for 1996 is "Envisioning the World in the Year 2025." Deadline June 25. Prose entries (essays, short stories, etc.) limited to 750 words; poems less than 30 lines; original artwork (drawings, cartoons, paintings or photo essays with captions) limited to 8 plates. Include name, age, school and home address on each page. Send entry with a cover letter, a certificate of originality (from a parent or teacher), SASE and a $3 entry fee. Youth organizations also invited to enter by telling how their club or group works locally to (1) enhance the quality of life for low-income, minority or disabled people; (2) preserve nature and ecology; or (3) improve racial or cultural harmony in your school or community. Send entries with same information and fee as above. Send SASE for complete information.

Prizes: Ten awards are given to student groups and youth under age 16. Everyone entering contest will receive the autumn issue containing the ten winning entries.

Sponsor's Remarks: "The goal of *Skipping Stones* is to reach children around the world, in economically disadvantaged as well as privileged families, including underrepresented and special populations within North America. *Skipping Stones* encourages cooperation, creativity and celebration of cultural and environmental richness. It provides a playful forum for sharing ideas and experiences among children from different lands and backgrounds."

Subscription Rates: In the U.S.: one year $20; institutions $30; foreign $30 in U.S. funds. Third World libraries and schools or low-income U.S. families may purchase one-year subscription for $15. Free subscriptions available when situation warrants. Contact editorial office for information.

[**Author's Note:** Low-income entrants and subscribers are eligible for one free entry to contest. Contact *Skipping Stones* editorial office for information.]

✔‡$ **STEGNER FELLOWSHIPS**, Program Coordinator, Creative Writing Program, Stanford University, Stanford, CA

94305-2087. Ten fellowships awarded in both fiction and poetry categories each year. Program celebrated its 50th anniversary in 1995.

General Info: Completed application must include a manuscript, a brief statement of writing plans, mailing labels and a processing fee. Submission for poetry fellowships include a manuscript of poems, 10-15 pages in length. Submission of fiction should include a manuscript (standard typed format) of no more than 9,000 words, either two stories (three if they are very short) or up to 40 pages of a novel. Manuscripts are not returned. Send SASE for complete information and application form.

Prizes: Fellows receive a living stipend of $13,000 and required workshop tuition of nearly $5,000, totaling $36,000 for the two-year period.

Sponsor's Remarks: "In awarding fellowships, we consider the quality of the candidate's creative work, potential for growth and ability to contribute to and profit from our writing workshops. We do not require a degree for admission; no school of writing is favored over any other. The Stanford Creative Writing Program provides new writers with the company of their peers and the instruction of accomplished writers."

[**Author's Note:** The awarding of a fellowship such as this is much different than accepting a traditional writing competition award. Only serious teen and young adult writers should consider submitting. Be sure you understand the policies for both application and acceptance of a fellowship before entering.]

*$ TAWC SPRING WRITING CONTEST, P.O. Box 27, Sandusky, MI 48471. Sponsored by the Thumb Area Writer's Club for amateur writers in Michigan.

General Info: You must be an amateur writer residing in Michigan to enter. For this contest, amateur means (1) one who is not currently employed as a writer in the category that he/she enters and (2) one who has not sold a book or published more than three articles, poems or short stories in a paying market in the category entered. Each entrant may submit work in all three categories; short stories (1,500 words maximum), nonfiction (1,000 words maximum), poetry (64 lines maximum). You may submit up to three manuscripts in each category. Cost is $2 per each manuscript entered. Entries must be typed and follow standard format. Rules and deadlines available for SASE. Include SASE with entry for return of manuscript.

Prizes: The number of entries will determine the amount of the awards. Typical prizes are: $15 first place, $10 second place, $5 third place, plus several honorable mentions. Winning entries may be published in TAWC newsletter, *Thumbprints*.

Sponsor's Remarks: "In the past, several of our place winners and honorable mention winners have been teens."

Subscription Rates: One year for nonmember $9. Single issue of *Thumbprints* $.75.

[**Author's Note:** You *must* be a resident of Michigan to enter this contest.]

* TEEN POWER STORY AND POETRY CONTESTS, P.O. Box 632, Glen Ellyn, IL 60138.
Sponsored through *Teen Power*, a Sunday School take-home paper published quarterly. Open to 12-16 year olds.

General Info: True stories and poems must have a clear, evangelical Christian theme. Stories should be between 600 and 1,000 words. Send SASE for contest guidelines. Annual deadlines: True Story—May 31; Poetry—first Friday in January.

Prizes: True story winners: first place $100; second place $75; third place $50. Winning entries published in September quarter. Poetry winners: first place $50; second place $40; third place $30. Winning entries published in March quarter.

Sponsor's Remarks: "We are looking for personal experience stories of how teens have seen God work in their own lives. Poems should reflect a teen's relationship with God."

Subscription Rates: One year $9.95. Slightly higher in Canada.

✔* TIMES HERALD YOUNG WRITERS CONTESTS, % Michael Eckert, *Times Herald*, P.O. Box 5009, Port Huron, MI 48061-5009.
Open to students in newspaper's circulation area.

General Info: Various essay and short story contests sponsored periodically for students. Watch for details in newspaper.

Prizes: Publication of winning entries, usually on the special "Eye Page," featured in Wednesday editions. "Eye Page" subtitled: "A closer look at what's happening from a younger point of view."

[**Author's Note:** See profiles of Michael Eckert (chapter eight) and Alicia Gauthier (chapter seven).]

✔* THE VEGETARIAN RESOURCE GROUP ESSAY CONTEST, P.O. Box 1463, Baltimore, MD 21203. Open to children 18 and under.

General Info: Separate contest categories for students ages 14-18, ages 9-13 and ages 8 and under. Entrants should base their 2-3 page essays on interviewing, research and/or personal opinion. You do not need to be a vegetarian to enter. Essays can be on any aspect of vegetarianism. All essays become property of The Vegetarian Resource Group. Each essay needs to include the author's name, age, grade, school and teacher's name. Entries must be postmarked by May 1 of contest year. Send SASE for contest guidelines.

Prizes: A $50 savings bond is awarded in each category. Plus winning entries are published in *The Vegetarian Journal*.

Sponsor's Remarks: "Vegetarianism is not eating meat, fish and birds (for example, chicken or duck). Among the many reasons for being a vegetarian are beliefs about ethics, culture, health, aesthetics, religion, world peace, economics, world hunger and the environment."

Subscription Rates: Membership includes subscription. Student rate for one year $14.40.

✔* VOICE OF DEMOCRACY AUDIO ESSAY SCHOLARSHIP COMPETITION, contact the local VFW Post in your community or your State VFW Headquarters. U.S. high school students in grades 10, 11 and 12 eligible. Program began in 1946 and was originally sponsored by the National Association of Broadcasters with assistance from the Veterans of Foreign Wars of the United States.

General Info: Eligible students must be in 10th, 11th or 12th grade and properly enrolled in a public, private or parochial high school in the U.S., its territories and possessions or in an overseas school as a dependent of U.S. military or U.S. civilian personnel. (Foreign Exchange students are excluded.) Entries are submitted in both typed format and as audio recording (not less than three minutes or more than five minutes in length). Check with your school counselor or local VFW Post for details and application forms and deadlines. Local winners advance to next competition level; state winners compete at national level. Theme for 1994-95 competition was "My Vision for America."

Prizes: Scholarships at national level include: first place $20,000; second place $15,000; third place $10,000; fourth place $6,000; fifth place $5,000; sixth place $4,000; seventh place $3,000; eighth place $2,500; ninth place $2,000; tenth through sixteenth place $1,500; all additional scholarships $1,000. State winners are required to attend the National Finals Program in its entirety in Washington D.C. as the guest of the VFW National Organization.

Sponsor's Remarks: "The Veterans of Foreign Wars of the United States and its Ladies Auxiliary hope that every high school in the country will provide the opportunity for its students to take part in this program. Through classroom study projects and special assignments, students will be motivated, while writing and speaking, to express their opinion about their personal responsibilities and understanding of the rights and responsibilities of being an American."

‡$ WELLSPRING SHORT FICTION CONTEST, 770 Tonkawa Rd., Long Lake, MN 55356.

General Info: Submit one double-spaced typed entry, 2,000 words maximum. No limit on entries, but *each* story must be accompanied by a $10 entry fee. Entries judged on intriguing, well-crafted work. Do not staple or fold entries. Annual deadlines: January 1 and July 1. Entries received after deadline will be judged for subsequent issue. Sample copies of *Wellspring Magazine* available for $5.50. Manuscripts are not returned.

Prizes: Awards of $100, $75, $25, plus publication in *Wellspring Magazine*.

Sponsor's Remarks: "Nominee for *Writer's Digest*'s Fiction Fifty List."

Subscription Rates: For two issues $8. For four issues $15.

[**Author's Note:** Suitable for mature teens. It would be best to study past issues.]

*$ WRITER'S EXCHANGE POETRY CONTEST,

P.O. Box 394, Society Hill, SC 29593. Ongoing contest sponsored throughout the year by the *Writer's Exchange* newsletter.

General Info: Poems of all styles (traditional, free verse, rhyme, haiku and other forms) may be entered. All subjects and themes (family relationships, friendship, nature, inspirational, thought-provoking issues, humor, etc.) are welcome. Poems are judged by the editor (Gene Boone) on originality and presentation of idea as well as technique and overall effect. Poems must not be longer than 24 lines. Entries must be in standard manuscript format with poet's name and address in upper left-hand corner. Entries will not be returned. Entry fee is $1. Enclose SASE for guidelines and with entry to receive winners' list. Deadline is open; with an open deadline poems are gathered and winners published in the issue that goes to press at the date closest to which poems were received. Late entries are not disqualified. All entrants receive a complimentary copy of the *Writer's Exchange* newsletter.

Prizes: Poet whose poem is judged best overall will receive 50 percent of contest proceeds (the amount is usually $25 or more). Second and third place as well as five honorable mentions receive surprise gifts—usually a book or other award of interest to poets. Winning poem and two runners-up published in *Writer's Exchange*.

Sponsor's Remarks: "Our mission is to encourage new poets, with an emphasis on poets who are just beginning and those who are seeking publication. Poets of all ages may enter poems in our contests."

Subscription Rates: One year (four issues) $8. Sample copy is $2.

[**Author's Note:** Note the low entry fee required.]

* WRITERS' INTERNATIONAL FORUM ANNUAL CONTESTS, P.O. Box 516, Tracyton, WA 98393-0516.

Publication bringing writers of all ages together to exchange ideas and improve their skills and marketability as writers. (Formerly known as *Writers' Open Forum*.)

General Info: Send #10 SASE to receive current contest information.

Subscription Rates: One year (six issues) $14; $24 in U.S. funds for foreign destinations.

[**Author's Note:** Be sure to see profile of editor Sandra Haven in chapter eight.]

* WRITING CONTESTS, The Writing Conference, Inc., P.O. Box 664, Ottawa, KS 66067.

Contests sponsored by The Writing Conference, a nonprofit organization that provides services to children, young adults and teachers with interests in reading and writing.

General Info: Students in grades 3-12 are invited to submit poetry, narration or exposition on selected topics each year. Send SASE in August to receive yearly topics and guidelines. Deadline is January.

Prizes: Winners in each category receive plaque. In addition, these winners have their writing published in *The Writers' Slate*. First-place winners, their parents and their teachers are guests at the Saturday luncheon of the Annual Conference on Writing and Literature, held every spring in Kansas City.

Sponsor's Remarks: "The goal is the improvement of writing and reading skills of young people."

Subscription Rates: One year (three issues to *The Writers' Slate*) for students $10; for teachers and other adults $12.95.

* WYOMING VALLEY POETRY SOCIETY, % Michelle Santiglia, 10 E. South St., #140, Wilkes-Barre, PA 18701.

Contest sponsored by WVPS for students in grades 1-12.

General Info: Held annually in conjunction with the Fine Arts Fiesta held in Wilkes-Barre, Pennsylvania in May/June. Open to students in local area (Northeastern Pennsylvania, primarily in Luzerne County). Contest details, including deadlines, are listed in local newspapers each year and are available at local libraries and from English teachers. Students participate with others in their grade range: Grades 1-3, 4-6, 7-9 or 10-12.

Prizes: Certificates presented for first place, second place, third place and honorable mentions in each of the grade ranges. Students read their winning entries on the stage in the Public Square, Wilkes-Barre, on the last day of the Fiesta.

Sponsor's Remarks: "Some of the children have participated in the contest on a yearly basis. A number of English teachers are also involved in the contest by having their students write poems, and these in turn are submitted to the contest judge."

* YOUNG PLAYWRIGHTS PROGRAM, Very Special Arts, Education Office, The John F. Kennedy Center for the Performing Arts, Washington, DC 20566. VSA is an international organization that provides opportunities through the arts for people with disabilities, especially children and youth. Founded in 1974 by Jean Kennedy Smith as an affiliate of the J.F.K. Center for Performing Arts, the organization offers programs in creative writing, dance, drama, music and visual arts. Students ages 12-18 may apply.

General Info: Scripts must explore an aspect of disability. Entries may be the work of an individual student or a collaboration by a group or class of students. Submit three typed copies of each script to the Young Playwrights Coordinator. Scripts must include a cover sheet including the title, author name(s), birth date, grade, home address, phone number, school name and address, teacher's name and a 250-word autobiographical description. If there is more than one author per script, include full information for each. While most submissions are one-act plays, full-length plays are accepted. Top scripts are reviewed by a panel of well-known theatre professionals. Write for detailed brochure and current deadline. A hands-on Teacher's Guide is also available.

Prizes: Expense-paid trip to Washington, DC, for winner and a chaperone to participate in rehearsals and be a guest at the premiere production of his/her play at The John F. Kennedy Center for the Performing Arts. If the chosen script is written by multiple authors, VSA will assist with financial support for the trip.

Sponsor's Remarks: "Although the play must address or otherwise incorporate some aspect of disability, the choice of theme, setting and style is up to you. You may want to write from your own experience or write a play about some experience in the life of another person. Students with and without disabilities are encouraged to participate."

* YOUNG PUBLISH-A-BOOK CONTEST, Raintree/ Steck-Vaughn, P.O. Box 27010, Austin, TX 78755. Yearly contest for children in grades 2-3 in U.S. and Canada.

General Info: New theme announced each fall. Stories, 300-500 words in length, must relate to year's theme and be written by children in grades 2-3. *Entrants must be enrolled full time in an accredited public or private school.* Each student must be sponsored by a teacher or school or public librarian. All entries become the property of the publisher and will not be returned. Sponsors should submit children's stories in typed, double-spaced format. Illustrations are not accepted. Cover sheet should include all information (name, address, grade level, school and telephone number) for both young author and sponsor. Judging criteria includes adherence to theme, potential for illustration, use of language, etc. Rules (poster format) are available free by calling (800) 531-5015 or writing to above address. Submission deadline January 31.

Prizes: One grand-prize-winning entry will be published in professionally illustrated, hardcover book form and become part of the current series bearing the contest name. Winners also receive a $500 advance against royalties, as well as ten copies of their published books. The sponsor named on each of the winning entries receives twenty free books from the Raintree/Steck-Vaughn Library catalog. Ten honorable mention young authors each receive $25; their sponsors receive ten free books.

Sponsor's Remarks: "Teachers and librarians may sponsor as many children as they wish in the PAB contest. We encourage teachers and librarians to use the contest as a classroom activity or to encourage a young writer. A photo and biography of the author is given in the back of each of the winning entries. Authors are invited to dedicate their books to special people in their lives."

*$ YOUNG SALVATIONIST MAGAZINE—CONTEST, % Lesa Salyer, P.O. Box 269, Alexandria, VA 22313. Published monthly except summer for high school/early college aged youth by The Salvation Army.

General Info: Open only to young members of The Salvation Army under the age of 23. Send SASE to above address for further details.

Subscription Rates: One year $4 (U.S. funds).

Appendix A

Sandy Asher Talks About Writing Plays

S ince I personally know next to nothing about play and script writing, I have asked Sandy Asher, writer-in-residence at Drury College (Springfield, Missouri) and an award-winning children's book writer and playwright to share some tips and resources. Here are her comments:

First and foremost, young playwrights should get involved with theater groups at school and in the community. The theater presents challenges and limitations that you simply have to experience and understand! It's not necessary to perform. Playwrights need to know how things work backstage, too! Any job that allows you to watch and become involved in rehearsals and performances will give you a feel for what does and doesn't work well in the theater.

Second, attend plays and read plays as often as you can. For junior and senior high students, I especially recommend the Dell series of plays from the Young Playwrights Festival, Inc. (321 West 44th St., Suite 906, New York, NY 10036) sponsored by the Dramatists Guild. Two titles I have on hand are *Sparks in the Park* and *Hey Little Walker*.

Third, read Carol Korty's excellent book *Writing Your Own Plays: Creating, Adapting, Improvising* (Scribner, 1986). Another good sourcebook is *Putting on a Play, A Guide to Writing and Producing Neighborhood Drama*, by Susan and Stephen Judy (sometimes spelled Tchudi), also from Scribner, 1982.

The Playwright's Companion (updated each year) is the

best marketing guide I've found and lists many contests, workshops and other opportunities for young playwrights, but you have to read all the entries carefully to ferret out those meant for young people. It's worth the trouble, though, because competing with adults in contests such as the one we sponsor at Drury College will generally result in disappointment. We received over 500 submissions in 1993. The competition is very stiff, so increase your odds by sticking with programs meant for your age group.

The Playwright's Companion also lists publishers from whom you can order catalogs and plays to read. I particularly recommend a look at Anchorage Press, Baker's Plays—which sponsors a high school playwriting contest—Dramatists Publishing Company, New Plays, Inc., Pioneer Drama Service, and Samuel French. *Playwright's Companion* is available from Feedback Theatrebooks, 305 Madison Avenue, Suite 1146, New York, NY 10165.

Many of the play publishers' catalogs also contain books of interest to teachers working with young playwrights, as does the Heinemann/Boynton-Cook catalog. Organizations of interest to teachers include ASSITEJ/USA (contact Amie Brockway, The Open Eye: New Stagings, 270 West 89th St., New York, NY 10024) and the American Alliance for Theatre and Education (Theatre Department, Arizona State University, Temple, AZ 85287-3411).

Plays need to be read aloud by actors and produced in informal workshop situations—often several times—before they're ready to win contests or be published. There's only so much you can do on your own. Those special problems and possibilities of the stage need to be dealt with "on the hoof"—with live actors and an audience interested in helping to develop works-in-progress. Again, school and community theater groups provide the best opportunities for getting your plays read aloud by actors, gathering reactions from supportive audiences, learning, experimenting and polishing your work. Many theaters, especially family theaters, such as The Coterie in Kansas City and the Kennedy Center in Washington, DC, conduct playwriting workshops for young people. Ask around! If your local theater group doesn't have a playwriting workshop, maybe you can help start one!

Hope I've been helpful!

Sandy Asher
Writer-in-Residence
Drury College

Among Ms. Asher's latest plays are *A Woman Called Truth* and *The Wise Men of Chelm* (both published by Dramatic Publishing Company), and her most recent book is *Out Of Here: A Senior Class Yearbook* (Dutton/Lodestar, July 1993).

INDEX